IMAGES
of America

BANDERA COUNTY

I0806421

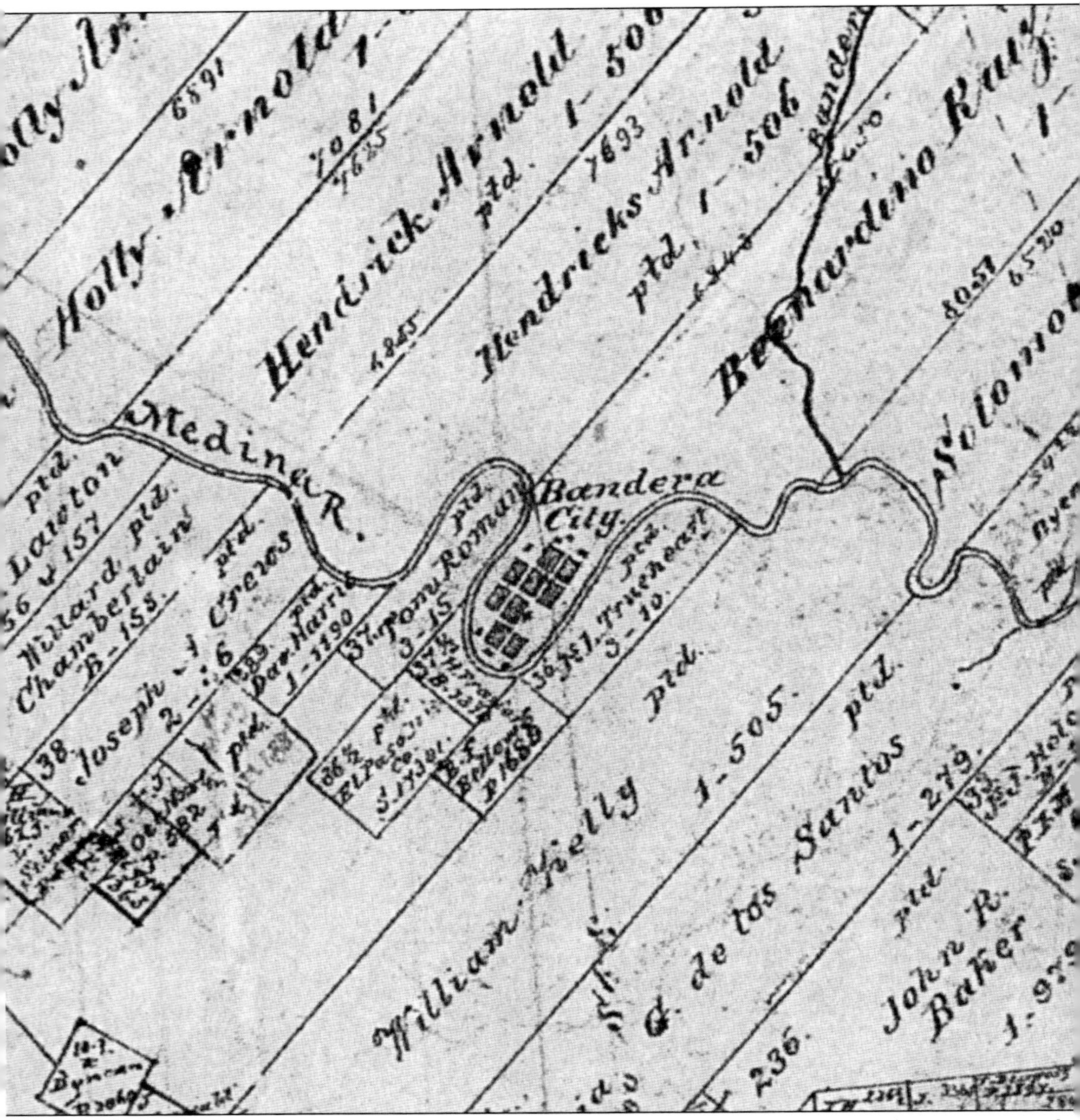

In 1856, the Texas state legislature marked off Bandera County from the northwest portion of Bexar County. Bandera, the county seat, was platted out on land within a bend of the Medina River, as shown in this 1862 map. Four prominent plats, clearly seen on the map, were given to Hendrick Arnold, an African American, as compensation for his services in the Texas Revolution against Mexico. (Courtesy of Lauren Langford.)

On the Cover: In close proximity to Bandera Pass, Bandera became a center of trade as settlers, cattle drives, the military, and freighters traversed across Bandera County. Former trail driver Lee Risinger opened a general merchandise business in 1886. This image was taken when Risinger arranged for a freighter to deliver much-needed supplies after a wet spell in 1910 made the roads into Bandera impassable. (Courtesy of the Frontier Times Museum Collection.)

IMAGES
of America

BANDERA COUNTY

Frontier Times Museum

ARCADIA
PUBLISHING

Copyright © 2010 by Frontier Times Museum
ISBN 978-0-7385-8554-3

Published by Arcadia Publishing
Charleston, South Carolina

Printed in the United States of America

Library of Congress Control Number: 2009938070

For all general information contact Arcadia Publishing at:
Telephone 843-853-2070
Fax 843-853-0044
E-mail sales@arcadiapublishing.com
For customer service and orders:
Toll-Free 1-888-313-2665

Visit us on the Internet at www.arcadiapublishing.com

In memory of Ray Marvin Hay,
whose footsteps through the museum
will keep him close in our hearts forever.

Contents

ACKNOWLEDGMENTS

The Frontier Times Museum Board of Trustees would like to acknowledge the following for their contributions. A special thank-you to Peggy Tobin for not only contributing to the introduction, but also for her dedication to preserving and documenting the history of Bandera County. Thank you to Rebecca Huffstutler Norton for her tireless efforts in gathering the photographs and researching and writing the narrative that provided insight into what makes this county unique and special. Rebecca is greatly indebted to trustee Claire Roberts and Lauren Langford for their assistance. We would like to recognize the efforts of museum staff Rose Greenawald, Richard Cage, and Jane Graham. Jane, our museum manager, did yeoman's duties in tracking down images and finding just the right person with the perfect photograph.

This book would not have been possible without the support of the Bandera County Historical Commission. Pres. Roy Dugosh's enthusiasm opened the door for us, and Merry Langlinais gave access to the commission's photograph archives and images of Medina Dam. Elenora Dugosh Goodley's work on the history of the Polish settlers is invaluable and without comparison. County commissioner Doug King's dedication to the history of the county courthouse shows his skill as a historian.

In San Antonio, Siri Lindholm lent her expertise with good humor, and Tom Shelton and Patrick Lemelle at the University of Texas at San Antonio's Institute of Texan Cultures provided hard-to-find treasures from their collection.

There were many in the community who provided information and support. A warm thank-you goes to the *Bandera County Courier* and the many families who trusted us with their memories. Annette Kalka-Schulte, Mary Margaret Anderson, Betty D'Spain, Bobby and Mary Stein, Judy Hicks, and trustee Theresa Helbert's family photographs were a treasure trove of Bandera history. Marlene Grothues and Burgin and Valli Johnson brought to life the pleasures of living on Medina Lake. Trustee Neal Dalton gathered old friends who brought fun images of dude ranches and colorful characters. Afternoons with rodeo champions Ray Wharton and Scooter Fries were time well spent with legends, truly something to remember. Most of all, thank you to Ruth Hay, whose guidance and knowledge made everything just right.

All dam construction photographs in chapter four are courtesy of Ed Burger and the Bexar, Medina, Atascosa Water Improvement District No. 1. All flood photographs in chapter five are courtesy of the Ray Marvin and Ruth Hay Collection. Unless otherwise noted, Stompede photographs are courtesy of San Antonio Light Collection of the University of Texas at San Antonio's Institute of Texan Culture, a gift of the Hearst Corporation.

INTRODUCTION

Bandera County in the Texas Hill Country is a place of contradictions and uniqueness. The splendor of green hills against the immense Texas sky is juxtaposed against a harsh landscape of limestone and rocky soil where making a living is not always easy. Those that live here know that their nirvana can be shaken by deadly floods as well as droughts that can last several years or until the next flood. Those that settled the area have traditionally been of hardy stock. They value hard work, individualism, and independence. The churches they built stand next to dance halls, and rowdy Saturday nights give way to quiet, reflective Sunday mornings.

The Tonkawa Indians first settled in the Medina River Valley, calling it the Valley of Paint. They were later driven out by the Lipan Apaches and Comanches. In 1737, Josef de la Urrutia returned from an expedition exploring the unknown territory to the northwest of San Antonio de Bexar. He reported that he had found the pass through which marauding Apaches were coming to raid Spanish settlements. He described a long range of hills following the Guadalupe River through which easy travel was made possible by the narrow pass. The pass was later identified on an 1842 Spanish map as *Puerto de Bandera*. The name *Bandera*, or banner, has had several unproven explanations, most having to do with Spanish-Indian encounters or battles at the site.

No record exists of any permanent European settlement in Bandera County until the mid-19th century. In 1852, John James, Charles DeMontel, and John Herndon entered into a partnership to acquire land along the Medina River in order to establish a town with a sawmill in which to make shingles from the plentiful cypress trees that grew along the riverbank. By 1853, a horse-powered sawmill and a commissary store were built. Thomas Odem, P. D. Saner, and A. M. Milstead, with their families, were the first to come to the camp along the river and worked in the sawmill making shingles. The same year, James and DeMontel surveyed and platted the town of Bandera, and the small village grew up in a bend of the river.

The first organized group of settlers to arrive in Bandera was Mormons. Led by Elder Lyman Wight, they came to Texas after breaking off from the main migration of Mormons from Illinois to Utah. Arriving in the spring of 1854, they camped on the north side of the Medina River across from the town. They later settled about 12 miles downstream in what became known as the Mormon Camp. They engaged in making and selling furniture, doing well until the death of Elder Wight in 1858. While many left the area, several families remained in Bandera County and later established a Reorganized Church of Jesus Christ of Latter Day Saints in Bandera.

The next group to arrive in Bandera was made up of Polish émigrés from Silesia, who had first settled in the Polish settlement of Panna Maria, southeast of San Antonio. The hardships were too great there, and a group of families moved on to Bandera in 1855 upon hearing the sawmill was in need of workers. Given homesites and the chance to buy farmland, the Polish settlers soon became a pivotal force in the community, building businesses and establishing the second-oldest Polish Catholic parish in the United States. The sawmill became a major operation, gaining many government contracts to provide shingles for army posts being built along the long trail to California.

Unlike the Polish immigrants and the Mormon colony, most settlers arrived as individuals to take up land grants. Nearby Pipe Creek and Privilege Creek received their names from local citizens making the long trip from Boerne or San Antonio, southwest of the area. One man lost, and later found, his pipe in a creek where the village of Pipe Creek grew. Another, admiring the countryside that another creek ran through, announced he wished to declare a homestead there, with the privilege of releasing his claim if he found something better farther north.

After the Civil War, Texas regained its economic health in part through the driving of herds of cattle from South Texas north to the railroads being extended across Kansas. Many drives came through Bandera, to follow the Western Trail up through Texas, to cross the Red River, and make it to Dodge City. Young men raised on farms became cowboys, going up the trail and learning the skills that would later bring nationwide recognition to local rodeo performers.

As the century moved along, named settlements grew up around the county, notably Medina and others such as Tarpley and Bug Scuffle, which townsfolk later named Vanderpool after their postmaster, P. M. Vanderpool. Sparked by the *c.* 1880 establishment of a general store, Medina became a well-populated town, with a robust commercial center and several churches. During the heyday of former frontier scout and minister Policarpo Rodriquez, his settlement of Polly, Texas, boasted a post office, a school, and a chapel that Rodriquez built and deeded to the Methodist Church. In 1912, with the construction of a dam in Box Canyon, Medina Lake was created. The old Mormon Camp was flooded, but new neighborhoods and the community of Lakehills grew up around the lake.

Bandera County went through a period of ranching and farming, in which cotton, wheat, oats, and sugar cane were grown. This proved to be difficult because of frequent droughts and shallow soil. The raising of sheep and goats on the hilly terrain proved to be easier and more profitable than cattle, and Bandera County became a leading export of wool and mohair. A major local business was the Wool Warehouse, owned by the Bandera County Ranchmen and Farmers Association, overlooking the Medina River. The building was stacked high with wool and mohair brought in to be sold to northern buyers.

As the economy began to decline by the beginning of the 20th century, the county's population thinned, the land was worn out from farming and overgrazing, and the price of wool and mohair dropped during the Great Depression. Local ranchers opened their properties to visitors, and the dude ranch business came into being. The first dude ranch, the Buck Ranch, opened in 1920, and was followed by the Bruce Ranch, the Dixie Dude Ranch, and many more. People from Houston commuted most weekends to the cool hills, as did many members of the armed forces stationed in San Antonio and Hondo to the west, which led to a boom time during World War II. The tourist industry became a major economic factor in the county, and dance halls and honky-tonks provided the entertainment.

Many vacationers decided to come to Bandera to live or retire, and the large ranches began to be subdivided into residential tracts. As of the 21st century, Bandera continues to flourish as a vacation and residential destination. Known as the "Cowboy Capital of the World," Bandera is the site of several rodeos throughout the year and is the home of many nationally recognized rodeo champions. The spirit of the independent individual continues to live on, creating a haven for characters and heroes.

One

Frontier Settlers

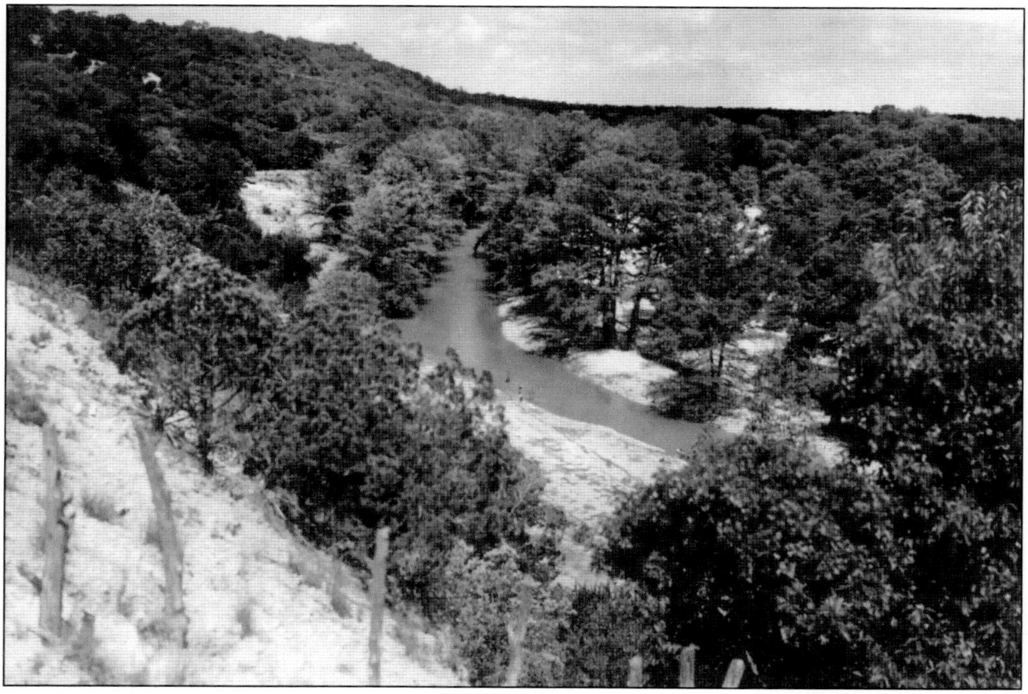

For those who settled along the Medina River and in the surrounding Hill Country, J. Marvin Hunter, a publisher and historian, recalled a local Native American legend. "He who once having drank from the waters of the Medina and goes away, will ever be athirst until he comes back to this valley. Banderaland!" (Courtesy of the Frontier Times Museum Collection.)

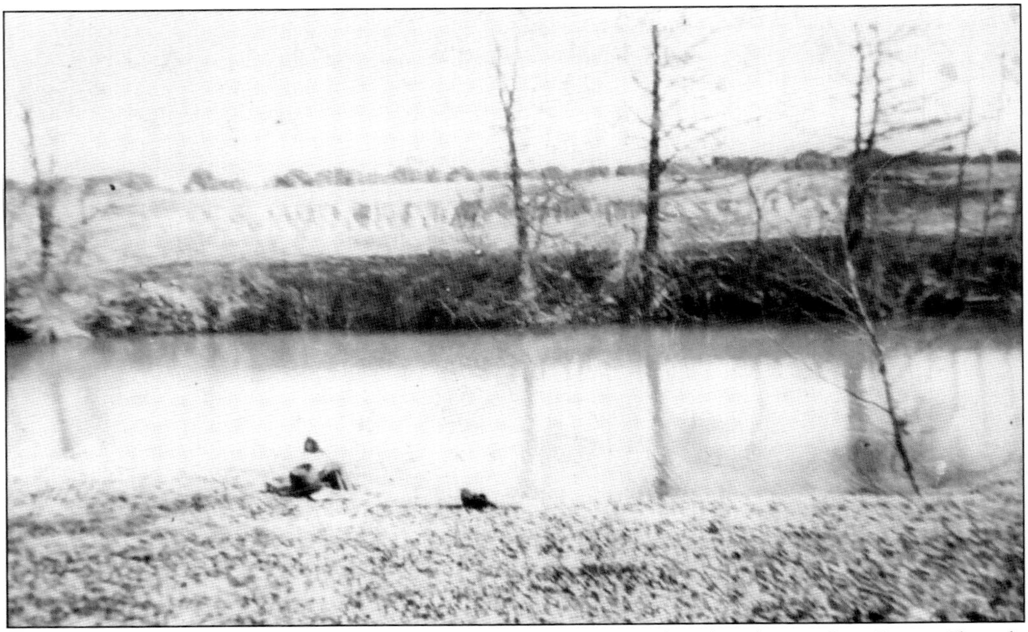

In 1852, the first shingle-making camp was established on this bend in the Medina River. Shingle making proved to be a profitable business. The shingles would be stacked in bundles of 1,000 and loaded onto ox wagons to bring to market in San Antonio. Up to 25,000 shingles would be loaded onto a single wagon. Going over hills and down poor roads, the trip would take several days. (Courtesy of Robin Shaw.)

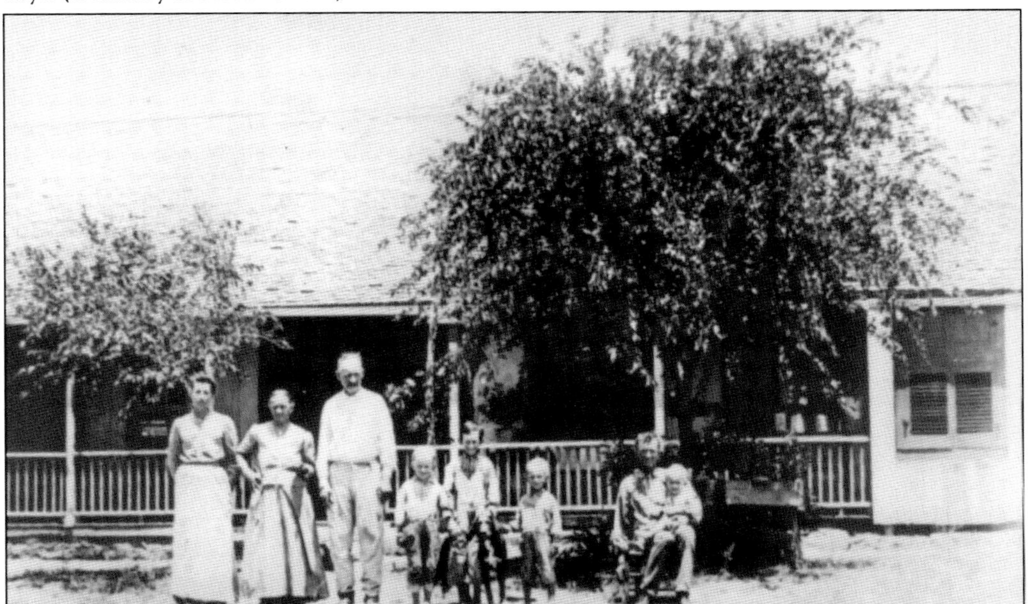

The original Polish families who came to Bandera to make shingles were each given a lot to build their homestead. Pictured in front of his family home, Coustian Dugosh arrived in Bandera with his parents, Johann and Franciska. Johann, a carpenter by trade, built Bandera's first store and post office with cypress lumber from the mill for August Klappenbach, a German settler. (Courtesy of Elenora Dugosh Goodley.)

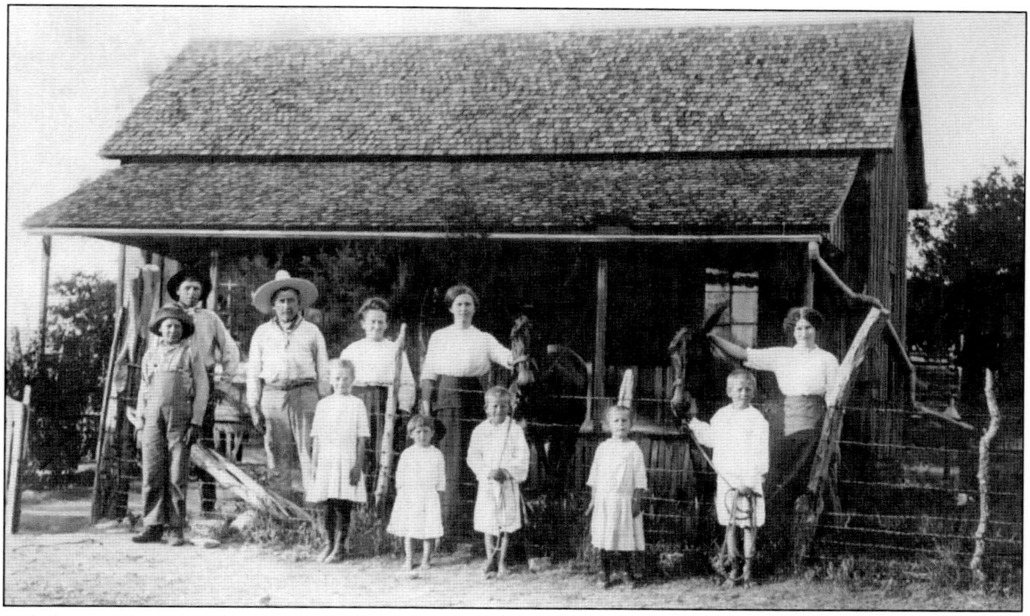

Polish settlers faced isolation and numerous Native American attacks. While the men worked at the sawmill, the women helped clear land and dug the millrace for a gristmill. Early homes were built of wood from the mill, with thatch roofs similar to the ones they had in Poland. Louis Adamietz and his family, pictured here, were descendants of Albert Adamietz, an original settler. (Courtesy of Bobby and Mary Stein.)

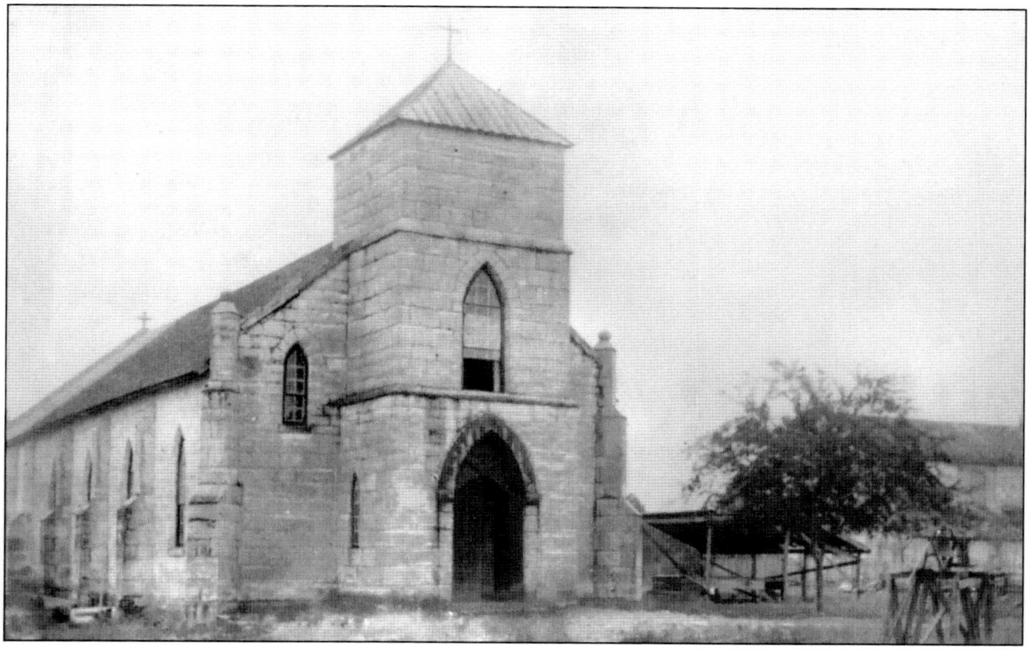

One of the first structures built in the new settlement was a church, a place to say the rosary and sing hymns. Three years after arriving in Bandera, the Polish settlers built their first church, St. Stanislaus, out of logs. Mass was held whenever a priest would arrive by horseback. In 1876, a larger stone chapel was built, along with a school and a convent. (Courtesy of Frontier Times Museum Collection.)

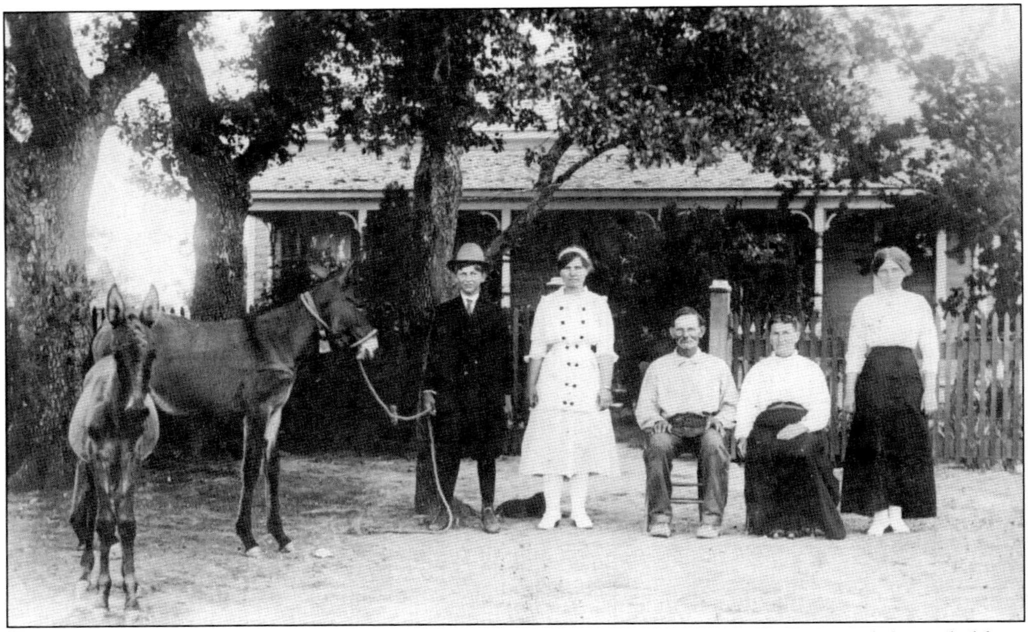

Life became easier for the children of the original settlers. Polish parents encouraged their children to speak English, and several schools were built throughout the county. They became town leaders, business owners, farmers, and ranchers, and their surnames are still prominent today. Frank Pyka (seated left), pictured with his family, was descended from John Pyka Sr., a signer of the 1855 petition to form Bandera County. (Courtesy of Theresa Helbert.)

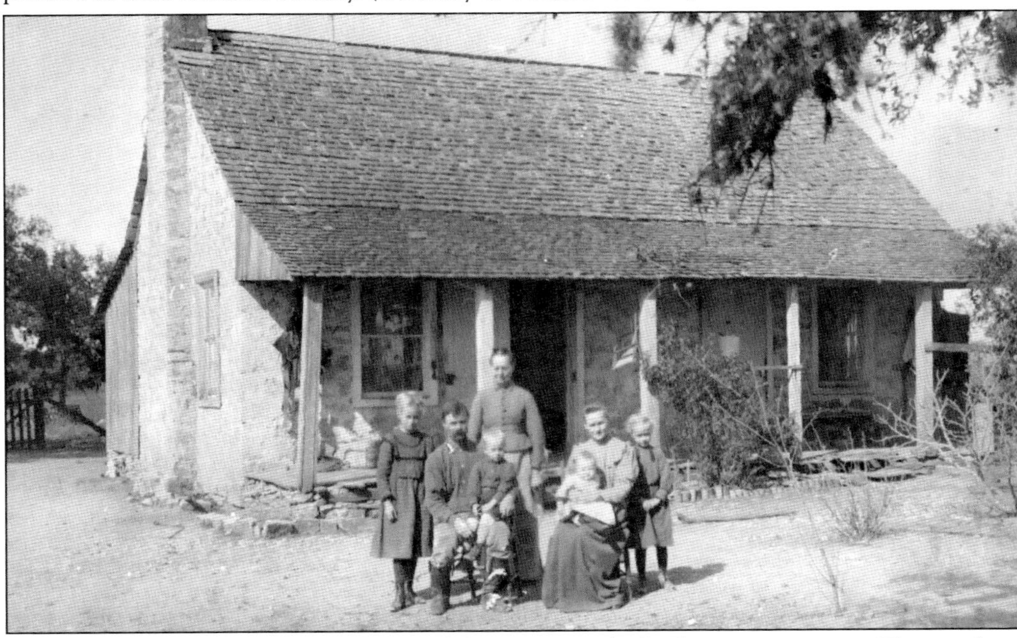

As letters arrived back in Poland, more Polish citizens made the decision to come to Texas seeking a better life. Frank Kalka came to Bandera in 1877 to escape oppression in his native Poland. He purchased acreage and began Oak Mound Farm, raising sugar cane, cotton, and livestock. His son Joe Frank (seated at left), pictured here with his wife, Mary Anderwald Kalka (seated at right), continued his father's operation. (Courtesy of Annette Kalka-Schulte.)

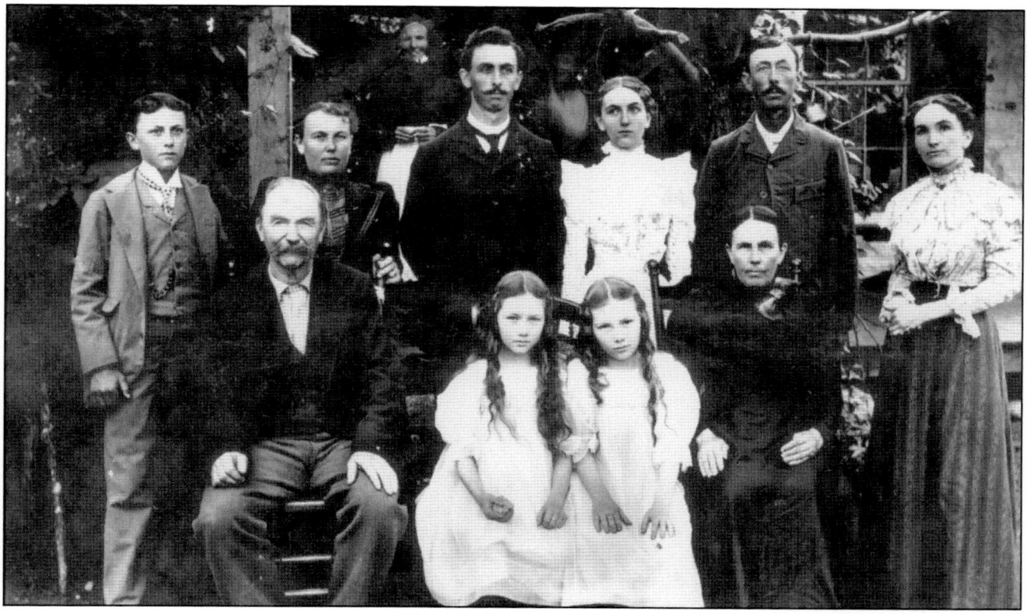

Seeking freedom from persecution, Elder Lyman Wight led a colony of about 250 Mormon settlers to Bandera in 1854. The settlers included doctors, teachers, millers, blacksmiths, and furniture makers. Joining the colony in Texas, the Hay family had been the first in their native Scotland to be baptized in the Mormon faith. George Hay, seated at far left, married fellow colony member Amanda Minear. After her death, he married Amanda's sister, Virginia, seated at far right. (Courtesy of Ruth Hay.)

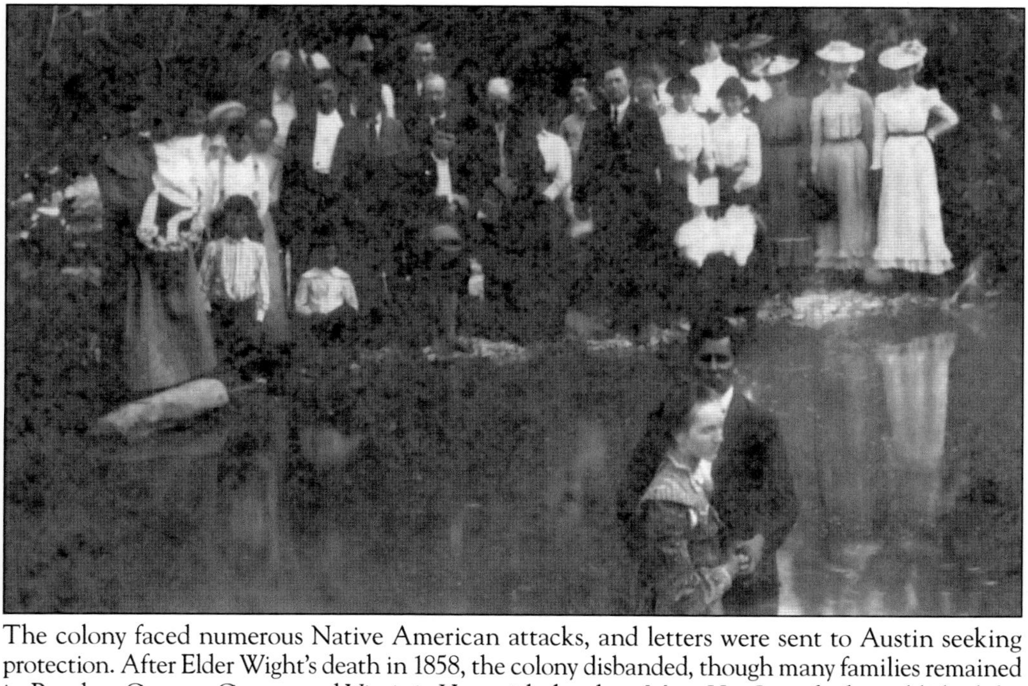

The colony faced numerous Native American attacks, and letters were sent to Austin seeking protection. After Elder Wight's death in 1858, the colony disbanded, though many families remained in Bandera County. George and Virginia Hay, with daughter Mary Hay Langford, established the Reorganized Church of Jesus Christ of Latter Day Saints in Bandera. Mary is shown here being baptized in the Medina River. (Courtesy of Lauren Langford.)

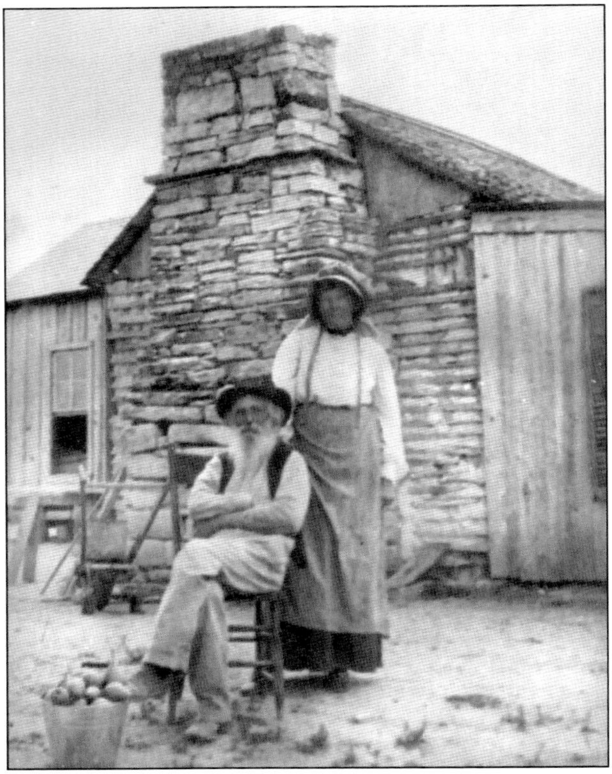

Amasa Clark was the first permanent settler to the area in 1852. He was the father of 19 children and had just about as many jobs in his long life. His served in the Mexican War in 1847 and went on to many adventures as a freighter, shingle maker, farmer, and camel herder, taking care of the army's camels at Camp Verde, near Bandera Pass. He is pictured at left with his wife, Francis. (Courtesy of the Frontier Times Museum Collection.)

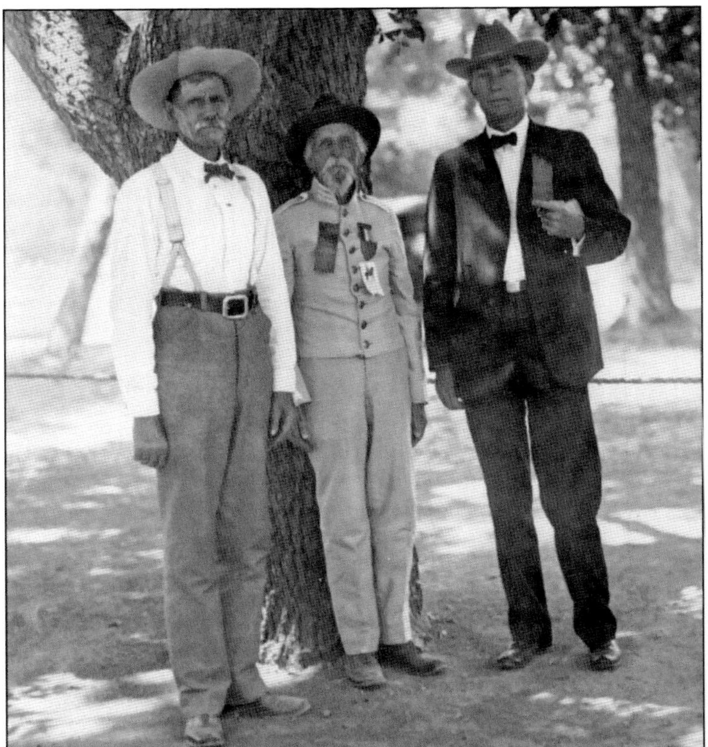

With his nephews Isaac Rhodes (left) and Harlow Rhodes (right), Amasa Clark celebrated his 100th birthday. He recalled caring for the camels at Camp Verde. They were to be used for transportation to bring supplies across the desert to western posts. Clark sheared some camels to make a mattress and two pillows with the hair. He lived to be 101 and was buried with one pillow beneath his head. (Courtesy of Bandera County Historical Commission.)

Born in Mexico, Policarpo Rodriquez moved to San Antonio with his family in 1841. As a government scout, he guided an expedition to establish a westward road from San Antonio to El Paso. While serving at Camp Verde, he came to Privilege Creek looking for camels that had strayed away from the camp. In 1858, he decided to settle there, purchasing 360 acres for $180. (Courtesy of the Frontier Times Museum Collection.)

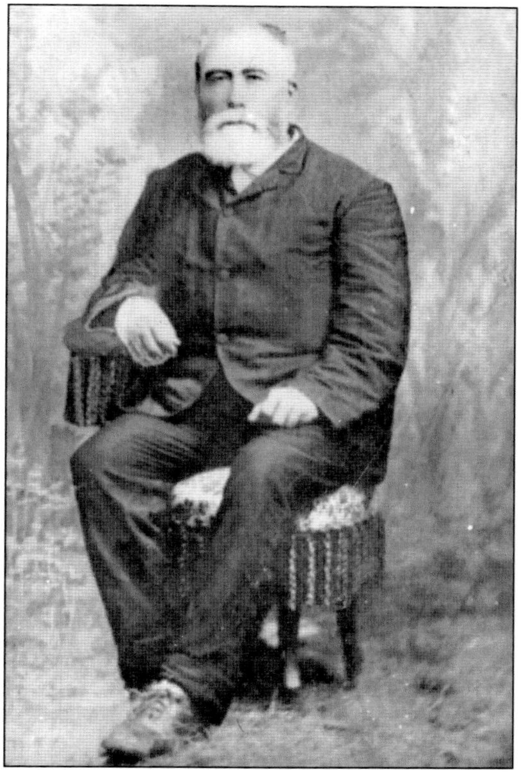

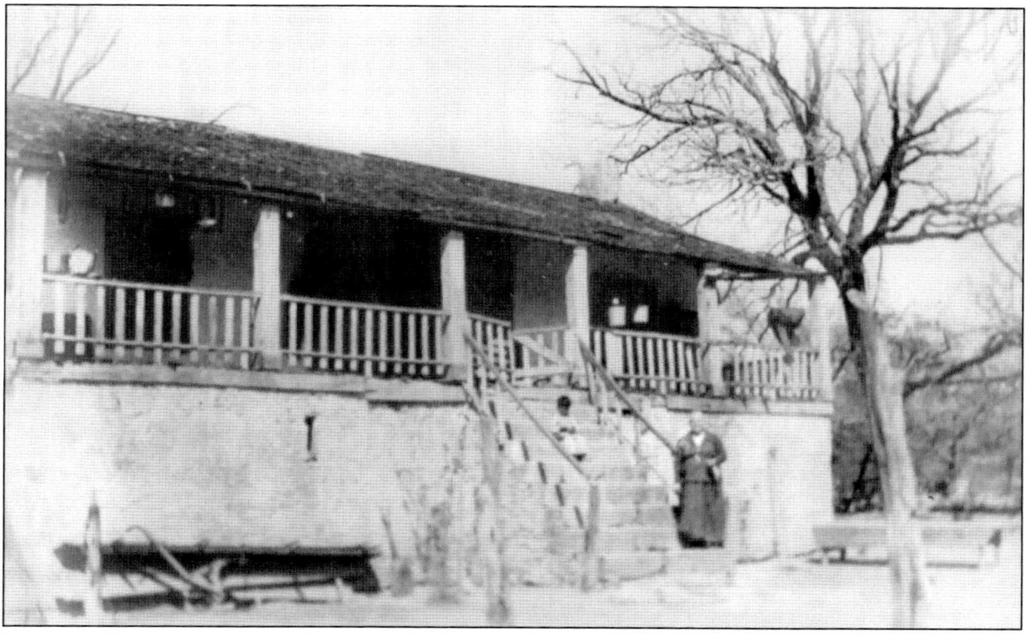

Policarpo built his limestone house with the first floor serving as a "fort," which featured narrow openings used for protection against Native Americans. Rodriquez developed the community of Polly. He built a Methodist church known as "Polly's Chapel" in which he preached for many years. In 1881, he petitioned the county to build a public school. It remained opened until 1942, when it was consolidated into the Bandera School. (Courtesy of the Frontier Times Museum Collection.)

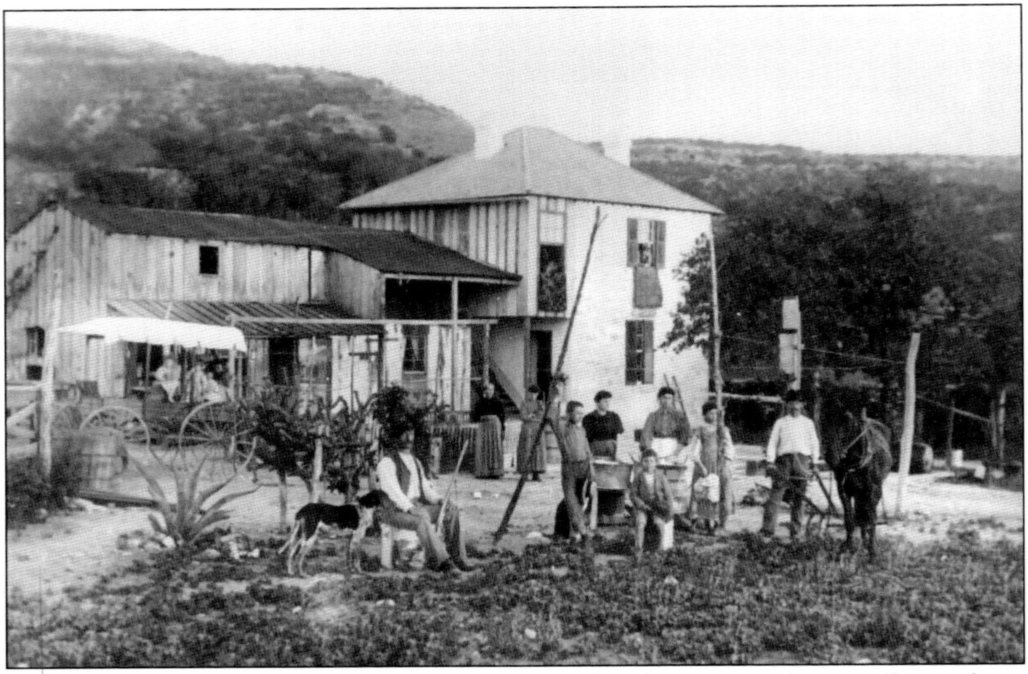

By 1880, Polly was primarily a Tejano settlement and included two Italian families and one Irish family. In 1885, Francisco Gerodetti, an Italian immigrant, purchased land from Policarpo Rodriquez and opened this store, selling supplies, groceries, and homemade wine. A post office was set up inside the store, and mail would be brought in by horseback from Pipe Creek, over the hills east of the store. (Courtesy of the Frontier Times Museum Collection.)

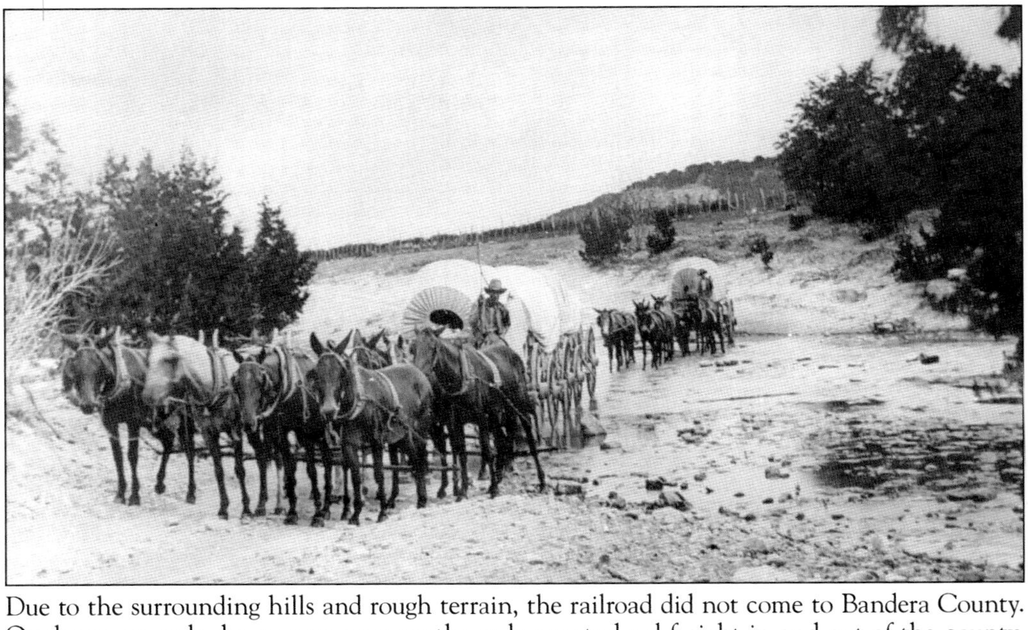

Due to the surrounding hills and rough terrain, the railroad did not come to Bandera County. Ox-drawn or mule-drawn wagons were the only way to haul freight in and out of the county. Freighters Ben and Frank Baker of Medina (the drivers pictured) were engaged for many years in hauling freight to Kerrville, Bandera, Rocksprings, and Junction. (Courtesy of the Frontier Times Museum Collection.)

Pipe Creek's first settler, Francis Marion Hodges, arrived in the area in 1868. Pipe Creek provided a stopping point for stagecoaches arriving from San Antonio, before moving on to Bandera. Andrew Prather, a preacher, arrived in the 1870s with his family. Prather's wife is shown here holding the family Bible, with her daughter and son-in-law. (Courtesy of Bandera County Historical Commission.)

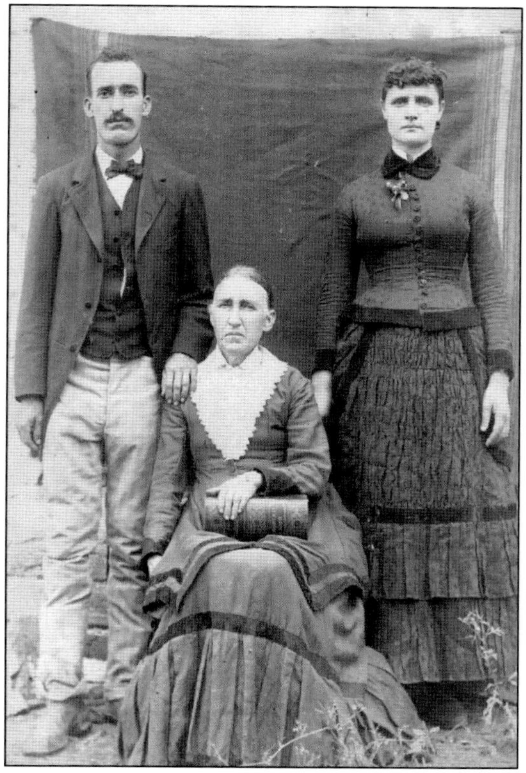

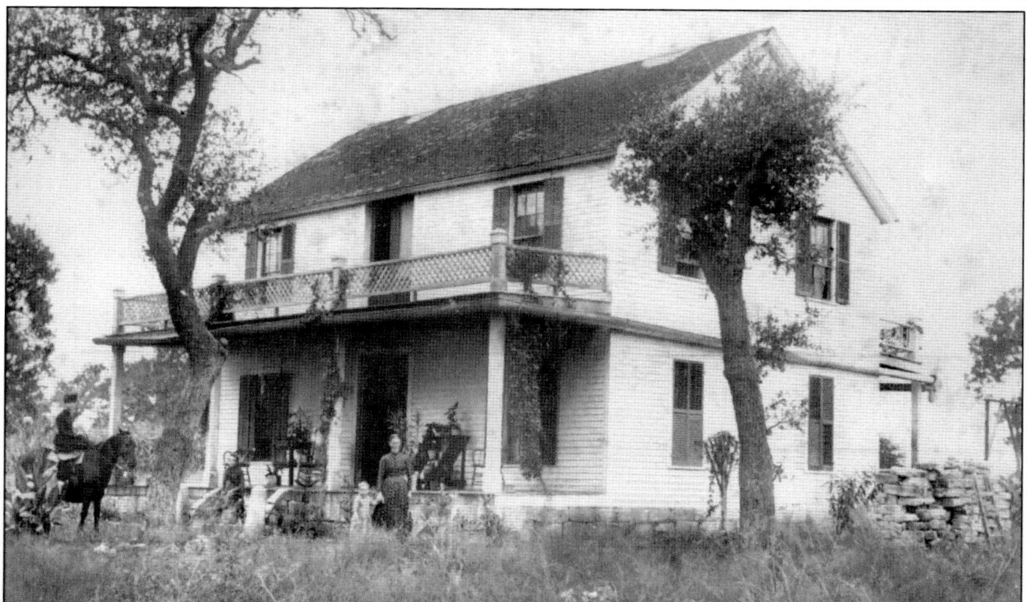

In the spring of 1871, the Stanard family arrived in Bandera County by carriage from Iowa. They settled on Laxson's Creek and procured a team of oxen to plow the land and start a farm. Sarah Stanard built a log schoolhouse and taught there for many years. The family eventually moved to Medina into this grand home, where family members continuously lived until the 1970s. (Courtesy of the Carr-Newcomer-Stanard family.)

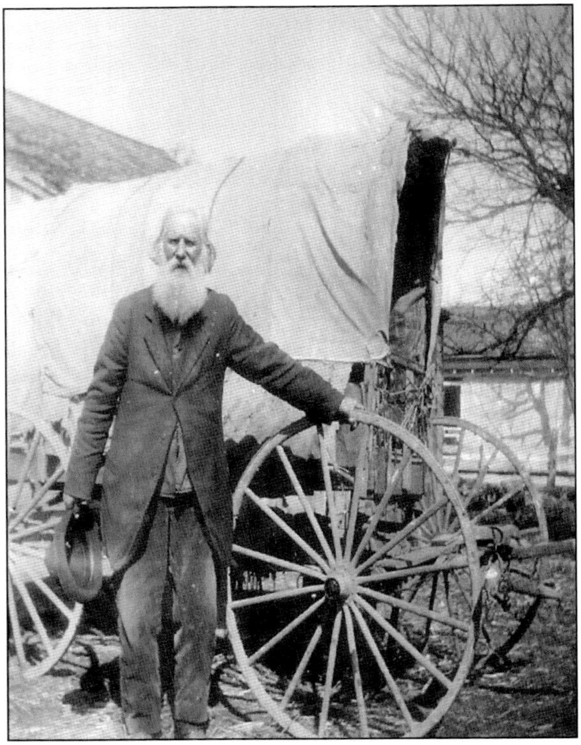

This old-timer proudly stands by his covered wagon, one way of getting around the Hill Country frontier. Distances between the small settlements throughout the county seemed even greater when hauling supplies across the hilly terrain and numerous creeks. The arrival of supplies was always a welcome sight, because it could also mean the arrival of gossip and news from far-flung friends and families. (Courtesy of Bandera County Historical Commission.)

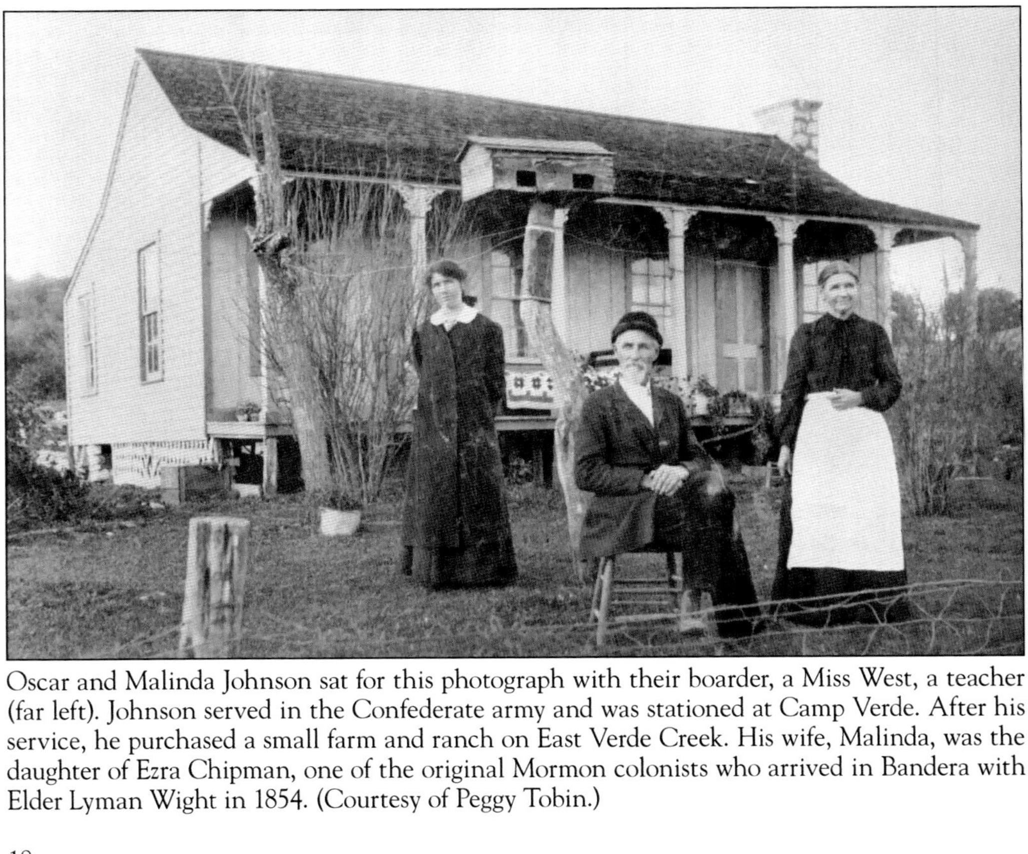

Oscar and Malinda Johnson sat for this photograph with their boarder, a Miss West, a teacher (far left). Johnson served in the Confederate army and was stationed at Camp Verde. After his service, he purchased a small farm and ranch on East Verde Creek. His wife, Malinda, was the daughter of Ezra Chipman, one of the original Mormon colonists who arrived in Bandera with Elder Lyman Wight in 1854. (Courtesy of Peggy Tobin.)

Two

Building Communities

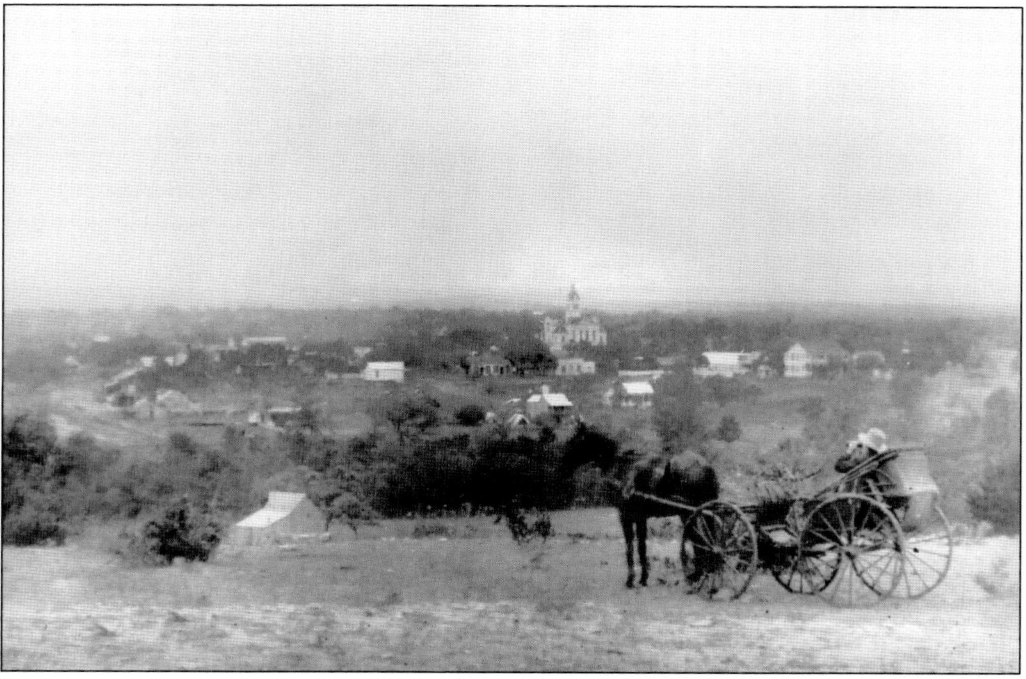

From his carriage, H. C. Duffy overlooks downtown Bandera and the new county courthouse. The decision to build a permanent courthouse in Bandera was met with conflict, as there were factions in the county who believed the county seat should be moved to a more centrally located town. Their petition was not successful. The new courthouse was completed in 1891 and is still in use today. (Courtesy of Christopher Baumle.)

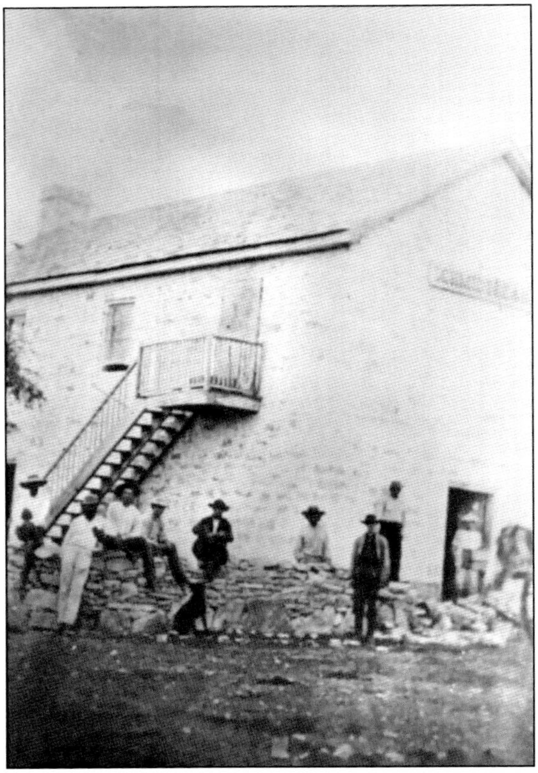

After Bandera County was created in 1856, there was no permanent building to house county offices. Offices and the court were held in buildings around town until the county commissioners purchased this building from the merchants Schmidtke and Hays in 1877. Built in 1869, a store, post office, and mill had occupied the first floor, and the Masonic Lodge met on the second floor. (Courtesy of the Bandera County Historical Commission.)

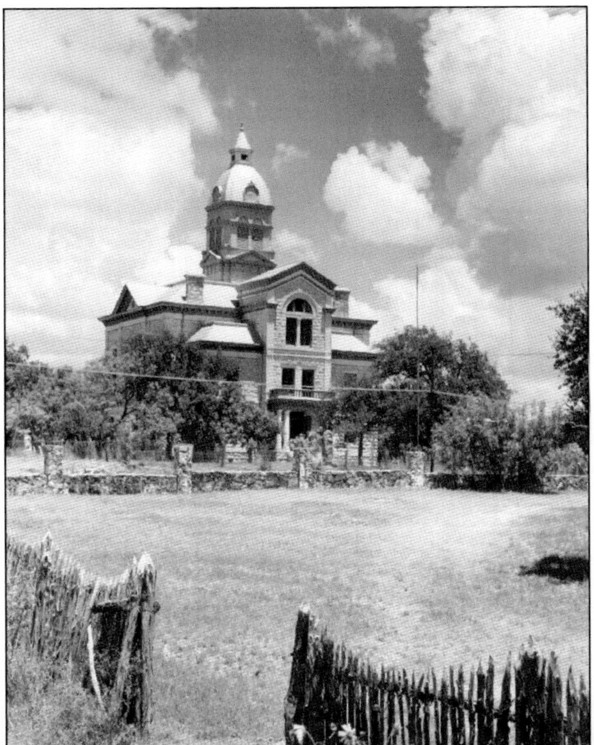

A more elaborate, Second Renaissance Revival–style limestone building was constructed to symbolize the town's growth and progress. Bandera was a boomtown in the 1880s, and the county commissioners were able to construct the new courthouse for almost $20,000. Soon after the building's completion in 1891, the county faced an economic downturn, and population declined. The elaborate courthouse sat for a time above unpaved roads and small farms that dotted downtown. (Courtesy of Ruth Hay.)

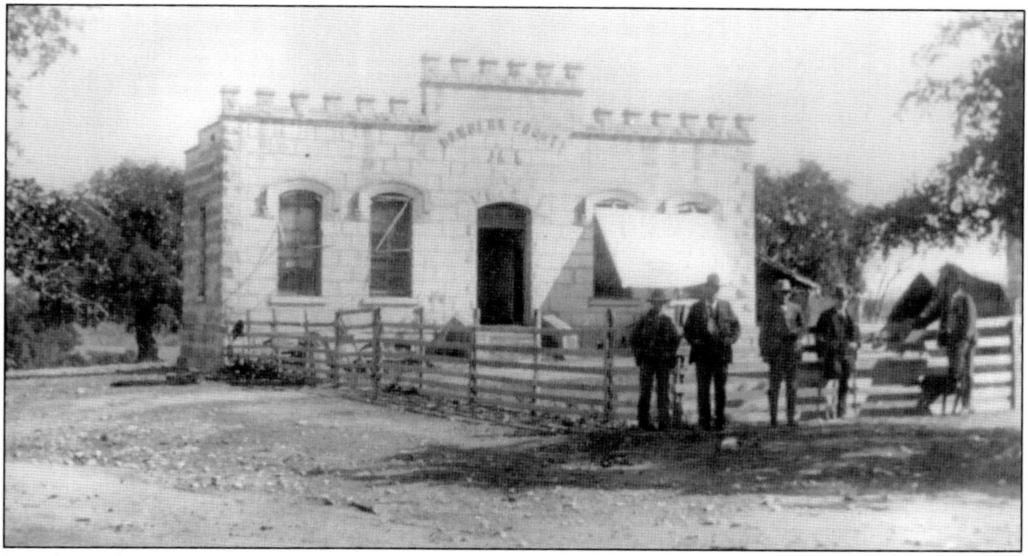

Bandera's first jail was a small room made of cypress timbers with an opening near the roof for ventilation. Prisoners were taken up on a ladder and brought through a trap door in the roof. The prisoner was chained to a ring bolted to the floor, and the ladder was removed. No one ever escaped. The new jail opened in 1881 and was considered a bit more civilized. (Courtesy of the Frontier Times Museum Collection.)

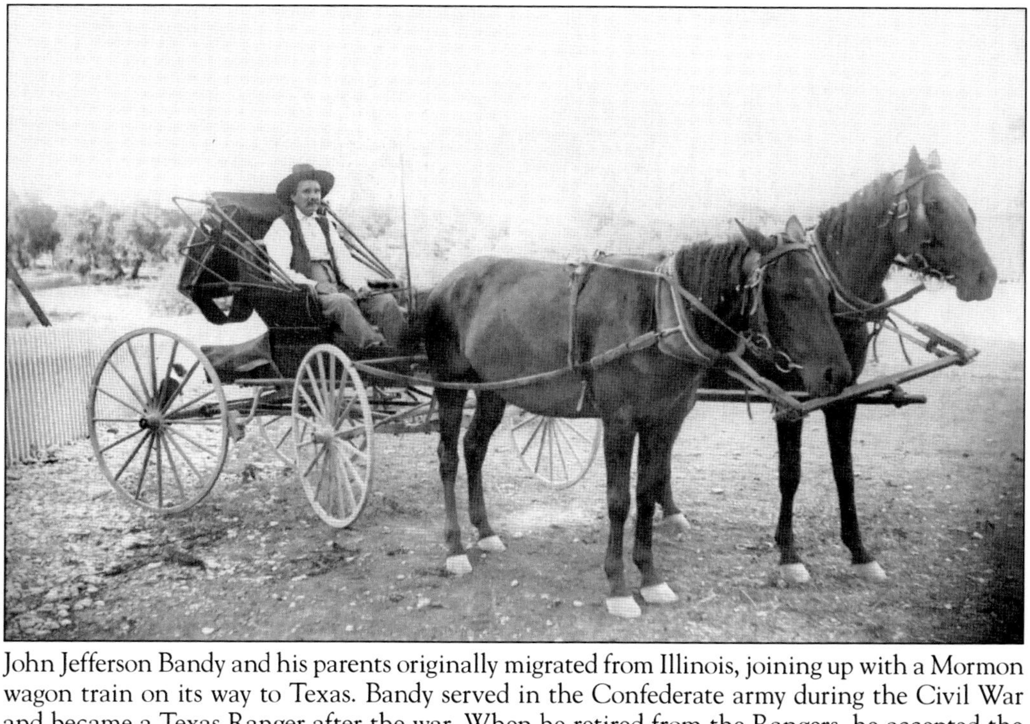

John Jefferson Bandy and his parents originally migrated from Illinois, joining up with a Mormon wagon train on its way to Texas. Bandy served in the Confederate army during the Civil War and became a Texas Ranger after the war. When he retired from the Rangers, he accepted the position of Bandera County tax assessor and collector for 16 years, from 1890 to 1906. (Courtesy of Lauren Langford.)

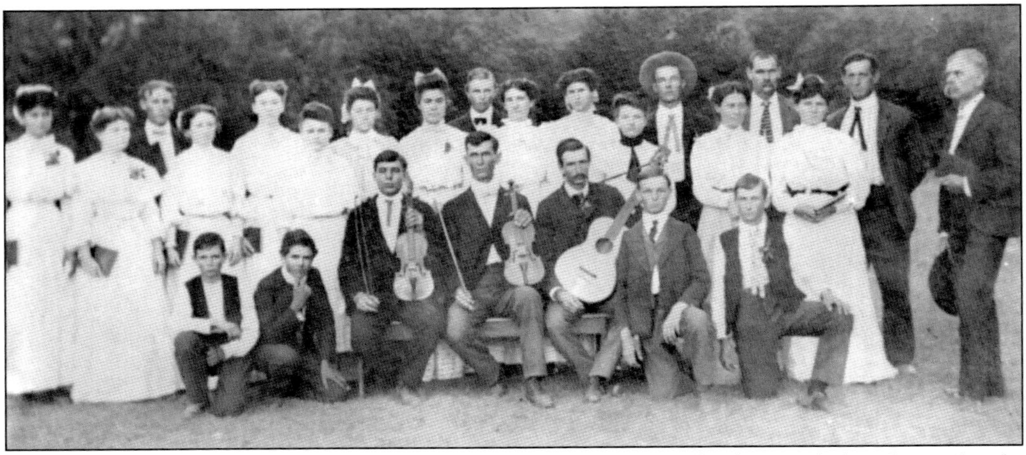

As communities developed, the area's social activities often revolved around churches, schools, and clubs. Cultural groups, such as this singing school from Vanderpool, arose to bring a bit of civilization to the frontier. Other groups included the Laxon Creek Literary Society and Ellen Maudsley Select School for Girls, dedicated to educating the daughters of prominent Bandera families. (Courtesy of the Frontier Times Museum Collection.)

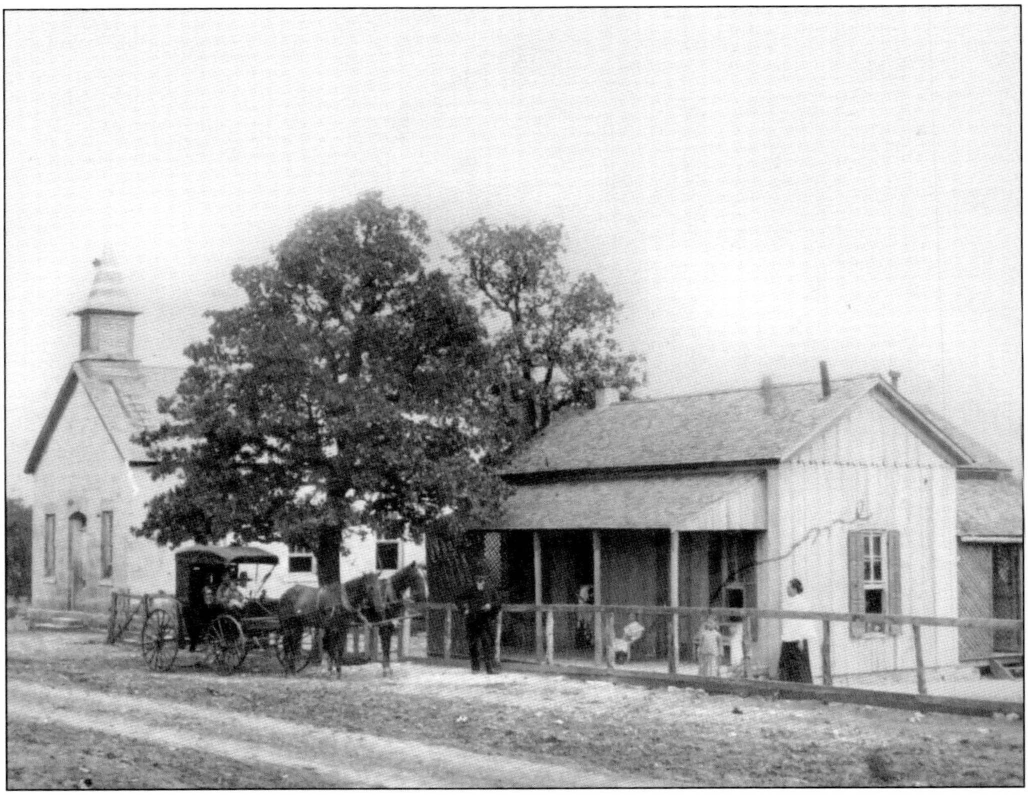

As was the case in many Western areas, one of the earliest Protestant denominations to organize was the Methodists. As early as the 1850s, the Reverend John Wesley DeVilbiss began circuit riding in Bandera and Medina. After years of meeting in homes, blacksmith shops, and brush arbors, the Bandera Methodist Church formally organized in 1867. Pictured above is the church and parsonage as they appeared in 1902. (Courtesy of Judy Goodenough.)

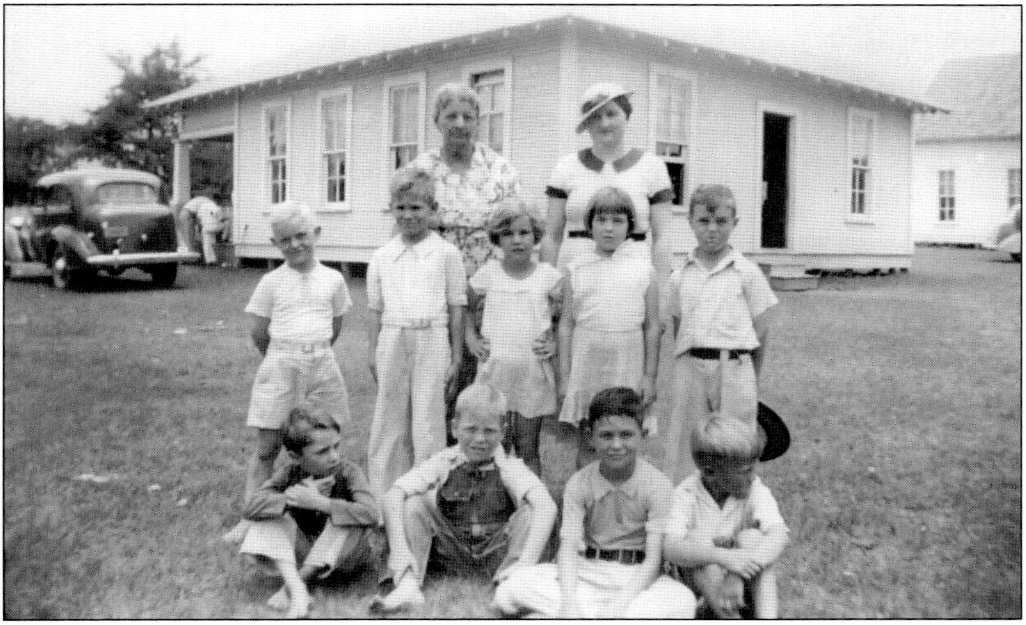

The three largest denominations in the county are Methodist, Baptist, and Catholic. The First Baptist Church, at the corner of Pecan and Thirteenth Streets, was founded in 1883. This group of youngsters posed on the church ground and includes Ray Marvin Hay (second row, far left), who would grow up to be Bandera's first mayor. (Courtesy of the Bandera County Historical Commission.)

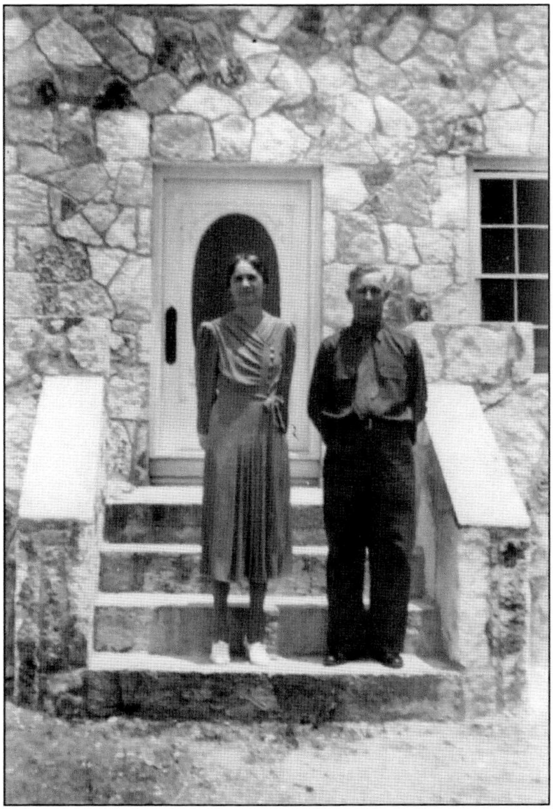

The Little Rock Church was built in 1931 on land Minnie Edwards had set aside to use for a church. Tommy and Myrtle Lewis are pictured on the church steps. Bandera County was without a Presbyterian church in 1985, when 10 families met to form a fellowship. In 1986, Lawrence Edwards gave approval for the use of the church, and the Pipe Creek Presbyterian Church was established. (Courtesy of Patsy Small.)

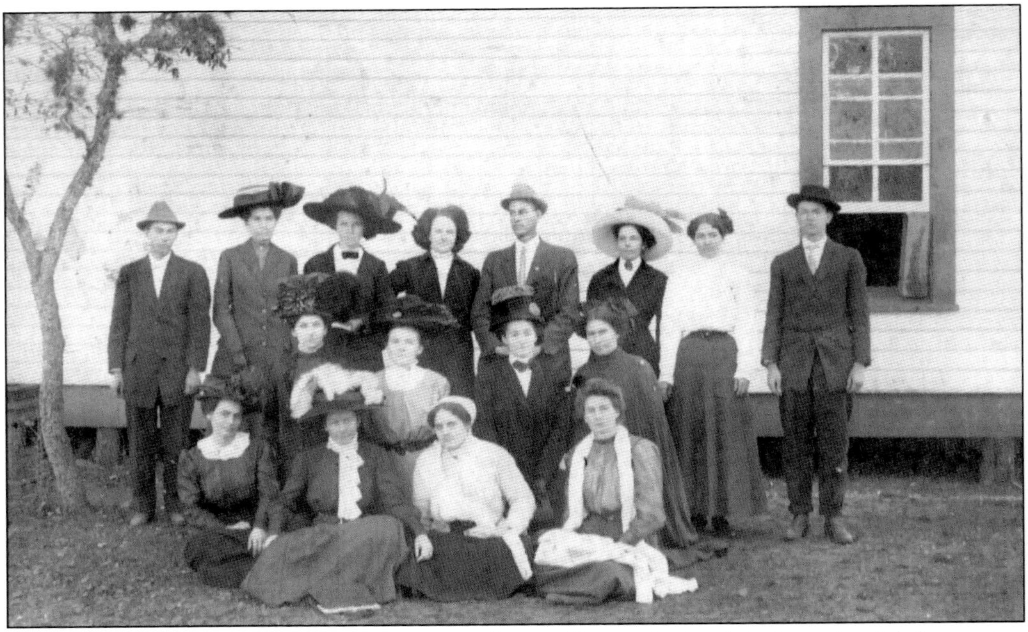

In the late 19th and early 20th centuries, teachers in Texas obtained their credentials by passing exams. To prepare for them, teachers from rural areas such as Bandera County would attend short courses and institutes sponsored by the county superintendent of schools. This 1910 photograph, identified as "Students of Bandera Public School Teaching," more than likely depicts one of those institutes. (Courtesy of Bandera County Historical Commission.)

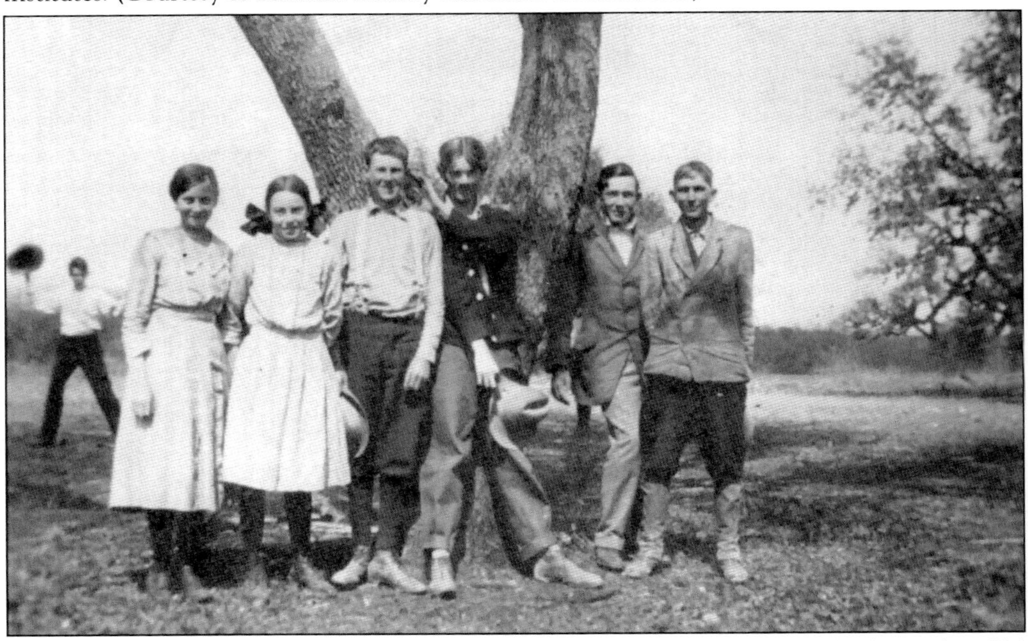

At one time, small schools were located throughout the county. Some schools had just a handful of students, such as this class from Winans Creek. Classes were often held in rough-hewn cabins that lacked indoor plumbing. Children walked long distances or, if they were lucky, rode horseback. By the mid-20th century, smaller schools were incorporated into the larger schools of Bandera and Medina. (Courtesy of Theresa Helbert.)

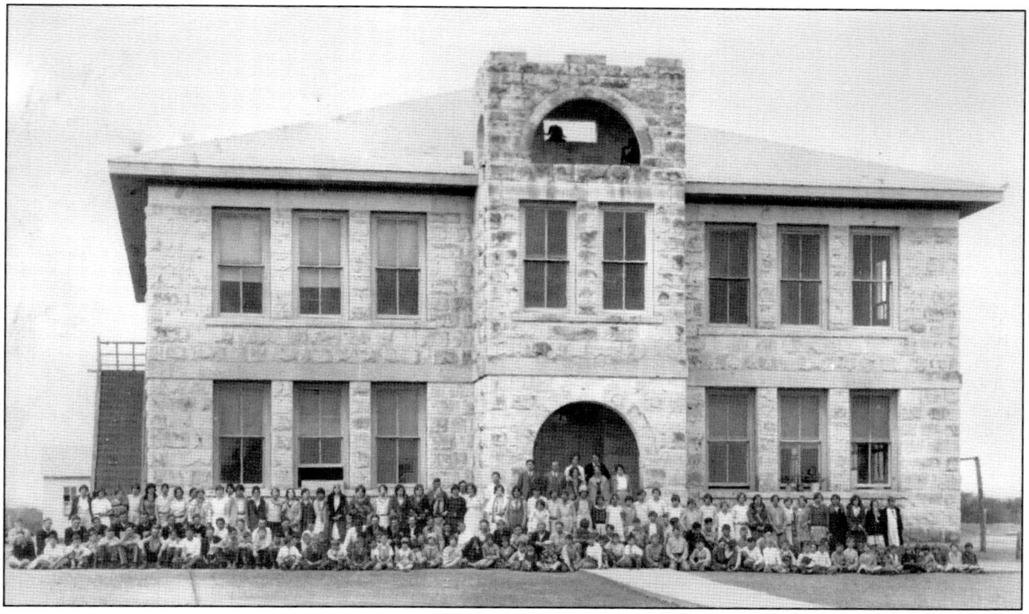

The "old rock building," as it was commonly referred to in Bandera, is situated on the current Bandera Middle School campus and was completed in 1910. For many years, it housed all of Bandera's students. During the Great Depression, the Works Progress Administration (WPA) added an additional structure nearby. A visit to Bandera's Independent School District's four modern campuses today would illustrate the tremendous growth of the past 100 years. (Courtesy of Bandera County Historical Commission.)

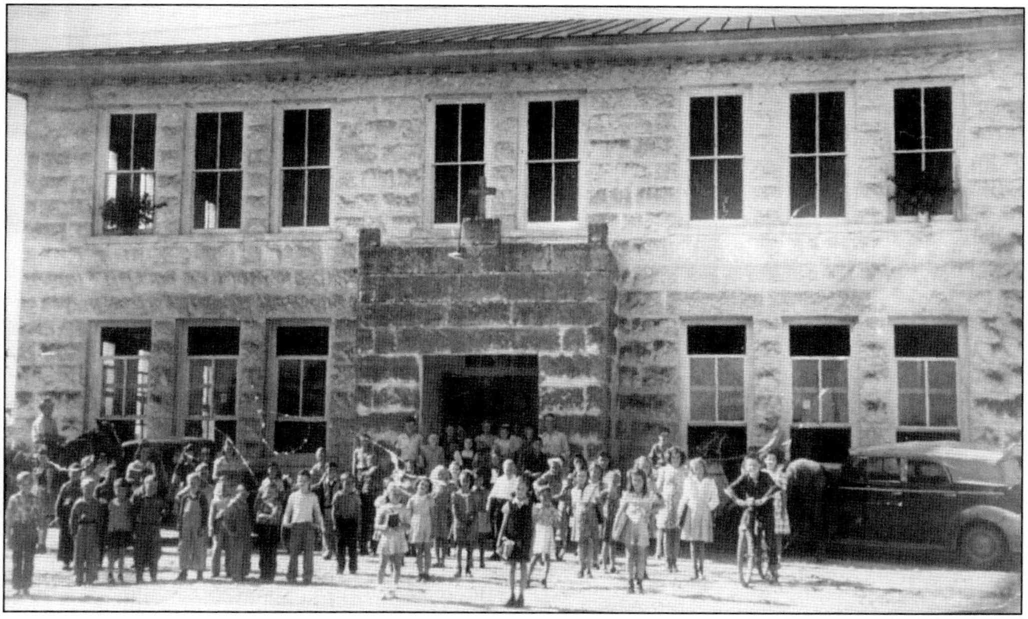

Compare this photograph of the St. Joseph School of St. Stanislaus to the one of the "old rock building," and notice the remarkable similarity. That is because the builder and contractor agreed to use the same set of plans to save the church money. Church members also donated their time and talents to complete the school in 1923, at a total cost of $9,684.12. (Courtesy of Elenora Dugosh Goodley.)

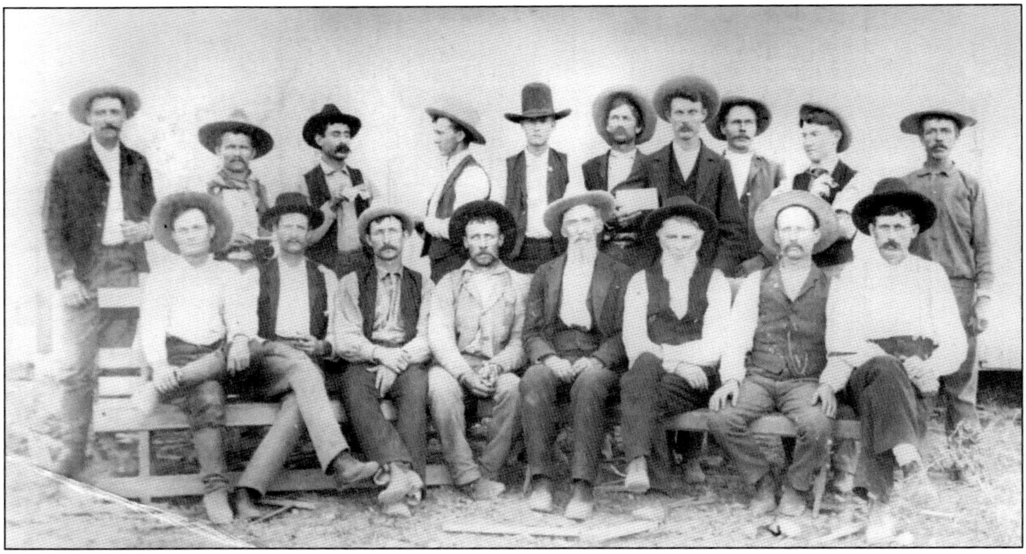

Stockman John W. Evans acquired the Polk horse ranch in Hondo Cañon in 1897, then opened it to stock farmers for settlement. By 1899, the settlers had established a cotton gin, a general store, and a school, and had named the town Tarpley. This group of gentlemen from Tarpley proudly had their picture taken on Election Day, no doubt to show their civic pride. (Courtesy of the Frontier Times Museum Collection.)

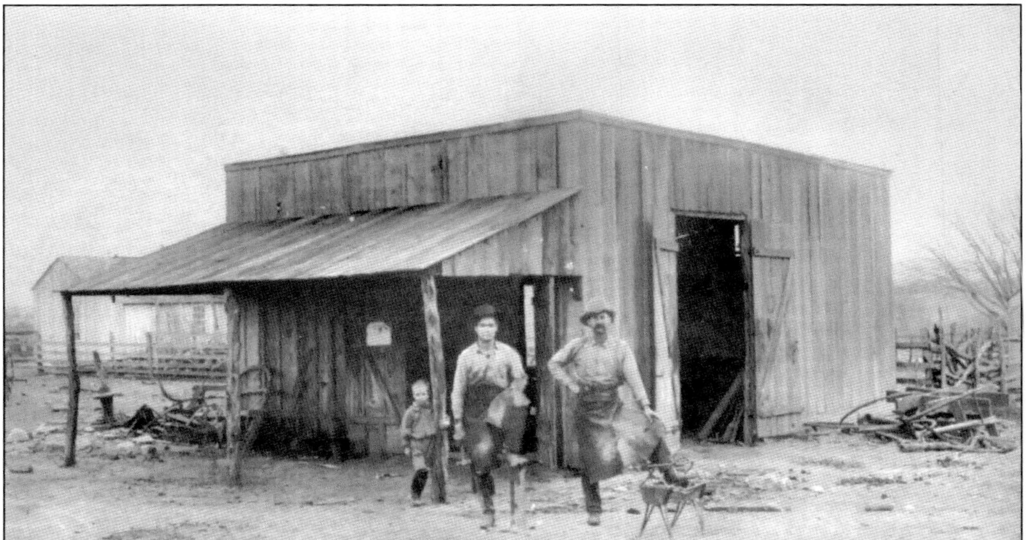

Blacksmith shops were found in most settlements throughout the county. This photograph shows Joseph "Dick" Johnston, George Johnston, and Bascom "Backy" Johnston at the blacksmith shop in Medina. Medina was a bustling town with a hotel, a cotton gin, a corn mill, general stores, a bank, and a saloon. Its population declined when Real County was created from a large section of northwestern Bandera County in 1913. (Courtesy of Linda Buckelew.)

Mr. and Mrs. Marion Van Cleave operated a gristmill on Mill Creek near Vanderpool. A dam above the mill caught the water that was channeled through a ditch to the waterwheel as soon as a gate in the ditch was opened. Farmers were left waiting to grind their corn if the water was not flowing. Waiting for the waters to rise could sometimes take days. (Courtesy of the Bandera County Historical Commission.)

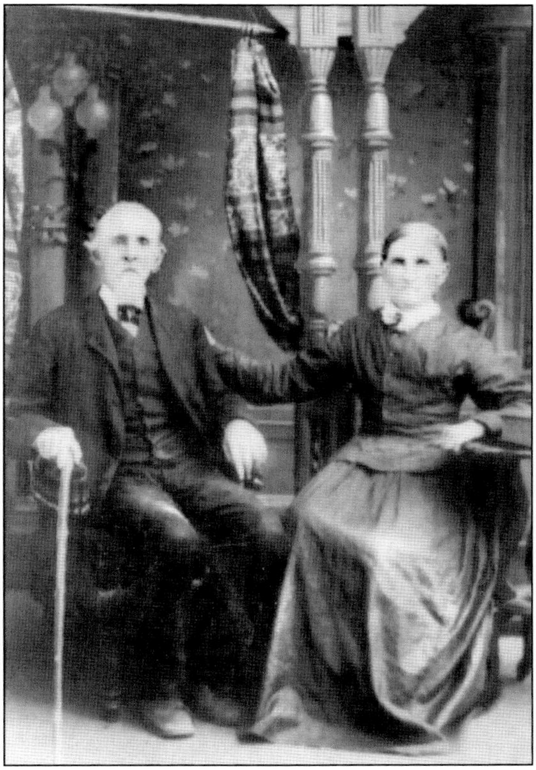

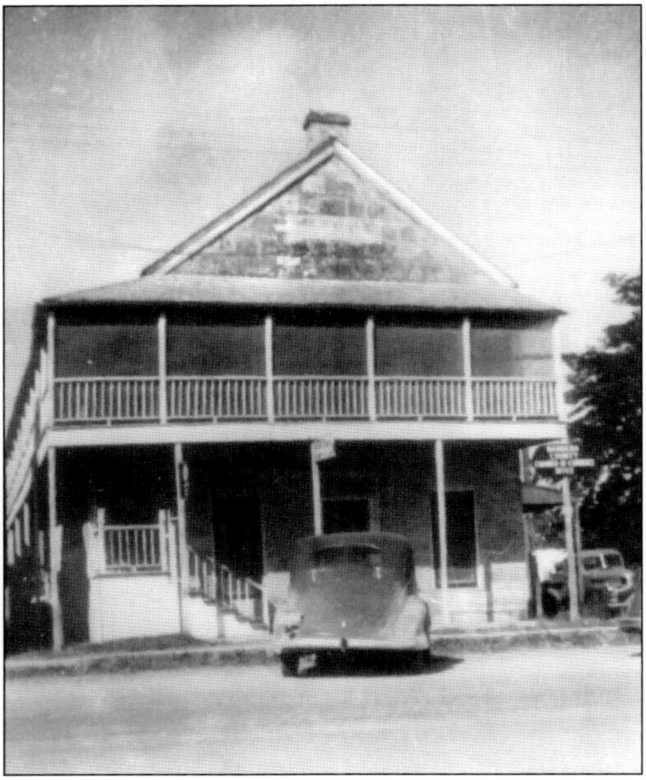

In 1906, the first bank of Bandera County opened in this rustic building on the corner of Eleventh and Cedar Streets, becoming First State Bank in 1910. Robbers hit the bank in 1932. Using a torch, they burned a hole in the top of the safe, grabbed $4,000, and left behind a single dollar bill. They were never caught, despite the best efforts of the Texas Rangers. (Courtesy of the Bandera County Historical Commission.)

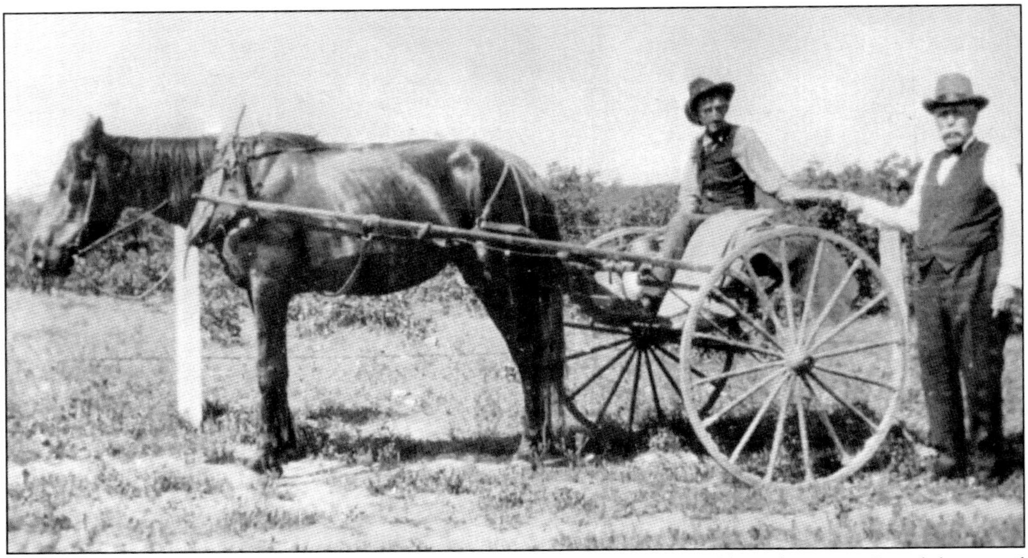

Bandera's first settlers received mail irregularly by way of Castroville. Christian Santleben and his son August were contracted to bring the mail to Bandera by horseback. Fourteen-year-old August carried a six-shooter for protection, since skirmishes with area Native Americans were still common. He recalled he made the 64-mile round-trip at least 100 times. Renne Allrid Sr. (seated in buggy), contracted to deliver the mail by buggy, certainly had better working conditions. (Courtesy of the Frontier Times Museum Collection.)

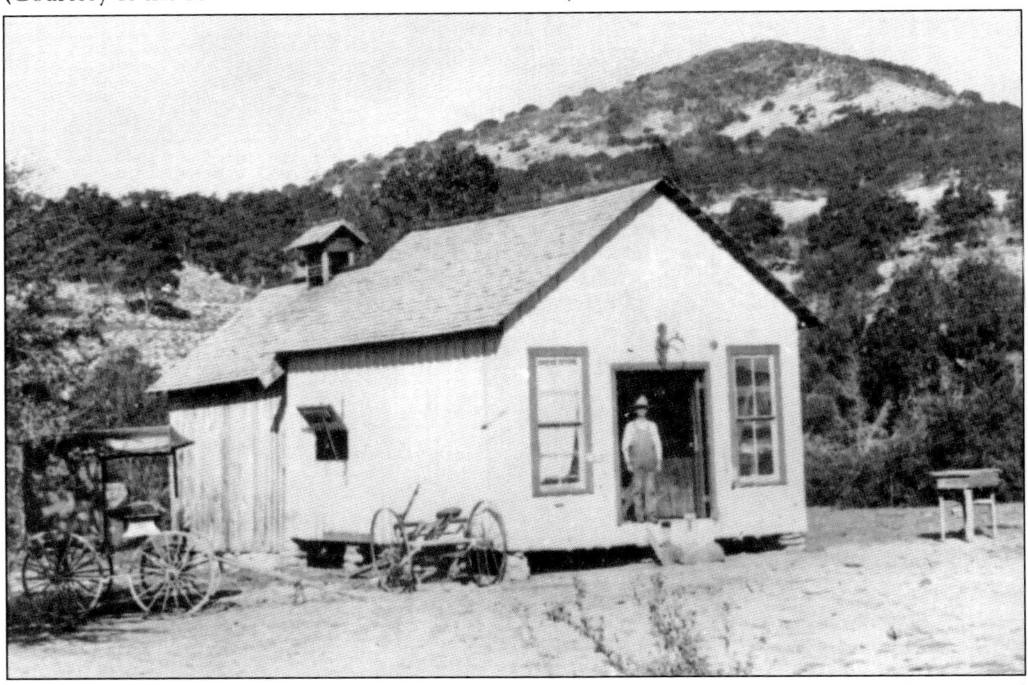

Many small settlements throughout Bandera County had their own post offices. The original post office serving a small settlement along Williams Creek was named Hondo Cañon and was established in 1878. In 1899, the post office was moved farther south, and Wiley John Prickett Jr. was made postmaster. The settlement was renamed Tarpley, which was a common family name in the Pickett family. (Courtesy of the Frontier Times Museum Collection.)

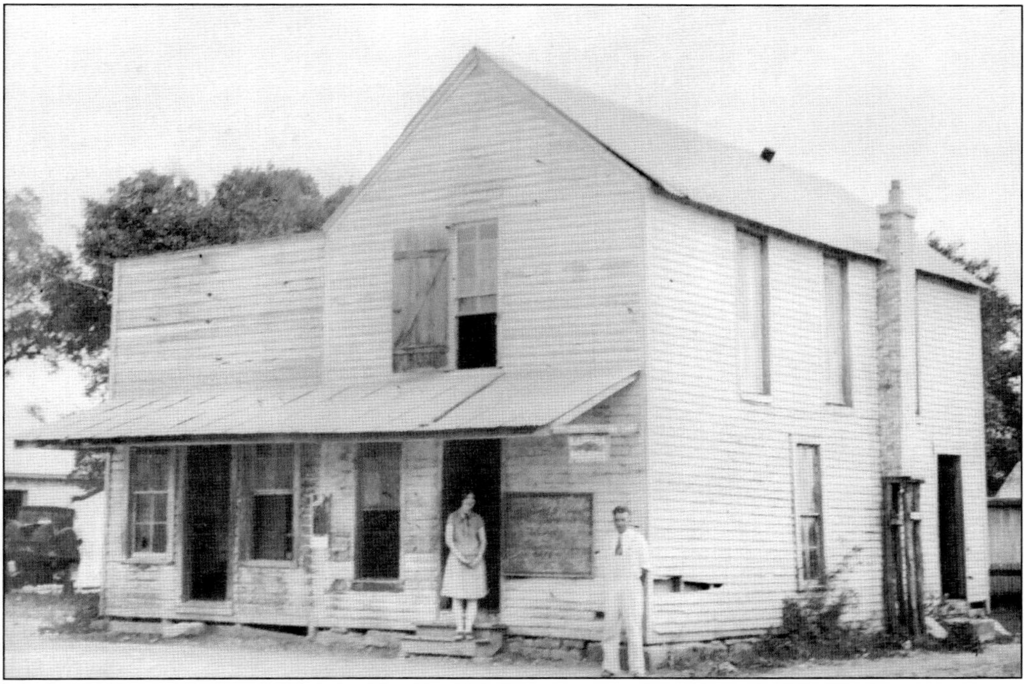

Since mail arrived only once a week, Amasa Clark described in his memoirs that he would read the Galveston newspaper a little at a time to make it last until the next mail delivery. Early Bandera merchants would set up makeshift post offices in their stores. This ramshackle building served as Bandera's first official post office when seven-day mail service was established in 1929. (Courtesy of Bandera County Historical Commission.)

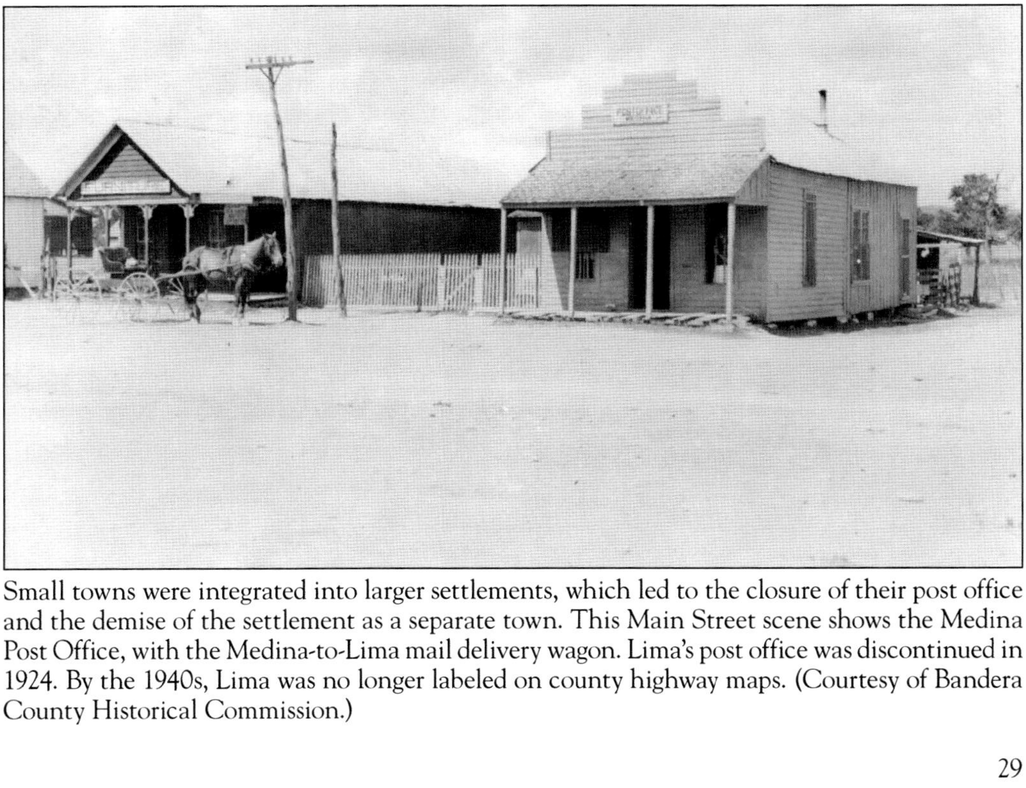

Small towns were integrated into larger settlements, which led to the closure of their post office and the demise of the settlement as a separate town. This Main Street scene shows the Medina Post Office, with the Medina-to-Lima mail delivery wagon. Lima's post office was discontinued in 1924. By the 1940s, Lima was no longer labeled on county highway maps. (Courtesy of Bandera County Historical Commission.)

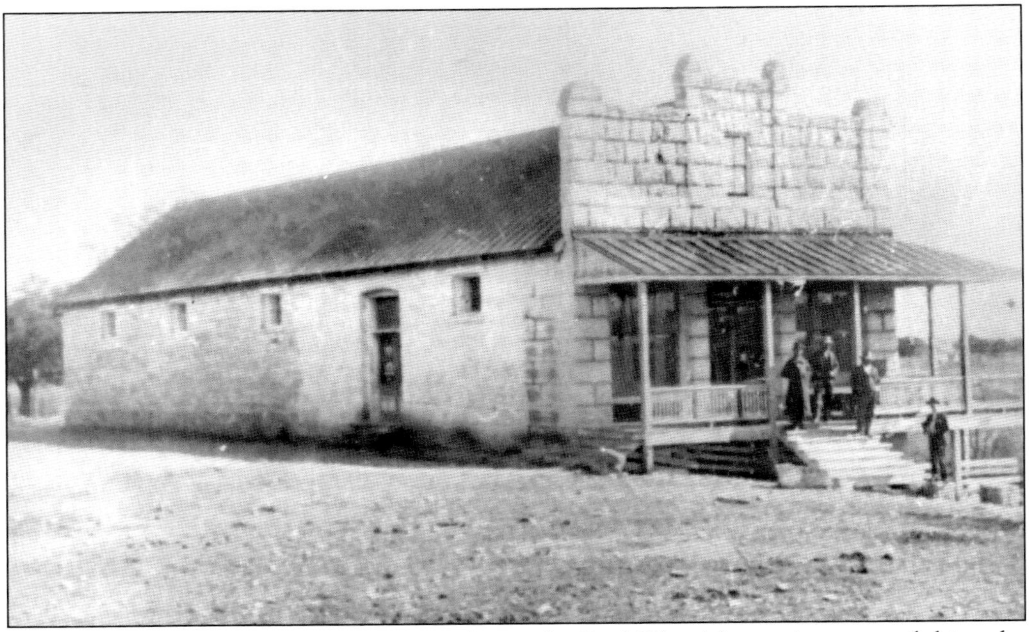

H. H. Carmichael came to Texas as a teen during the Civil War. After a stint as a trail driver, he opened a mercantile store in Bandera. During good times, he lived in a Southern-style mansion on Hackberry Street. He suffered great losses in the economic panic of 1893 and was forced to close the store. Today his home is a hotel. (Courtesy of the Frontier Times Museum Collection.)

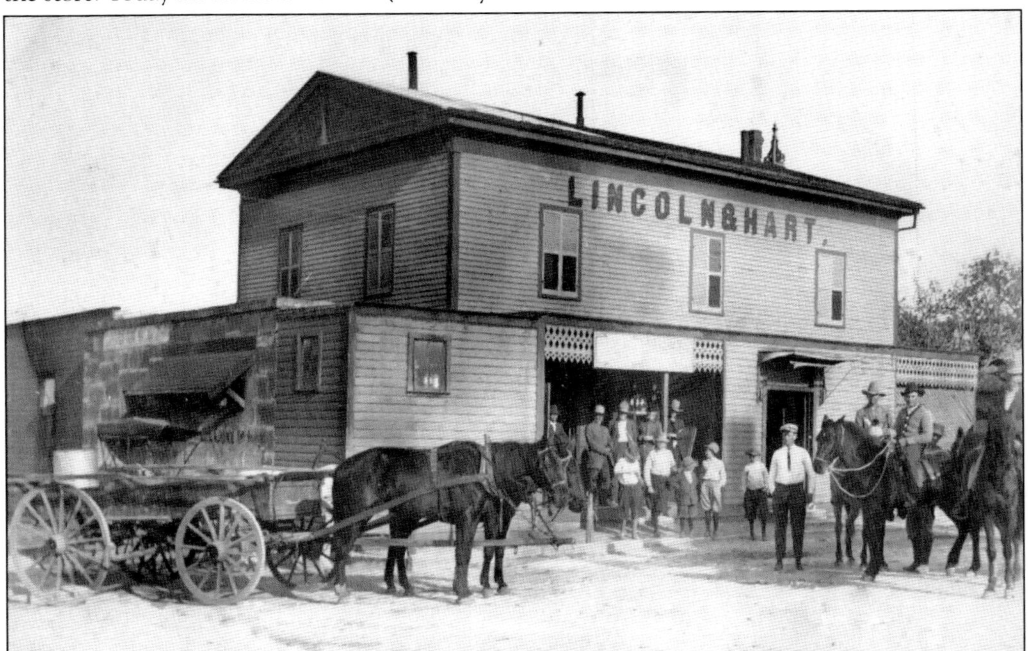

Judge George Lincoln and James Hart fancied themselves as sheep ranchers after arriving in Bandera in the 1870s. When they failed at this venture, Hart began work in the H. H. Carmichael store. When Carmichael closed the business, they bought his stock and opened Lincoln and Hart. Along with selling patented drugs, they sold their special screwworm killer, called "Hell on Screwworms." Sales were good, so it must have worked. (Courtesy of Annette Kalka-Schulte.)

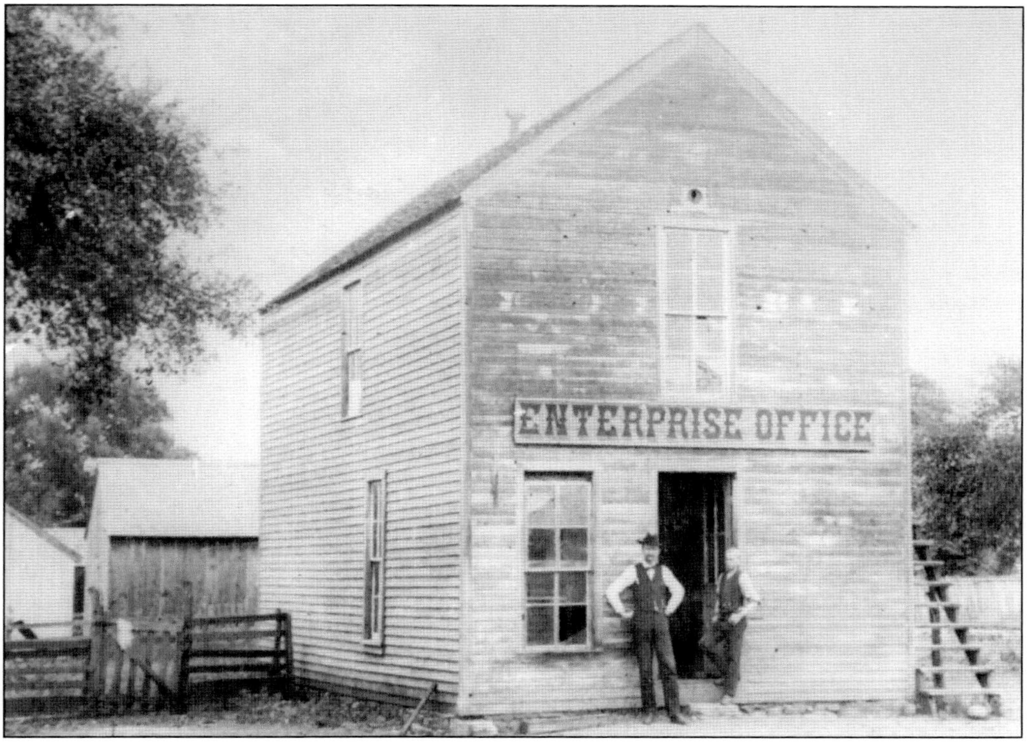

Bandera's first newspaper, the *Bandera Bugle*, was not published until 1880, twenty-seven years after the first settlers set up camp along the Medina River. In 1883, William Hudspeth and S. F. Chambers established the *Bandera Enterprise*, and since then, Bandera has been a two-newspaper town. The *Enterprise* went through several owners until the newspaper building burned down in 1915, and it ceased publication. (Courtesy of the Frontier Times Museum Collection.)

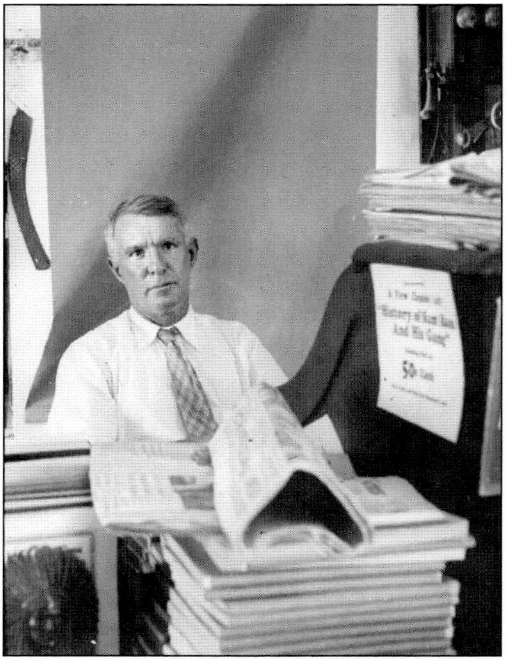

The *Bandera New Era* was established in 1916, and like the *Enterprise*, went through several owners until J. Marvin Hunter Sr. (pictured at right) moved to Bandera in 1921 and purchased the weekly newspaper. His *New Era* put community news items on the front page under clever headings like "Tuff Topics" and "Lima Lines," both towns that no longer exist. Hunter ceased *New Era* publication in 1935, but he started another newspaper, the *Bandera Bulletin*, in 1945. (Courtesy of the Frontier Times Museum Collection.)

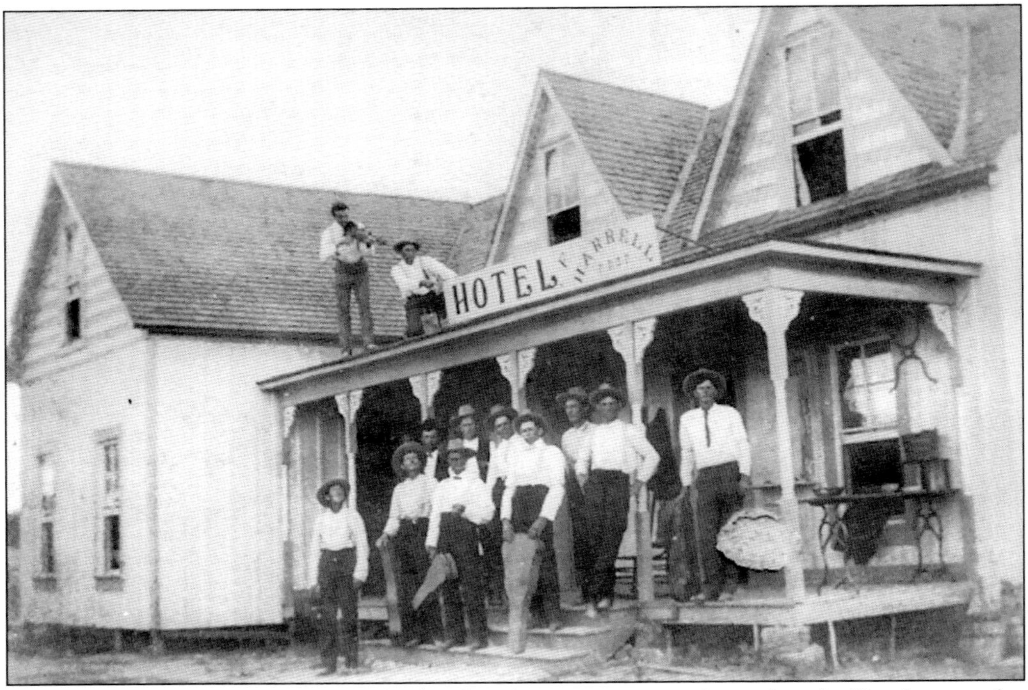

By the mid-1880s, Bandera was at the height of its prosperity with two hotels. Hotels were also opened in Medina and Tarpley. The first house built in Tarpley became a hotel in 1899 when the Buckner family began renting rooms in their home to travelers. A favored guest was Vice Pres. John Garner, who visited while traveling to his home in Uvalde, Texas. (Courtesy of the Bandera County Historical Commission.)

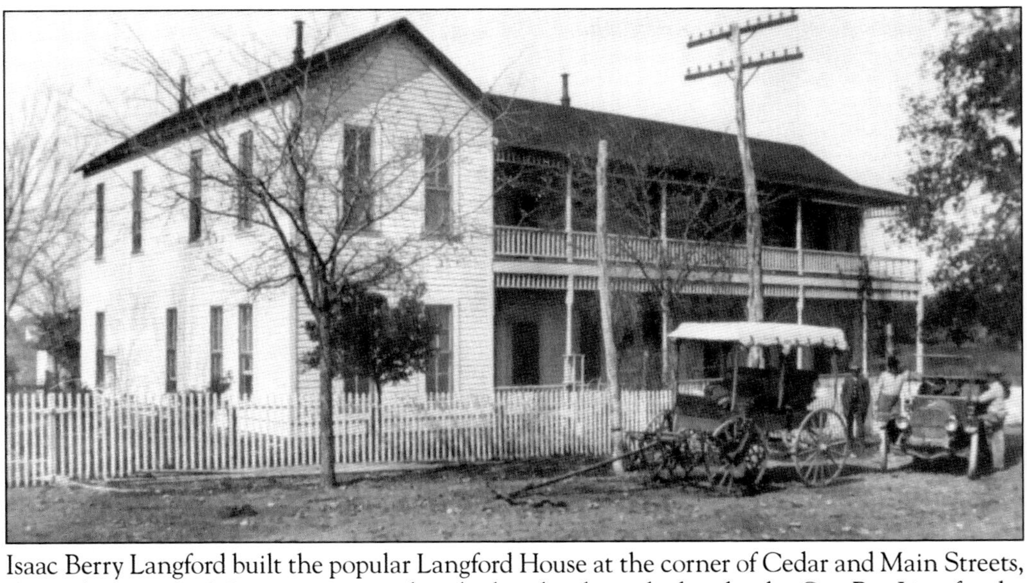

Isaac Berry Langford built the popular Langford House at the corner of Cedar and Main Streets, shown here in 1915. Passengers waited at the hotel to be picked up by the Cox Bus Line for the four-hour trip to San Antonio. The trip would take longer if the road was muddy. The bus would have to wait for mule teams to pull it through the bad spots. (Courtesy of Lauren Langford.)

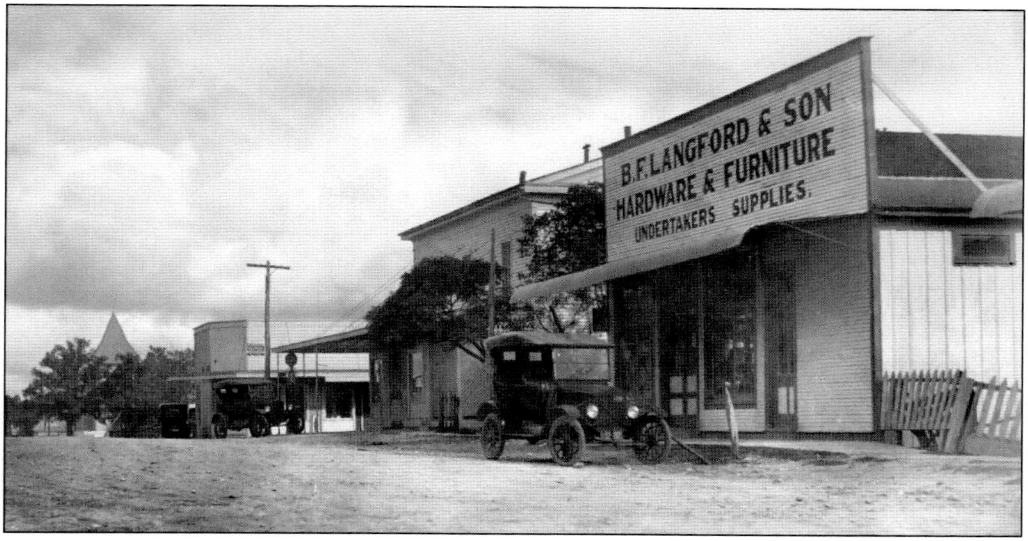

Isaac Langford was not only a hotel owner, but he was also Bandera's first undertaker. Along with his brother Benjamin, Isaac opened B. F. Langford and Son on Bandera's Eleventh Street. At the time, Eleventh Street was Bandera's Main Street. The store sold hardware, furniture, and undertaker supplies. In 1936, John Langford bought into the business and opened a funeral parlor next door. He also operated the county's first hearse ambulance service. (Courtesy of Bandera County Historical Commission.)

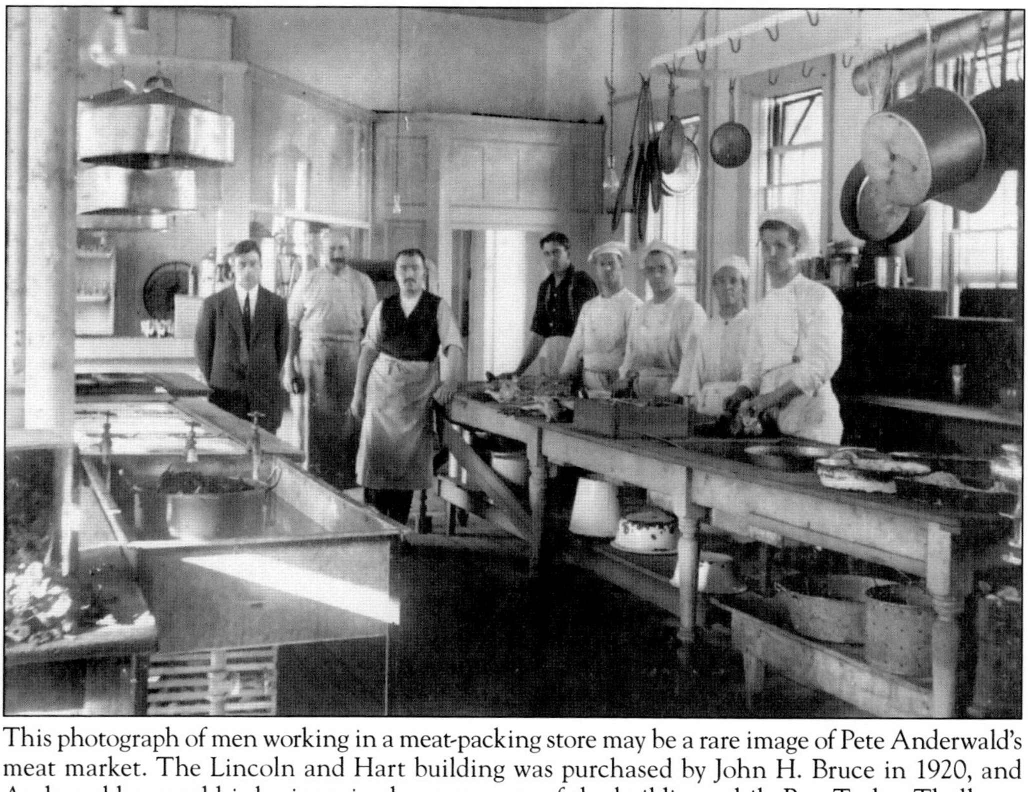

This photograph of men working in a meat-packing store may be a rare image of Pete Anderwald's meat market. The Lincoln and Hart building was purchased by John H. Bruce in 1920, and Anderwald opened his business in the west room of the building, while Roy Tucker Thallman had a cleaning and pressing shop in the lower east room. (Courtesy of Lauren Langford.)

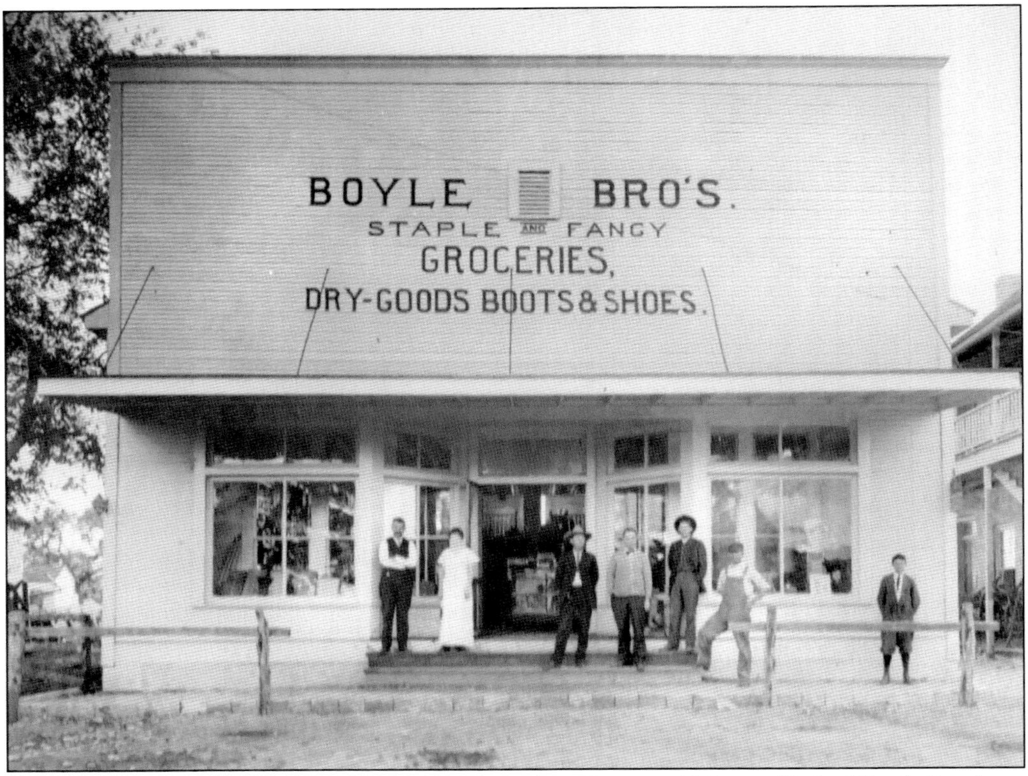

Jim and Mike Boyle, Irish immigrants who arrived in Texas in 1901, established Boyle Brothers. Tom joined his brothers in 1916. The woodstove in the back and the washer pitch out front were favorite gathering spots. The store contained a soda fountain and sold everything from saddles, to women's millinery, to fresh, butchered meat that was iced down with large blocks of ice from the local icehouse. (Courtesy of Johnny Boyle.)

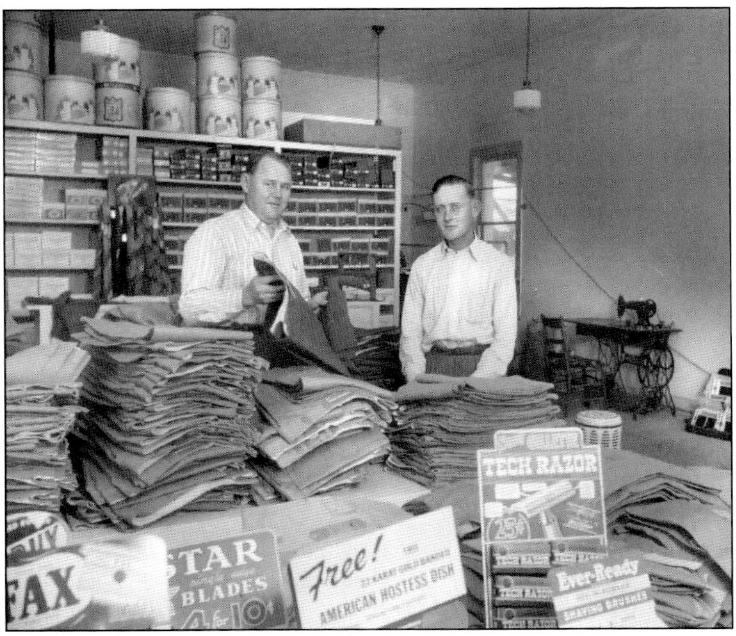

The building that now houses Stein's Clothiers was built around 1918 and was originally a grocery store operated by Henry Ward Stevens Jr. In 1941, Robert Stein (left) and Louis Stein opened their clothing store. Still operating today by Bobbie and Mary Stein, Stein's stocks Western clothing for local residents and was the first store in Bandera to carry Levi jeans, which cost $3.50 a pair. (Courtesy of Bobbie and Mary Stein.)

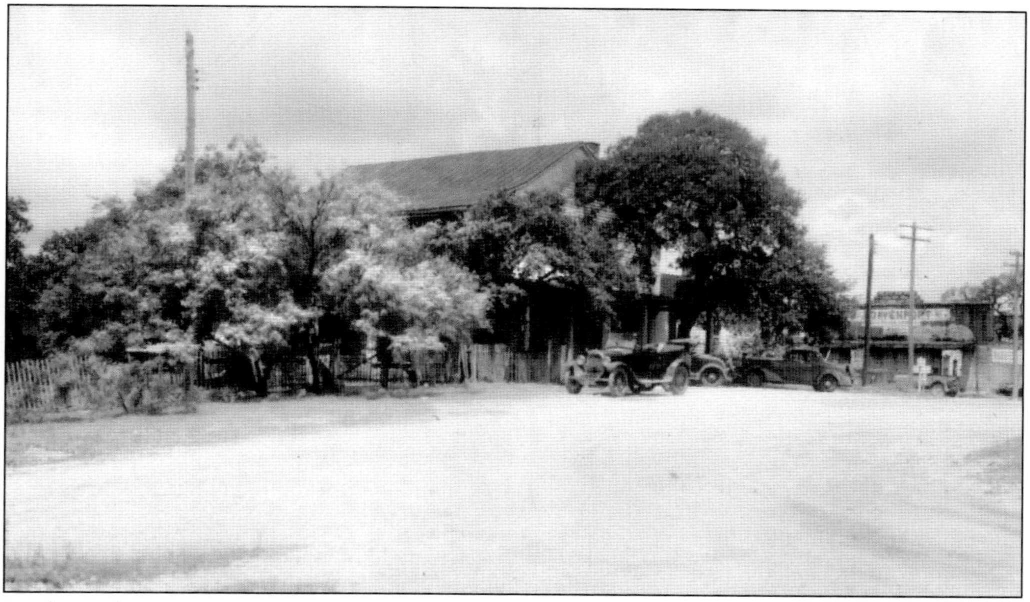

By the early 1900s, Bandera County began receiving modern amenities. The first electric light and power plant was installed in 1928. A waterworks system was installed in 1945, followed by a sewage system. With all the comforts brought by such modern amenities, the picture above shows that Bandera still maintained a rustic atmosphere for many years. (Courtesy of Christopher Baumle.)

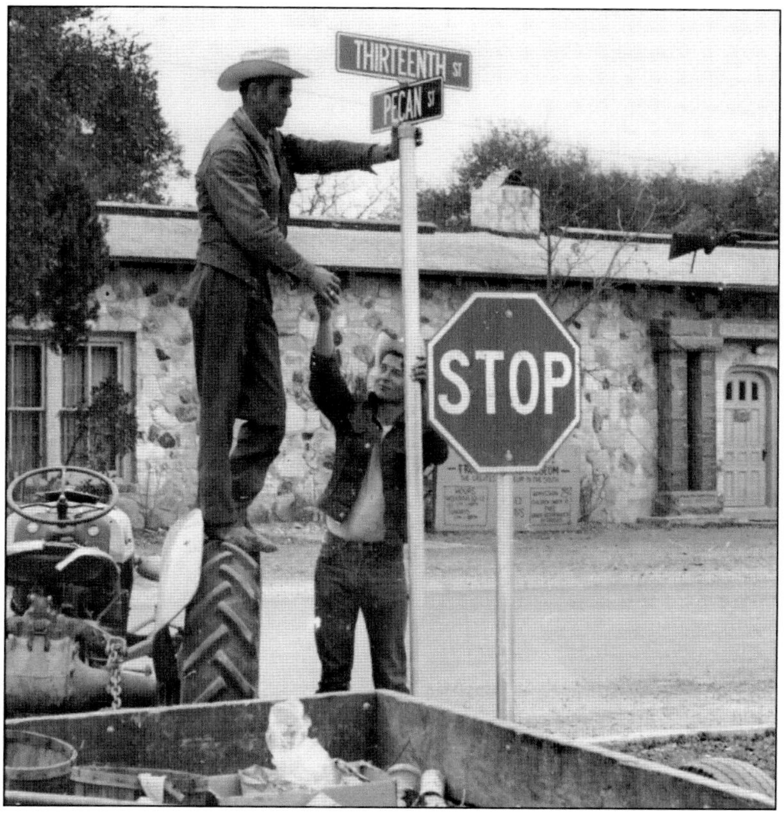

This photograph was labeled, "Street signs come to Bandera." Bandera values individual ruggedness and independence, so it was with a degree of wariness that incorporation of the city was approved. In 1964, residents elected their first mayor, Ray Marvin Hay, and their first city council. With incorporation came more development, such as paved roads throughout the city and street signs. (Courtesy of the Frontier Times Museum Collection.)

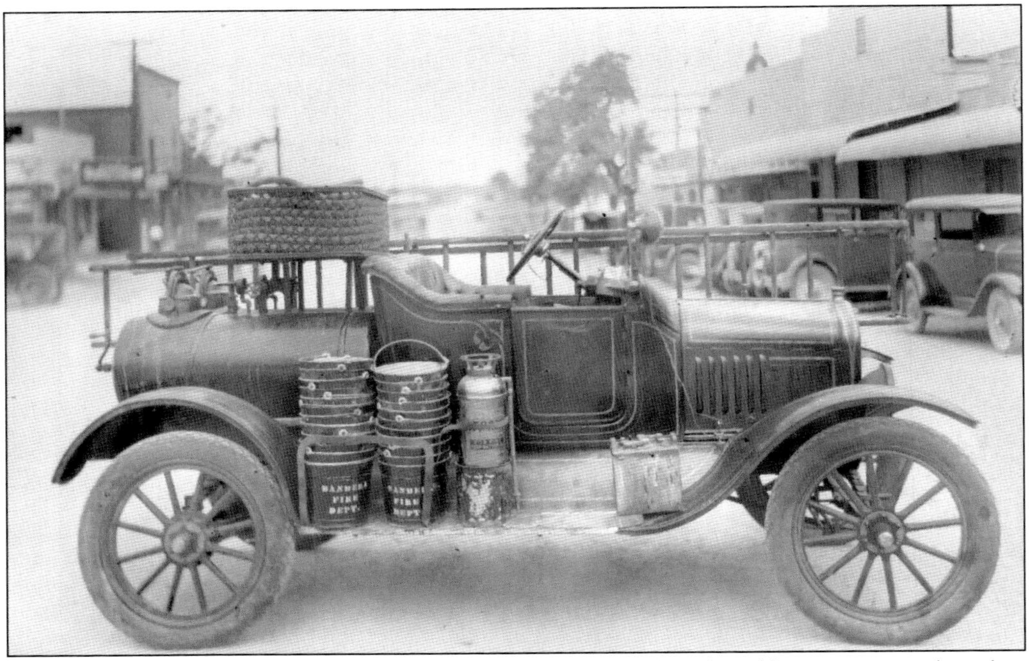

As towns grew, the need arose for residents to be provided with public services such as law enforcement and fire protection. In 1915, a fire destroyed several buildings in downtown Bandera, and a volunteer fire department was formed the next day. Frank Mansfield served as fire chief for many years. Firefighting is crucial in Bandera County, especially during times of drought. Today volunteer fire departments are established throughout the county. Bandera's volunteer fire department was in the forefront of firefighting technology when it purchased this early fire trunk. It appears from this photograph that buckets of water were the primary means of dousing a fire. By the 1940s, the fire department was ready to upgrade again and did so with a more modern and sleek fire trunk, shown below with Mansfield (left) and Walter Ruge. (Both, courtesy of Bandera County Historical Commission.)

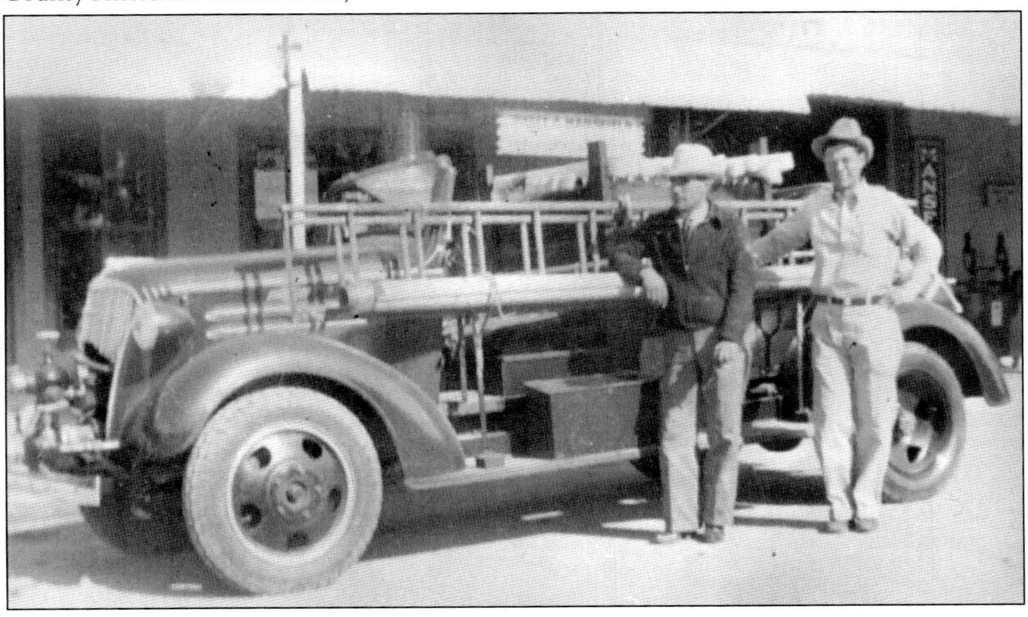

Three

LIVING OFF THE LAND

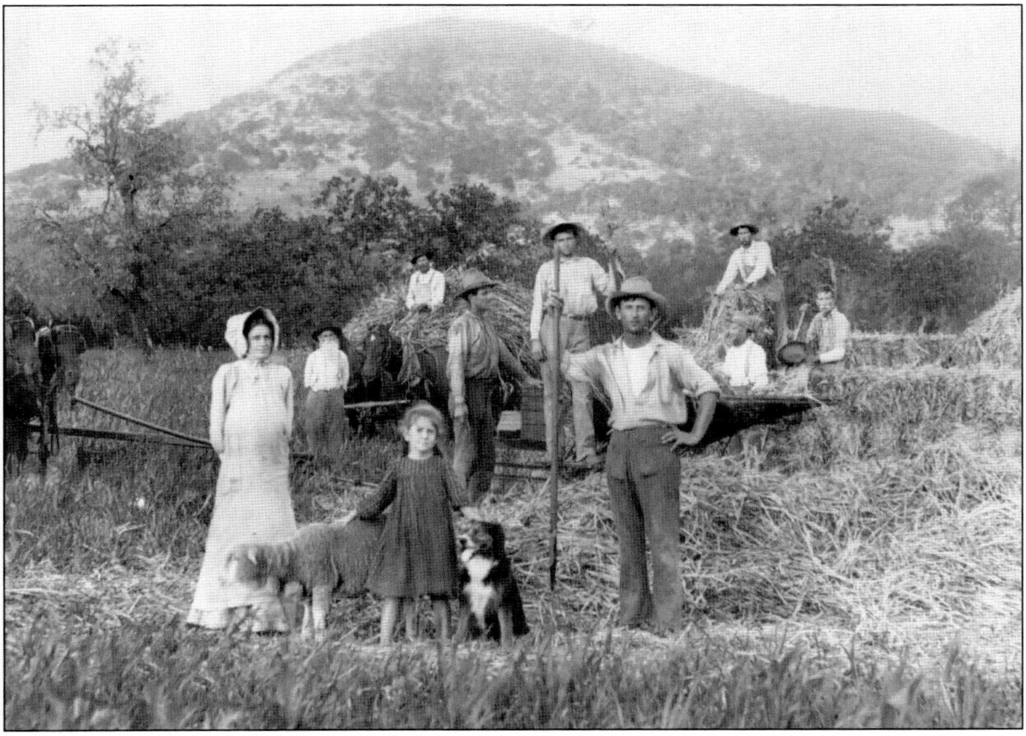

The relatively flat land of the valleys below the hills of Bandera County was used for farming. Neighbors and immigrant workers would help each farmer harvest their crops. In good years, farmers would bring their crops to San Antonio to sell and trade for supplies. As late as the 1920s, crops were loaded onto wagons to make the difficult journey over unpaved roads. (Courtesy of the Bandera County Historical Commission.)

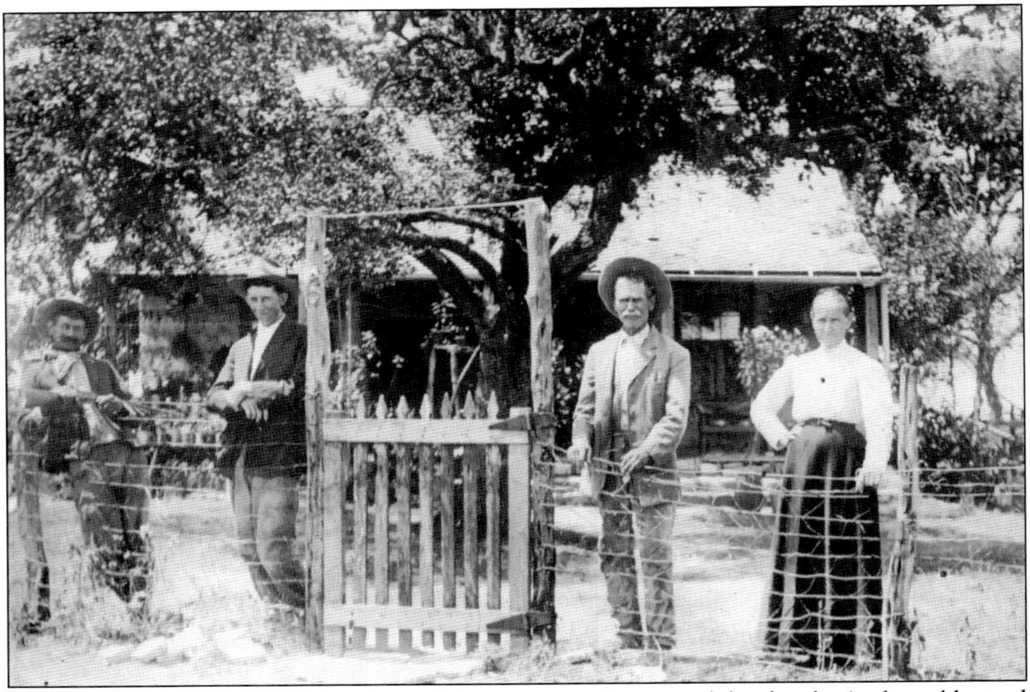

John C. Anderwald is pictured in front of the Anderwald home with his family. Anderwald raised livestock and grew tobacco and cotton. His brother Gabe helped John build his house, and Gabe later established his own Lazy "A" Ranch in 1874, where he grew cotton, tobacco, corn, sugarcane, and raised livestock. (Courtesy of Annette Kalka-Schulte.)

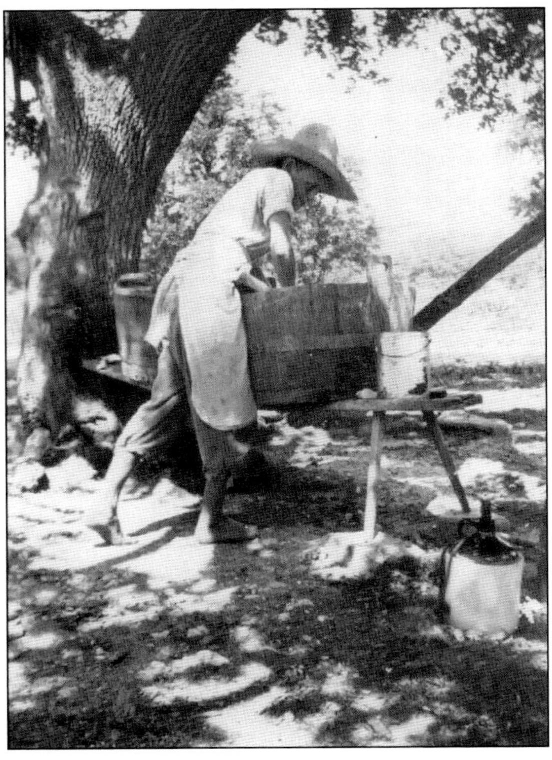

Everyone did chores on a farm, including Ignatius "Nick" Kalka, a third-generation family member on the Oak Mound Farm. He was caught by the camera doing his laundry. (Courtesy of Annette Kalka-Schulte.)

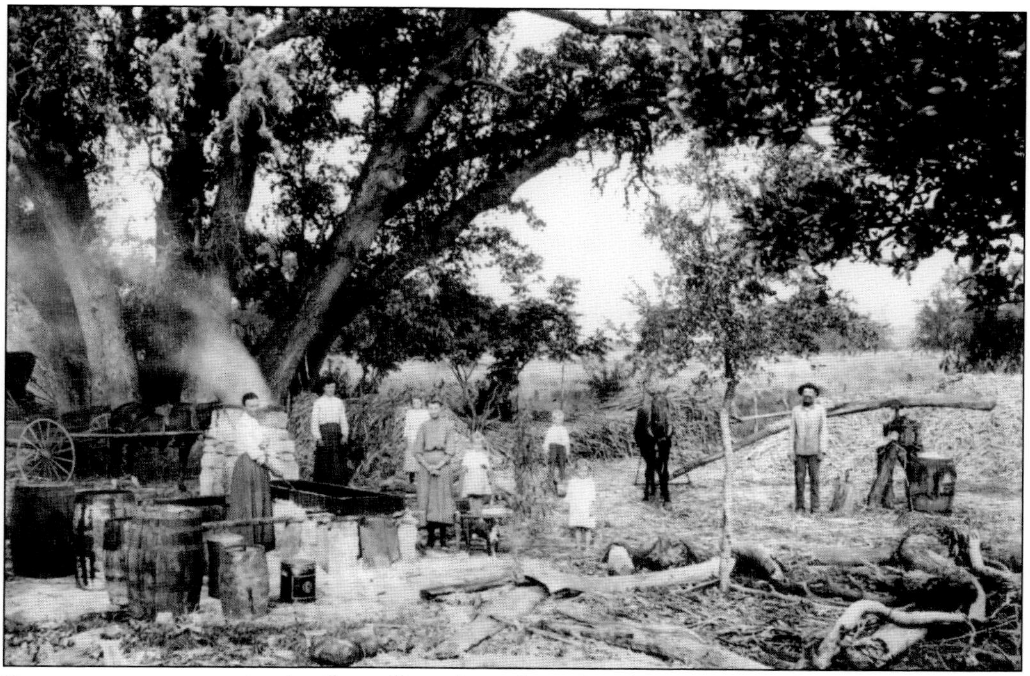

Sugarcane was grown in the flat valleys throughout Bandera County. John Dugosh produced molasses at his molasses pit on the Dugosh farm, located on San Julian Creek. This picture of the family hard at work was taken in the early 1900s. (Courtesy of the University of Texas at San Antonio's Institute of Texan Cultures.)

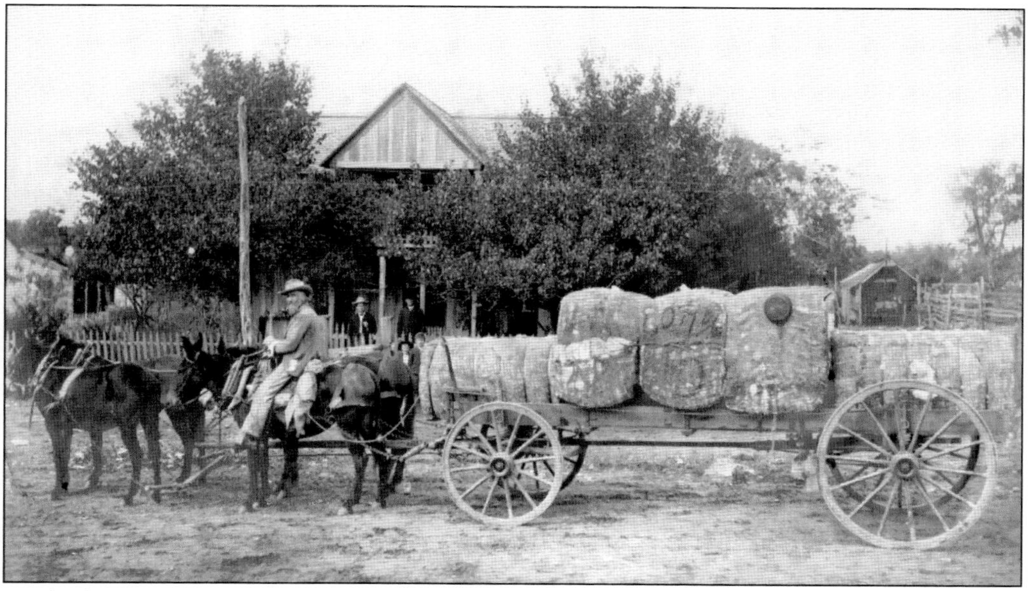

By the late 1800s, as large-scale farming was introduced, cotton became the third-largest crop grown in Bandera County. Around this time, the San Antonio and Aransas Pass Railroad extended its line to Center Point and Kerrville, northeast of Bandera. Wagons hauled cotton to gins and the railroad for distribution. Cotton remained profitable through World War I, but an infestation of boll weevils devastated the crops, and cotton was no longer cultivated. (Courtesy of Lauren Langford.)

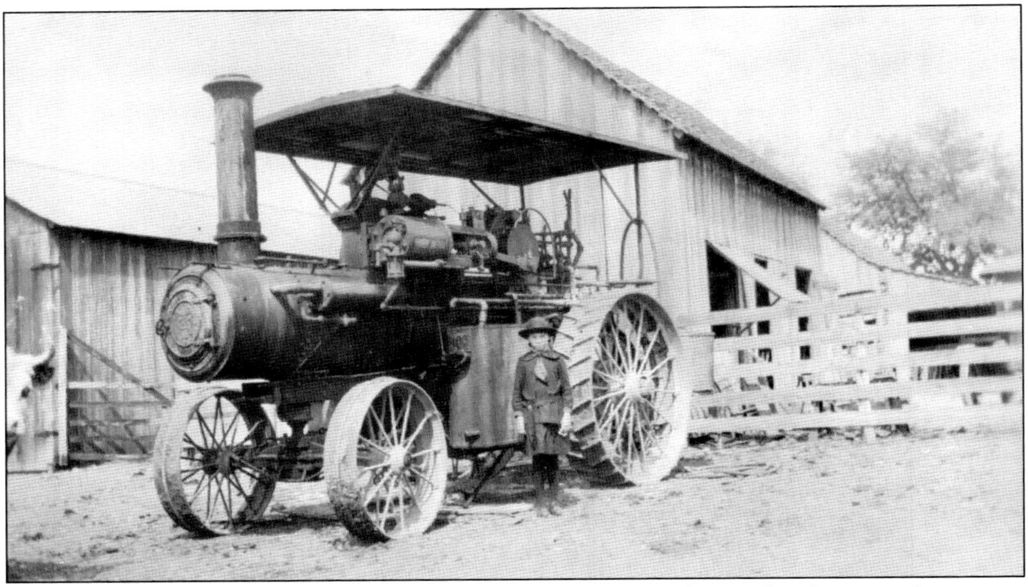

The Algueseva brothers were among the first to use a power-driven threshing machine, seen here in 1912. The Algueseva brothers traveled the county renting their services to local farmers. The thresher was driven by a big steam engine, which resembled a railroad locomotive. In a 1985 edition of the *Bandera County Historian*, Laura Newcomer Schott recalled that farmers often did not have money to give to the Alguesevas, so they were paid in shares—one half of the crop harvested. The farmer's share was placed in one stack and the thresher's share in the other stack. The arrival of the large machine was exciting enough for farmers to line their children in front of the thresher to take pictures. (Above, courtesy of Betty Laskowski D'Spain; below, courtesy of the Bandera County Historical Commission.)

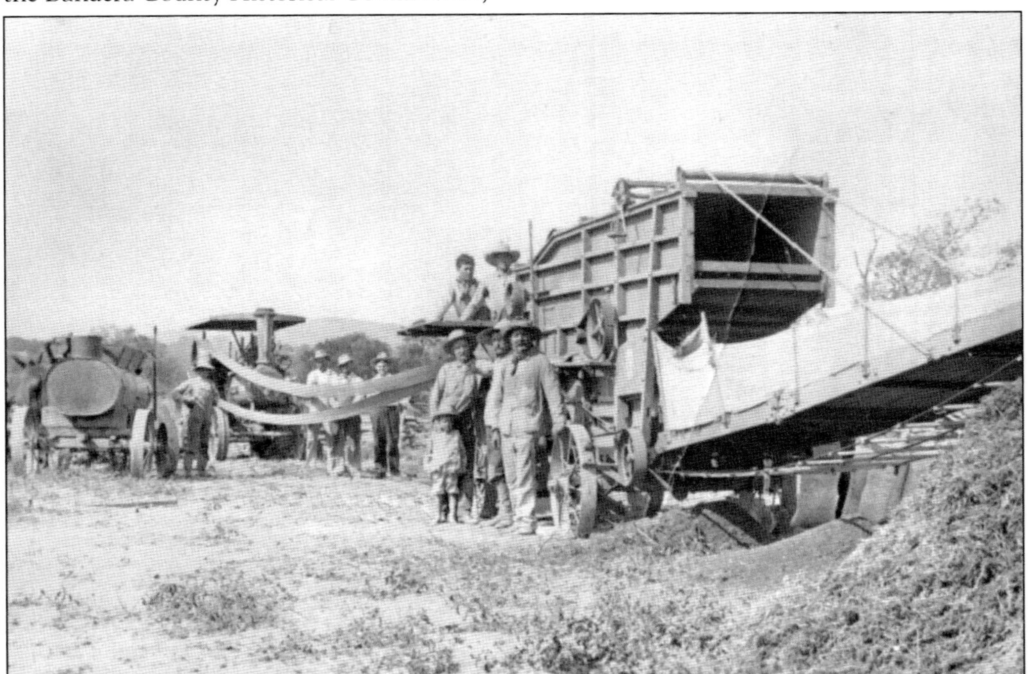

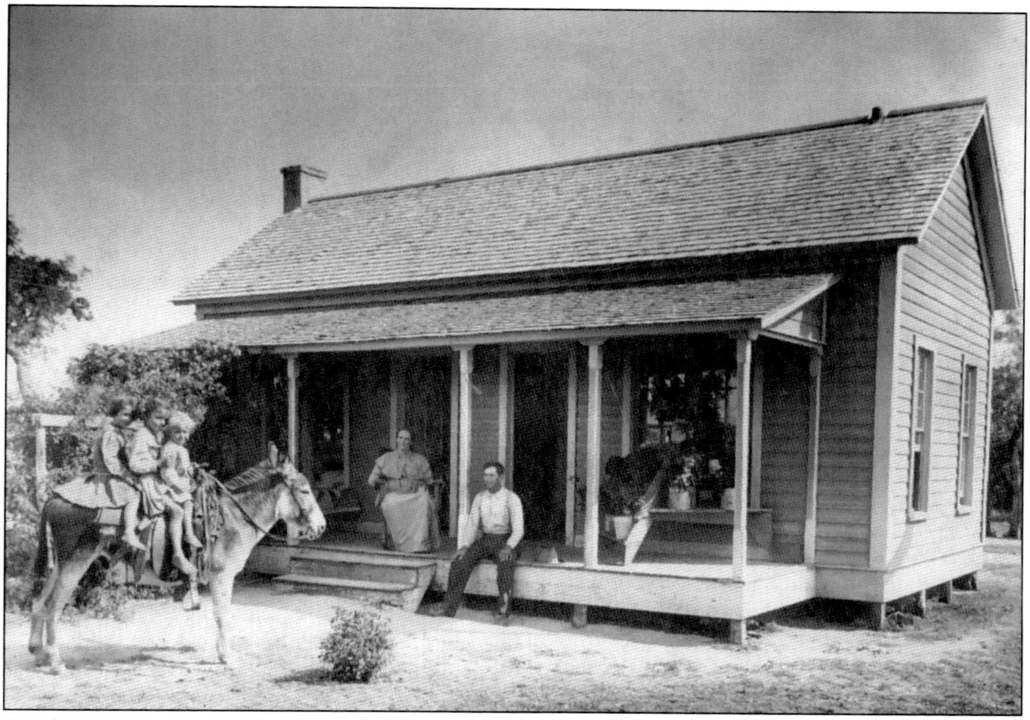

Cattle was raised throughout Bandera County, though the terrain was not suitable for large herds. Cattle raisers managed their herds and could be profitable if they were good businessmen. In this early photograph of Joe Newcomer, he sits on the porch of his home with his wife, Maud Alice, while their children enjoy a donkey ride. Newcomer would later become a leading cattleman, who was successful in raising and selling cattle. (Courtesy of the Carr-Newcomer-Stanard family.)

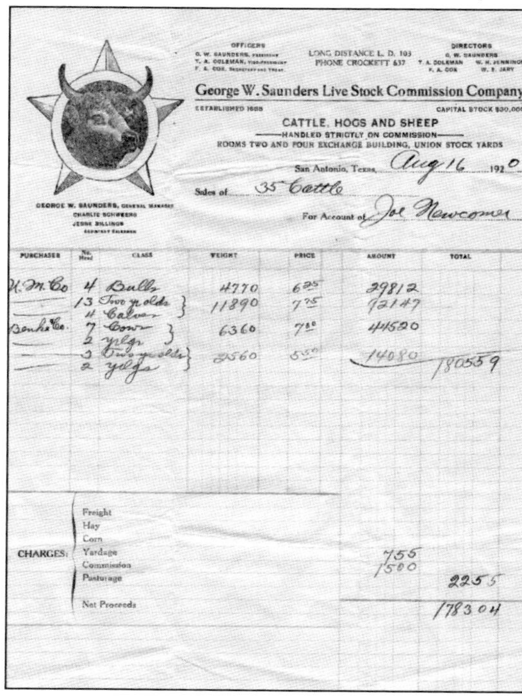

OFFICERS
LONG DISTANCE L. D. 103
PHONE CROCKETT 637
DIRECTORS

George W. Saunders Live Stock Commission Company

ESTABLISHED 1888
CAPITAL STOCK $30,000

CATTLE, HOGS AND SHEEP
HANDLED STRICTLY ON COMMISSION
ROOMS TWO AND FOUR EXCHANGE BUILDING, UNION STOCK YARDS

San Antonio, Texas, Aug 16 1920
Sales of 35 Cattle
For Account of Joe Newcomer

GEORGE W. SAUNDERS, GENERAL MANAGER
CHARLIE SCHWEERS
JESSE BILLINGS

PURCHASER	No. Head	CLASS	WEIGHT	PRICE	AMOUNT	TOTAL
U. M. Co	4	Bulls	4770	6.25	298.12	
	13	Two yr olds	11890	7.75	921.47	
	4	Calves				
Benke Co.	7	Cows	6360	7.50	415.20	
	2	ylgs				
	3	Two yr olds	2560	5.50	140.80	1805.59
	2	ylgs				

CHARGES: Freight, Hay, Corn, Yardage 7.55, Commission 15.00, Pasturage — 22.55
Net Proceeds 1783.04

Joe Newcomer did much of his business buying and selling cattle at the San Antonio Stockyard. This receipt, given to Newcomer, was from the George W. Saunders Livestock Commission. Saunders was a well-known cattleman whose company, at this time, was operating in Texas, Kansas, and Missouri. (Courtesy of the Carr-Newcomer-Stanard family.)

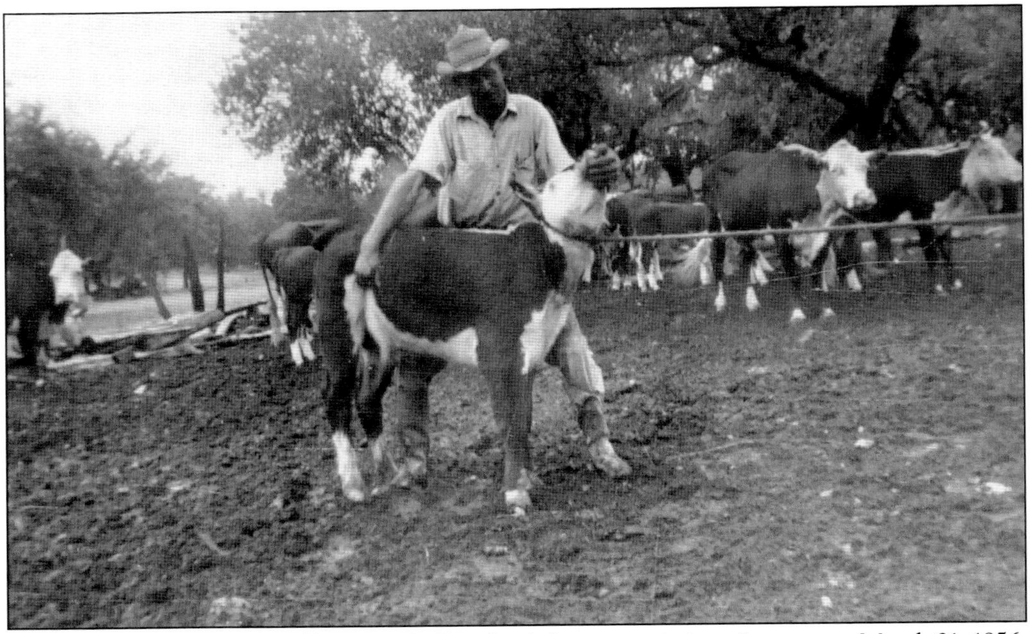

One of the primary orders of business for Bandera's first commissioner's court, on March 21, 1856, was to set up records for marks and brands to keep track of the cattle brought in by the early settlers. The registration fee of 50¢ was paid just three days later by the first person to register in the new county brand book, Abram Moncur, a member of the Mormon colony. He declared the Circle A brand to be his own. (Courtesy of the Bandera County Historical Commission.)

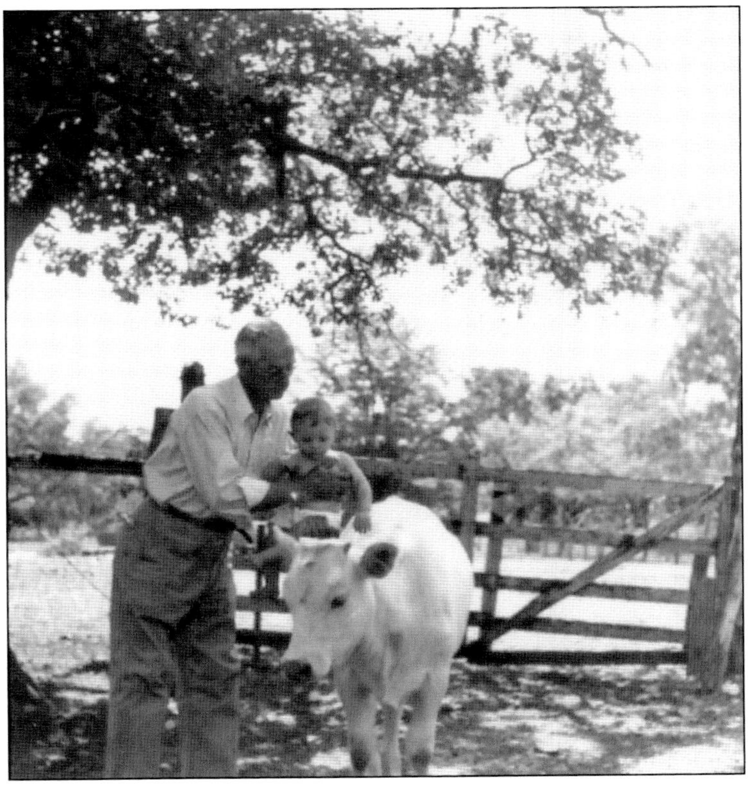

In 1936, the King Ranch brought the first Charolais cattle to the United States from Mexico. The Langford family of the Lazy L Ranches was a pioneer in developing the breed and exported the cattle all over the world. B. F. Langford Jr. and grandson Alan Langford are shown here in 1949 with one of the family's first Charolais heifers, Snow White. (Courtesy of Lauren Langford.)

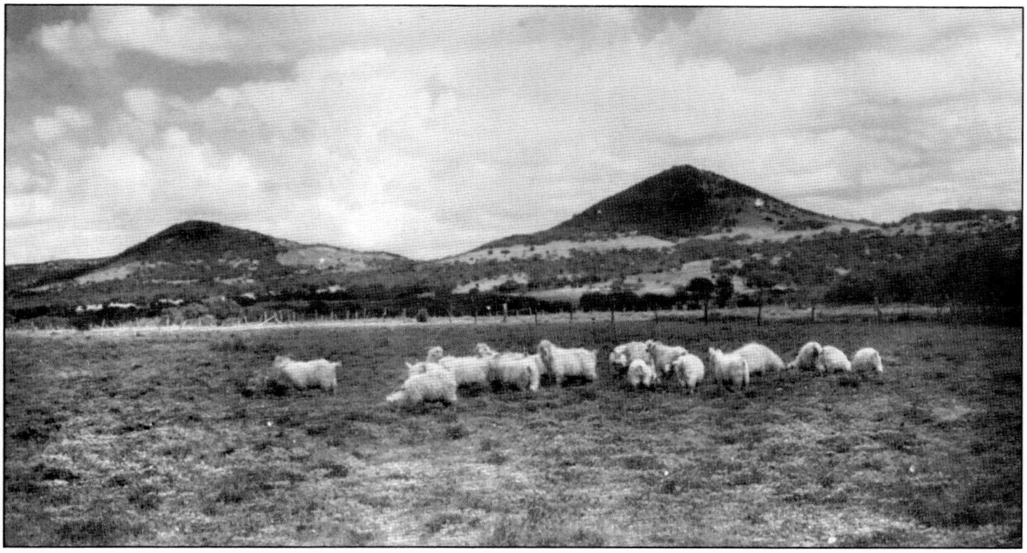

Mention Bandera County livestock and most would think "cattle." However, the land is better suited for sheep and goats. Shortly after the cattle-drive era, sheep replaced cattle as the primary livestock for the county. Bandera wool would be shipped to the railroad lines in Kerrville for sale and distribution. In the 1928 photograph above, goats from the R. N. Padgett ranch at Tarpley are pictured. (Courtesy of the Frontier Times Museum Collection.)

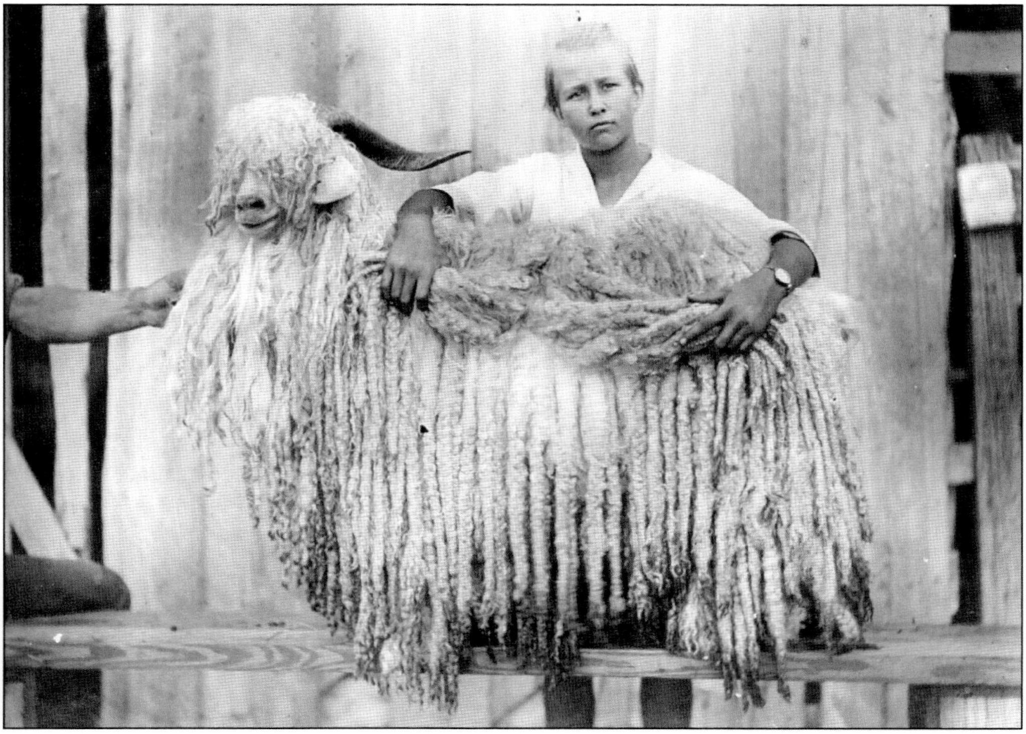

Angora goats thrived in Bandera County. It has even been suggested that a group of Basque herders settled here for that express purpose. Of prime importance was breeding to eliminate "kempiness"—the objectionable wiry fibers in mixed-breed goats. True mohair fibers are long and curly, as evidenced in the photograph above. (Courtesy of the Frontier Times Museum Collection.)

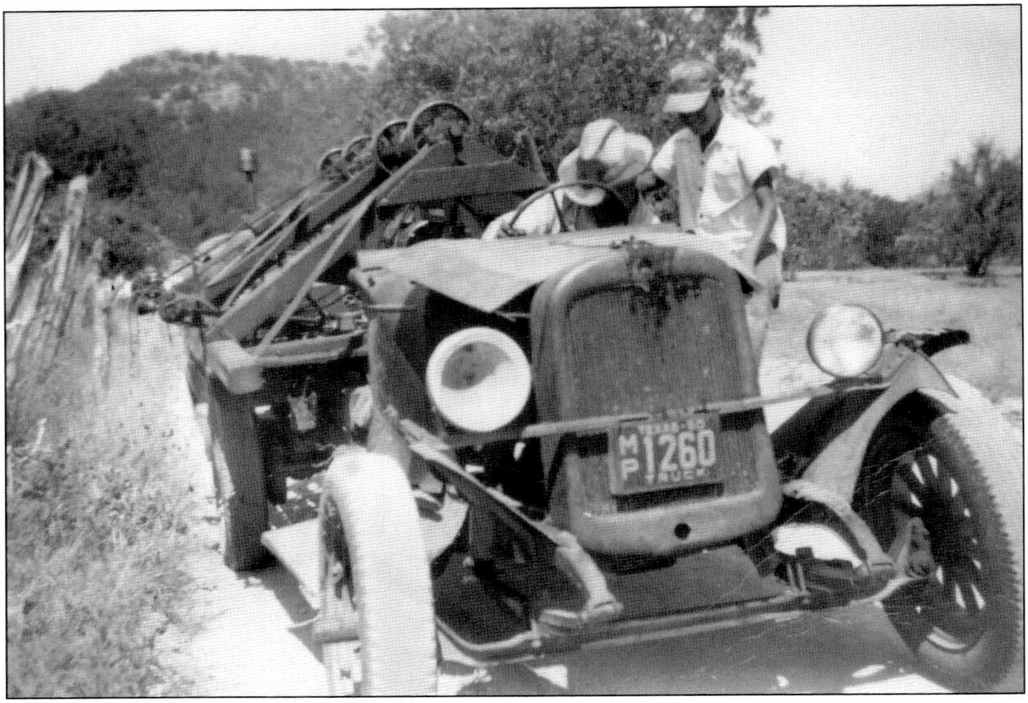

The Bandera County Ranchman and Farmers Association was organized in 1920 to expedite the selling of wool. In 1931, it was reported that 275,000 to 300,000 pounds of wool had been warehoused and shipped through the association. The demands of World War I and II increased the sale of wool, and Texas became the leading wool and mohair-producing state in the nation. The sheep and goats also provided a livelihood for people other than the county's ranchers. Crews would travel throughout the area to shear the livestock at the proper time. Raul Herrera and Paul Algueseva started their operation in 1950 and worked in Bandera and Medina. The photograph above shows their first shearing rig. Below, they are pictured in action. (Both, courtesy of Jerry Herrera.)

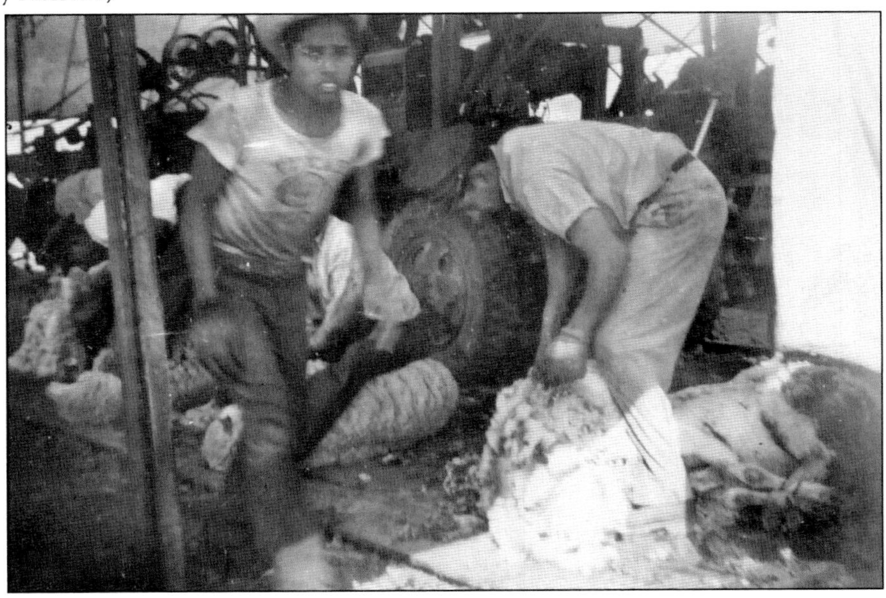

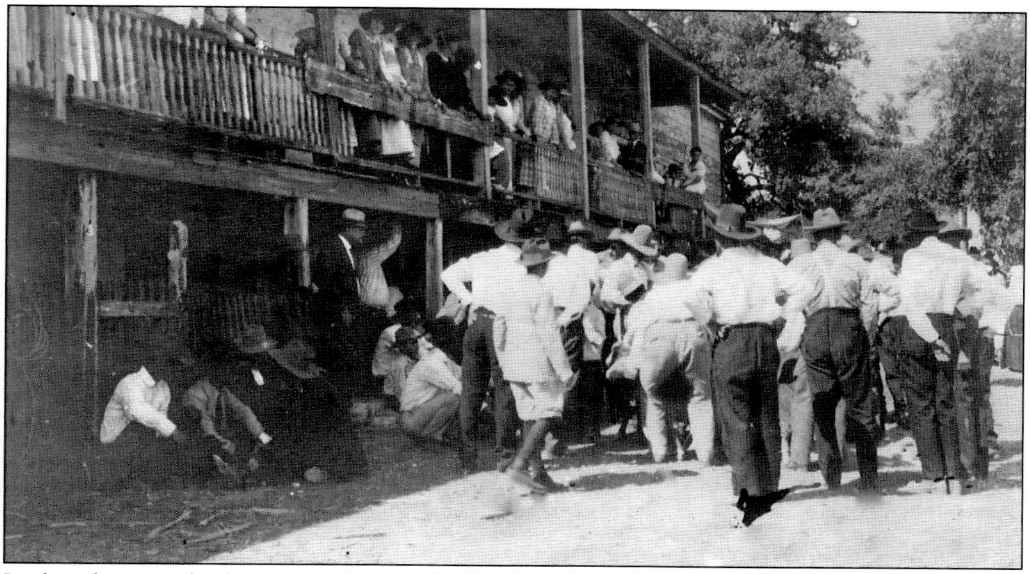

In this photograph, sheep are judged at the Bandera County Fair. Local sheep and goat ranchers entered their prize livestock in competitions held at the fair. Among the exciting, competitive events were density of fleece, oil in fleece, luster of fleece, and freeness from kemp. (Courtesy of the Bandera County Historical Commission.)

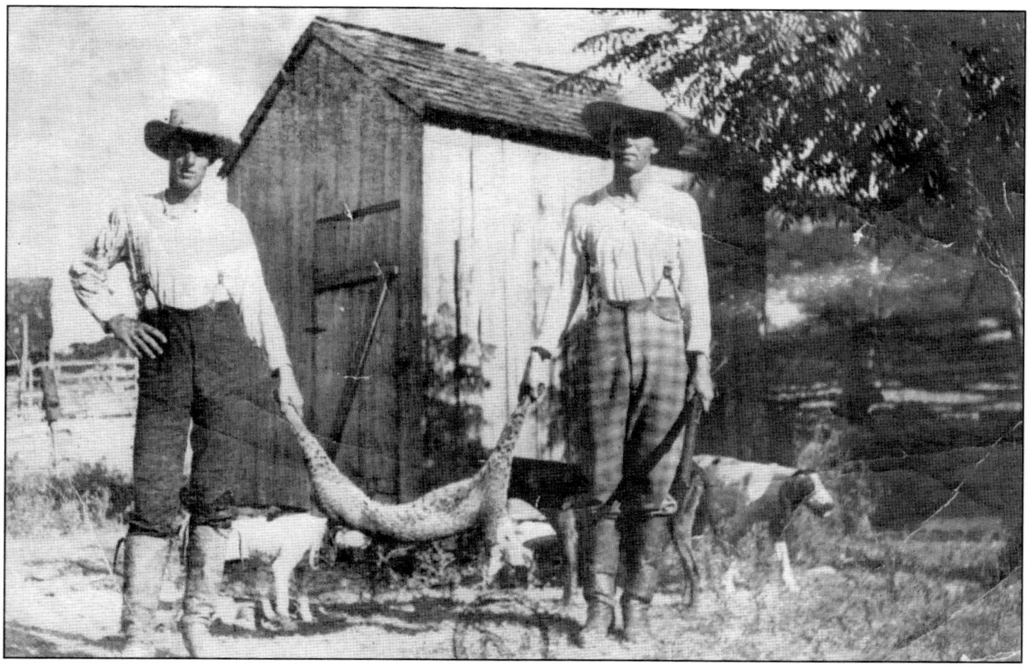

Predators were a constant threat to livestock, and ranchers were always on the lookout. Coyotes, mountain lions, and other wildcats roamed the hills, and livestock could be their next meal. County judge Arthur Pue (left) was also a sheep and goat rancher. He was photographed with his brother Percy, showing off the unfortunate intruder that was killed on their ranch. (Courtesy of the Carr-Newcomer-Stanard family.)

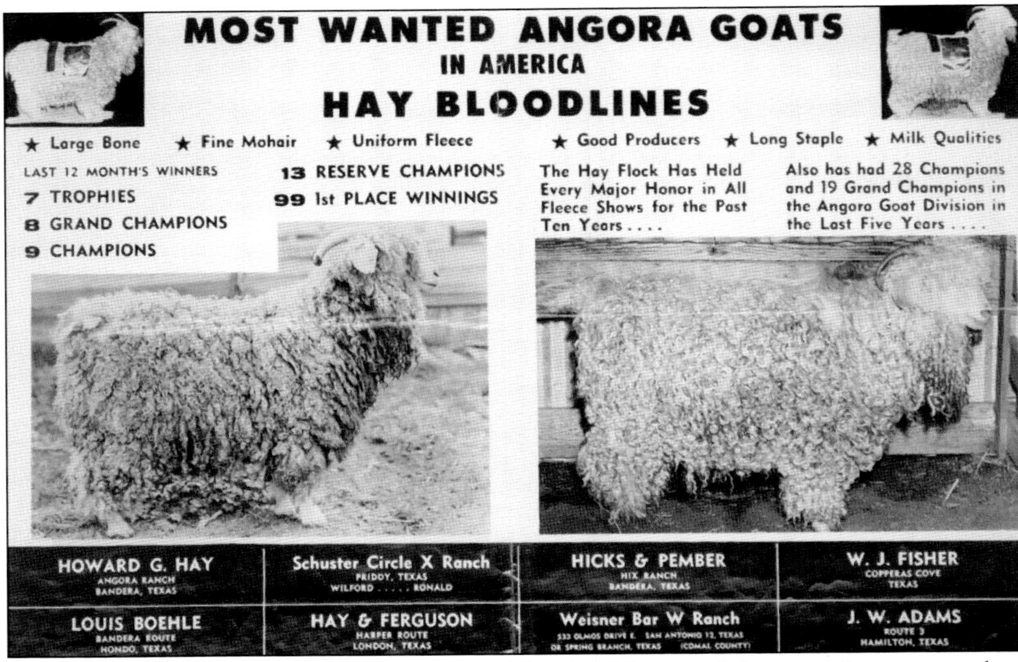

In the mid-20th century, one of the most successful and well known of the county's angora ranchers was Howard Hay. The Hay bloodlines could be traced to the Landrum herd, a Turkish import, shipped to Texas in 1897. It was reported that Hay's herd won more awards than any other in the United States at that time. (Courtesy of the Frontier Times Museum Collection.)

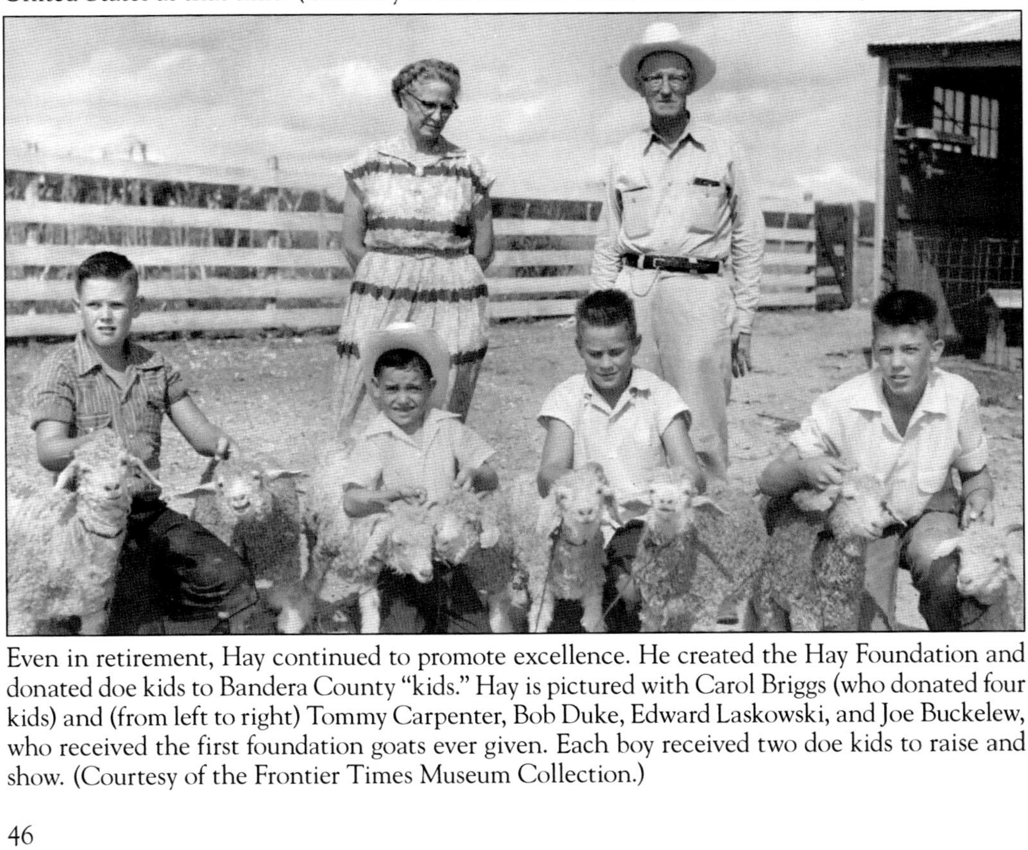

Even in retirement, Hay continued to promote excellence. He created the Hay Foundation and donated doe kids to Bandera County "kids." Hay is pictured with Carol Briggs (who donated four kids) and (from left to right) Tommy Carpenter, Bob Duke, Edward Laskowski, and Joe Buckelew, who received the first foundation goats ever given. Each boy received two doe kids to raise and show. (Courtesy of the Frontier Times Museum Collection.)

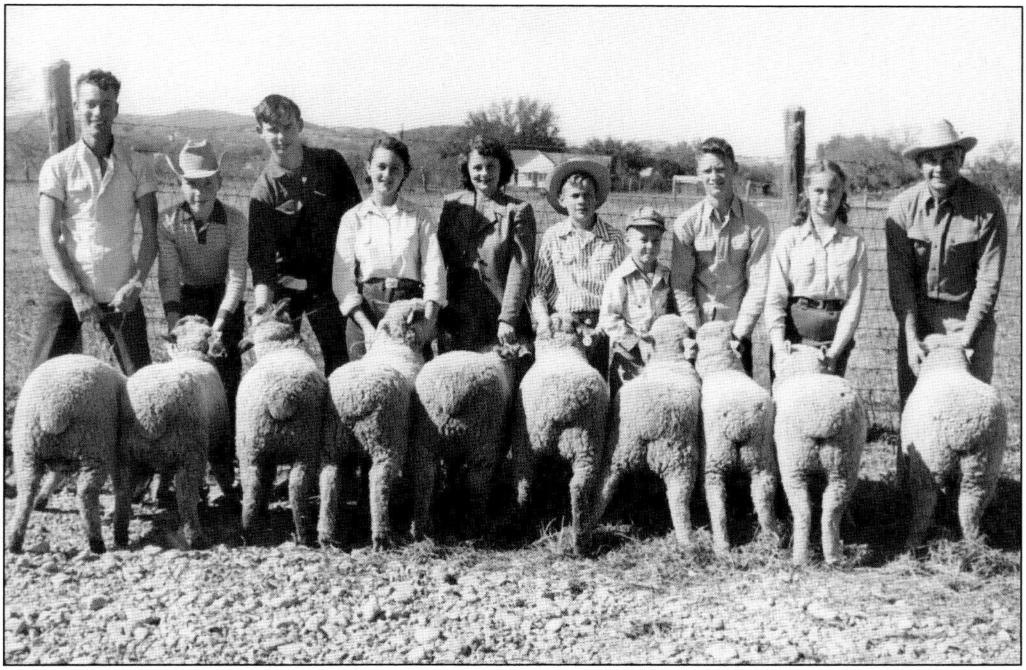

Underlining the county's importance in wool and mohair was the keen interest taken in these industries by students. Aspiring ranchers entered their animals in local competitions, which taught students animal husbandry skills and discipline. Unfortunately, these lambs did not win any prizes in the Medina Fat Lamb Show of 1954. Perhaps that is why they are not facing the camera. (Courtesy of Betty Laskowski D'Spain.)

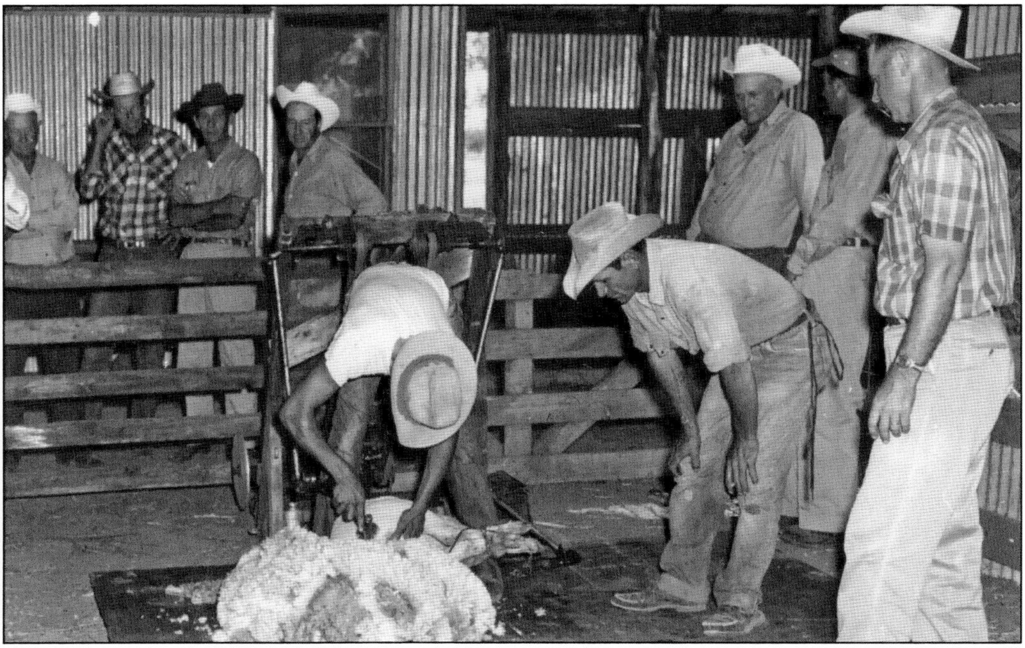

Wool and mohair shows were an important component to livestock shows and expositions. In addition to fleece judging, auctions were held, and livestock were sold to perpetuate prize lineages. (Courtesy of the Bandera County Historical Commission.)

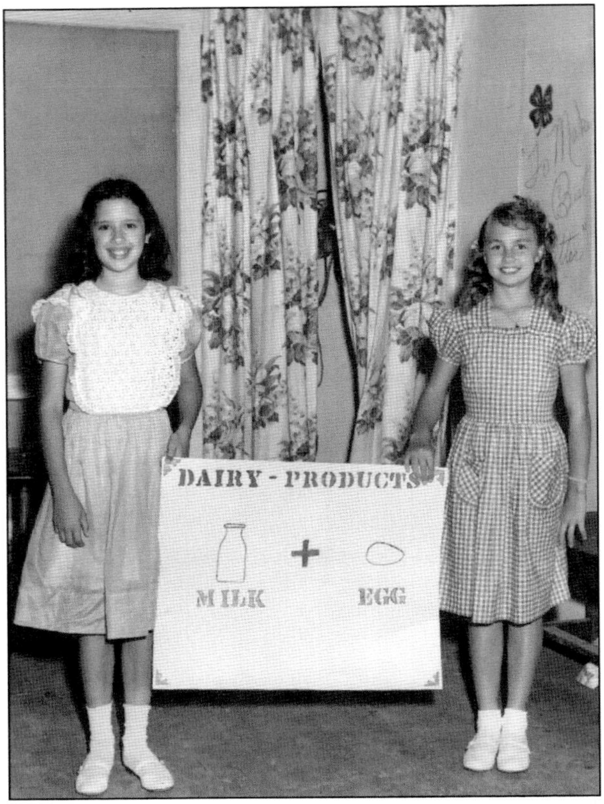

Along with the Future Farmers of America, the 4-H Club was a popular pastime for both girls and boys. By emphasizing "learning by doing," 4-H presented agricultural education to boys and girls, along with home-extension education for the girls. Students participated in a wide variety of projects that were aimed at teaching the skills needed to raise livestock, grow produce, farm, or those used in a home. A popular event for young ladies was the countywide dress revue, in which girls made and modeled dresses. The photograph at left shows Mary Sharman (left) and Betty Laskowski, who participated in the dairy food contest. Betty is also wearing a red gingham dress that she entered into the revue. Bandera's 4-H won many state and national awards in wool and livestock judging. (Left, courtesy of Betty Laskowski D'Spain; below, courtesy of the Bandera County Historical Commission.)

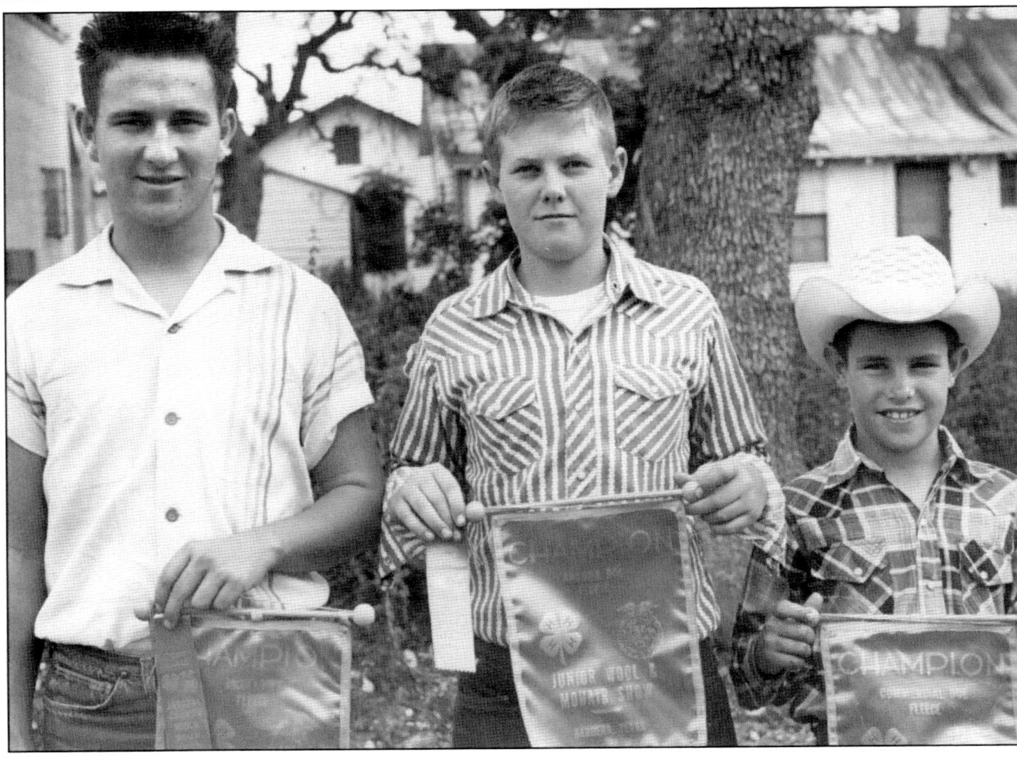

Four

A Lake Is Born

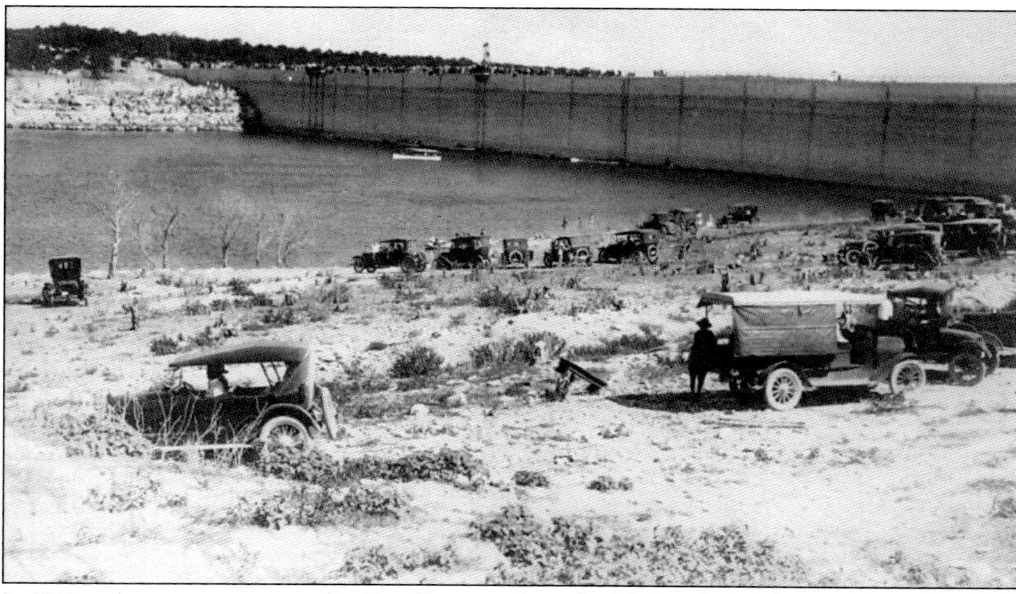

In 1912, a dam was constructed in Box Canyon where the Medina River flowed, creating Medina Lake. The lake was built to irrigate farmlands, but it became a much-loved recreational facility as communities grew up on its shores and individuals came to live amidst its beauty. Visitors have been attracted to its pristine waters and the promise of giant fish waiting to be caught. (Courtesy of Marlene Liepold Grothues.)

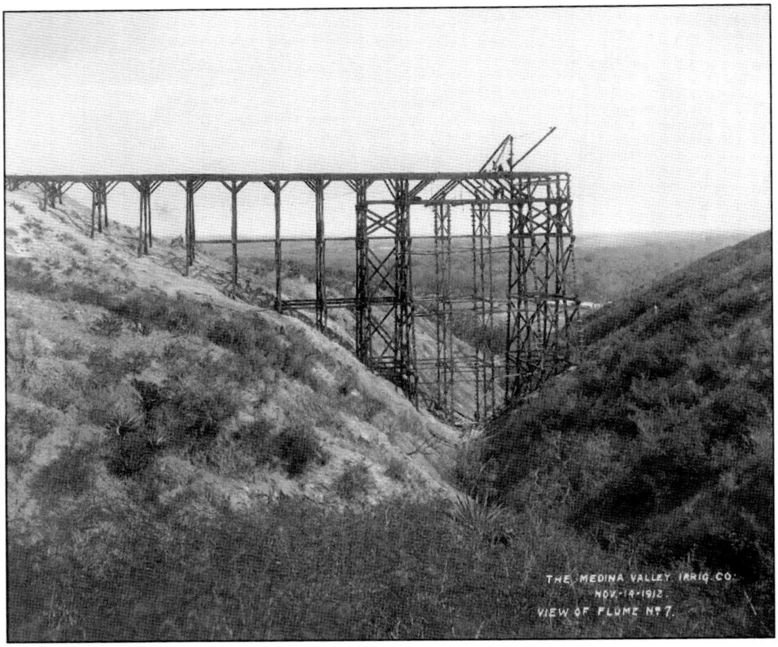

Henri Castro, an early colonist who brought over 600 families from Germany to Texas, first conceived the idea of an irrigation project along the Medina River. Noting the natural formation of the Medina Valley, Castro believed farms could be irrigated if some means could be found to hold the water that periodically flooded the Medina Canyon.

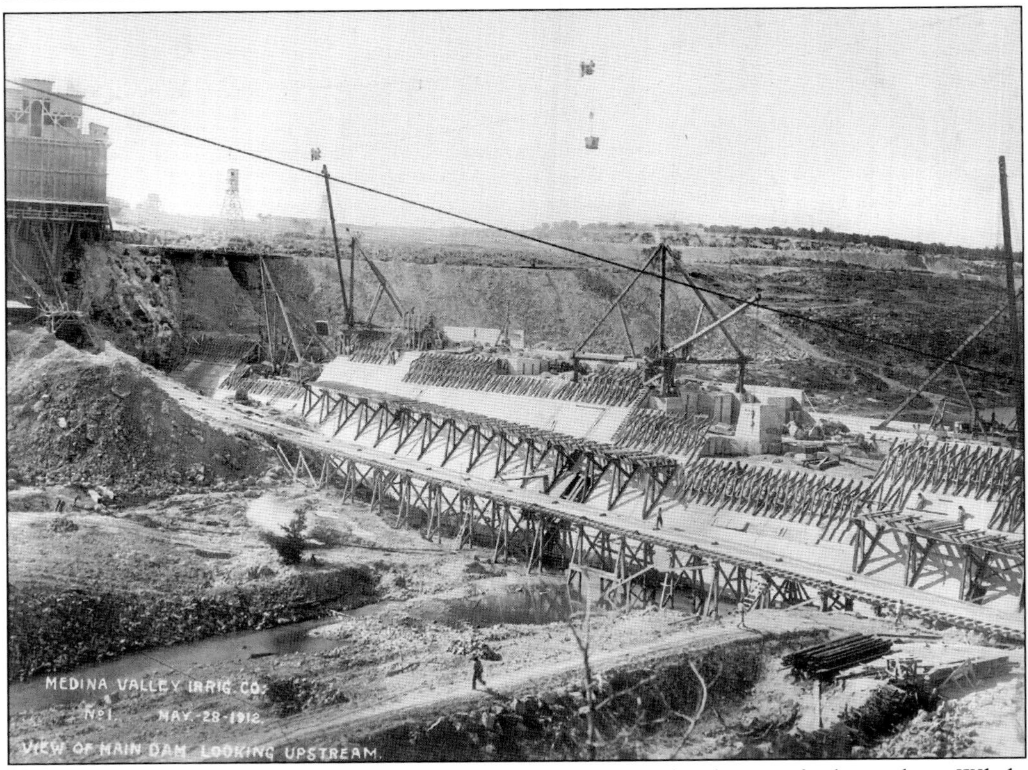

Alex Walton, a civil engineer from San Antonio, took up the dream of a large dam. While hunting in the "Box Canyon" of Medina River, he was impressed with the natural surroundings and envisioned the construction of a dam that would harness the periodic floodwaters that flowed through the rocky canyon in order to release the water as needed. In 1910, engineer Fred Pearson began raising money to make the dream a reality.

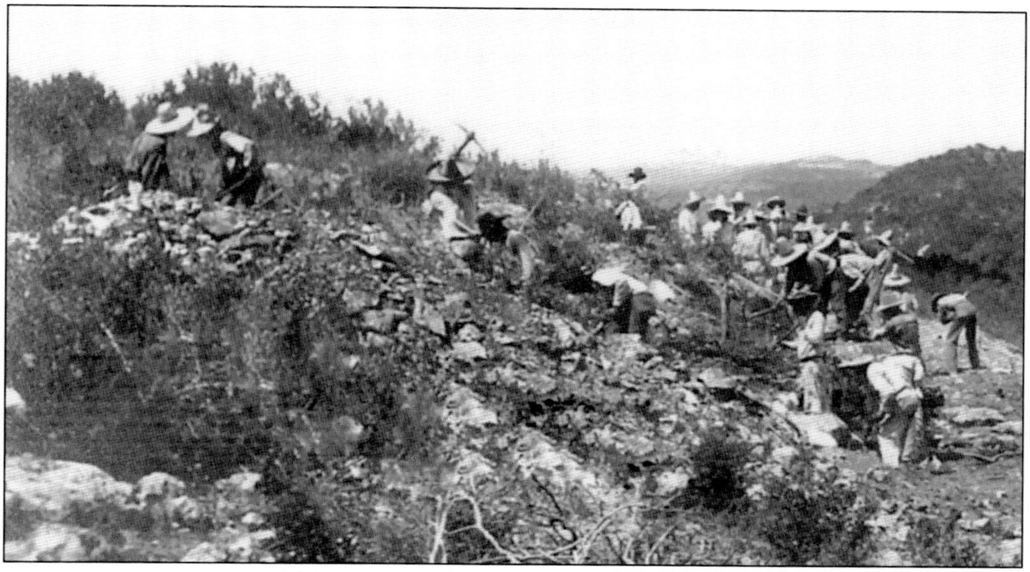

Pearson successfully raised $6 million to finance the dam and irrigation project for the Medina Valley Irrigation Company through the sale of bonds to British subscribers. In the spring of 1911, railroad tracks were laid to the construction site in southeast Bandera County. Pearson brought Mexican workers from a completed project in Mexico to work on the construction. African Americans and others willing to do the heavy manual labor joined them.

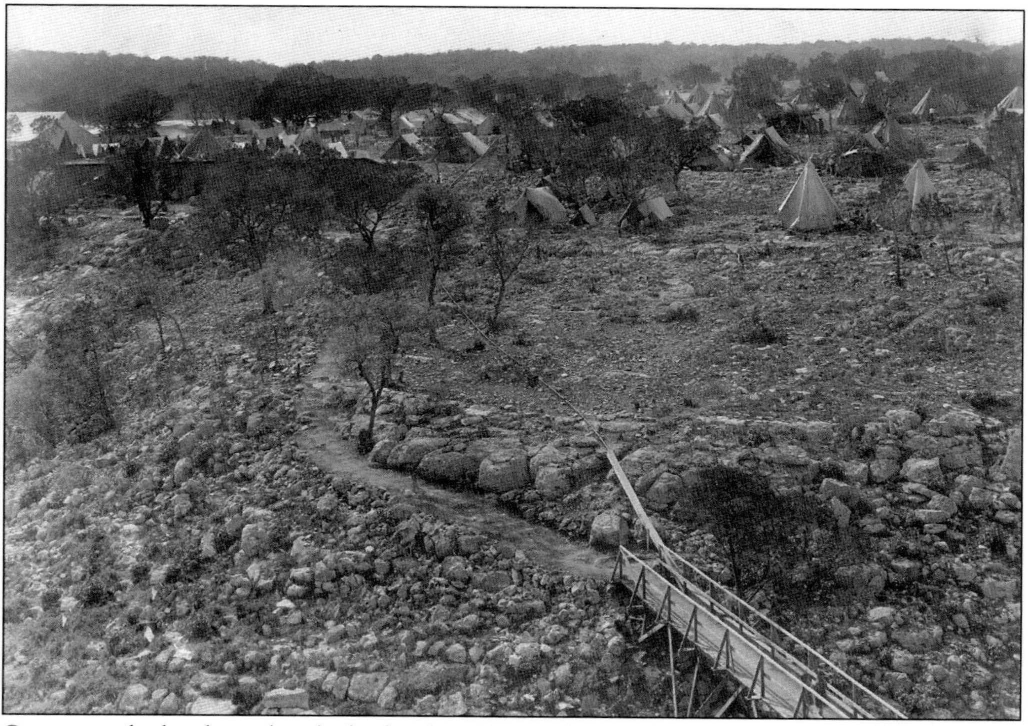

Camps were built to house hundreds of workers. Tents, cabins, and barracks served as makeshift homes. Some Mexican laborers and their families were said to have set up households in the caves along the cliff faces. Work went on around the clock, six days a week, with 10-hour shifts and one hour off for lunch and rest. With all the activity, the site became a popular destination for sightseers.

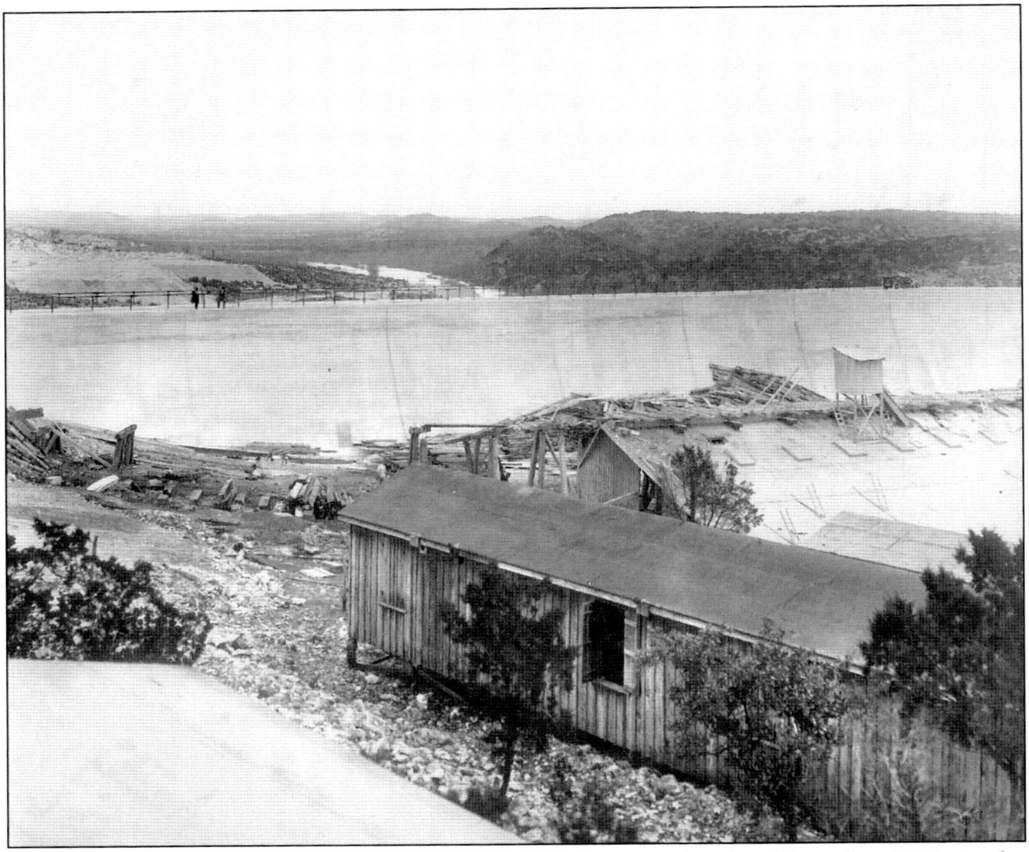

The construction began on November 10, 1911, and was completed in November 1912. At the time, the concrete dam was the largest dam in Texas and the fourth largest in the United States. At least 70 people lost their lives during the construction. Pearson and his wife lost their lives on the *Lusitania* as he was returning to Europe to raise more money for the project.

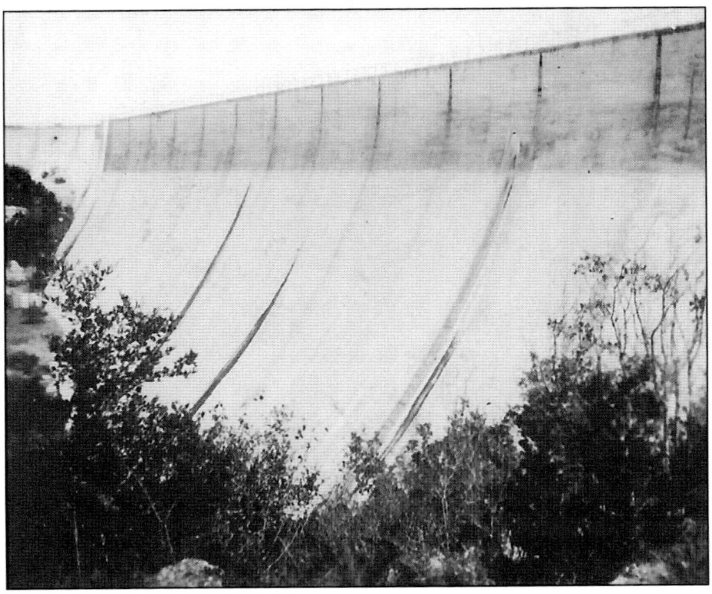

The landscape was forever changed as rising waters covered homes and places steeped in history and lore. A bronze plaque placed on the dam reads, "Before this dam was built there existed above this site a settlement known as Mountain Valley, established in 1854 by 16 families under the leadership of Lyman Wight. They abandoned their homes and mills in 1858 as a result of Indians depredations. Their lands are now beneath Medina Lake."

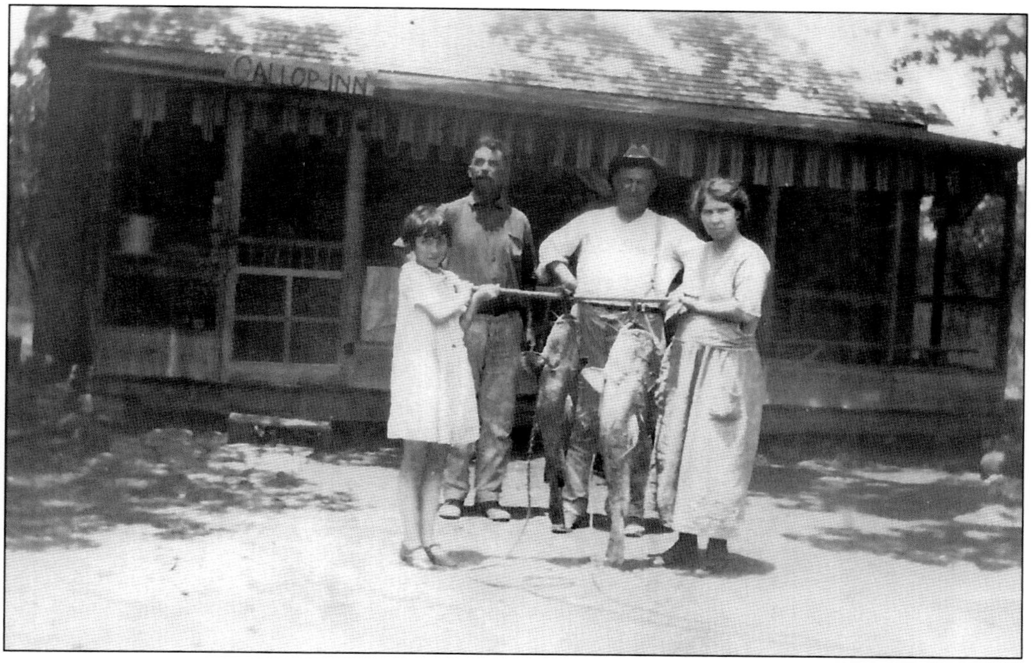

Anton Leibold's father, John, began the Leibold Ranch along the Medina River in 1882. Anton later built a ranch house in a pecan bottom, selling the pecans in San Antonio for extra money. With the construction of the dam, the family began building a second home on a hill. The home was not quite completed when the lake began to fill, and the family found themselves scrambling to move their belongings before the water rose too high. With the lake covering the fertile river bottomland, Anton needed to diversify. He opened the first fishing camp on the new lake. With his wife, Annie, he took in boarders for duck hunting and fishing. A bunkhouse and cabins were built to accommodate their guests. The family continues the tradition and recently opened the Medina Lake RV Park. (Both, courtesy of Marlene Leibold Grothues.)

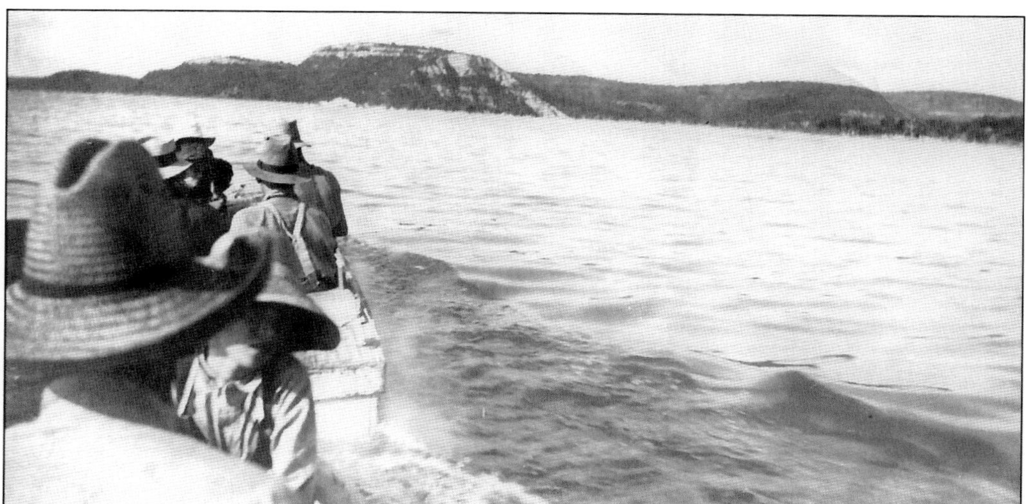

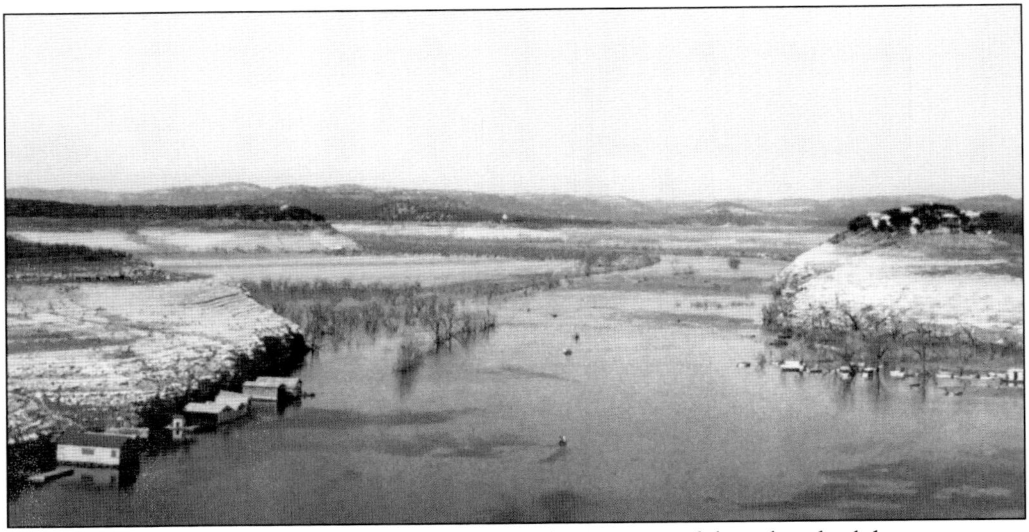

Medina Lake is known for fluctuating water levels. In times of drought, the lake can retreat hundreds of feet. During the severe drought of the 1950s, many farmed the fertile lake bottomland. Spring and fall grain crops used to feed livestock and hay for cattle were grown, along with the first commercial spinach crop. When the dam was first proposed, it was believed that the land that was to be flooded was of little value. Many landowners disagreed and were opposed to the sale of their bottomland. Many negotiated to retain the right to their property beneath the waterline once the lake was completed. The landscape around the shores of the lake becomes more dramatic as the water levels drop, as seen in the image above. Edward A. Johnson (below) is measuring how tall the millet grew in the fertile lake soil. (Above, courtesy of Doug King; below, courtesy of Burgin and Valli Johnson.)

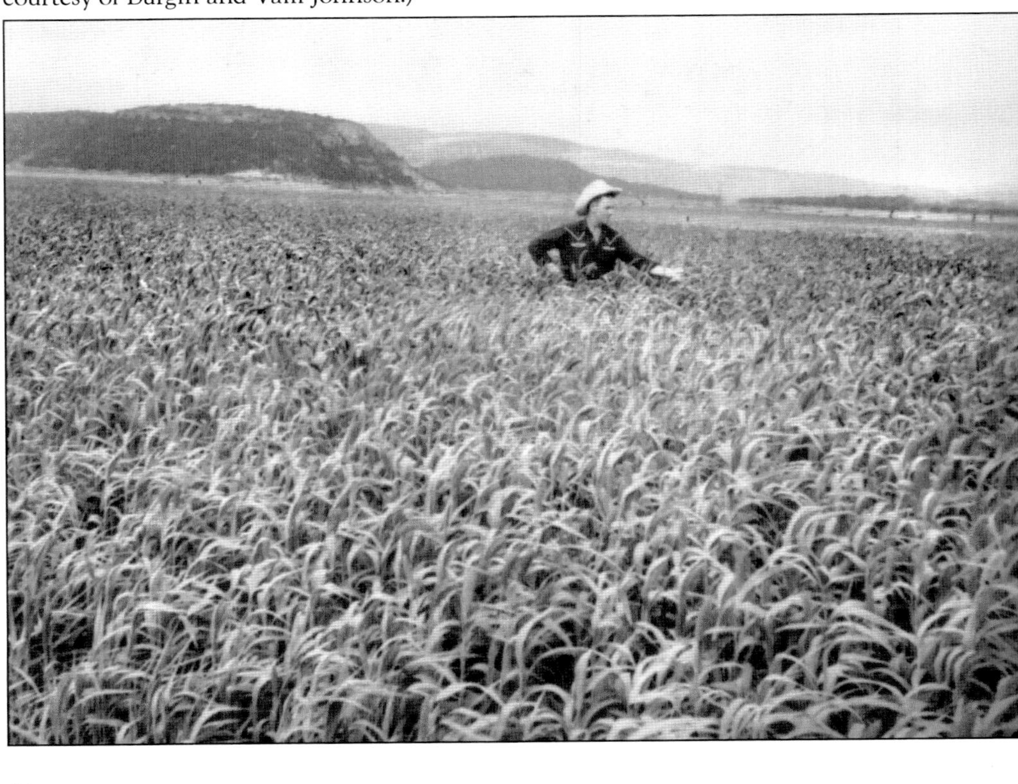

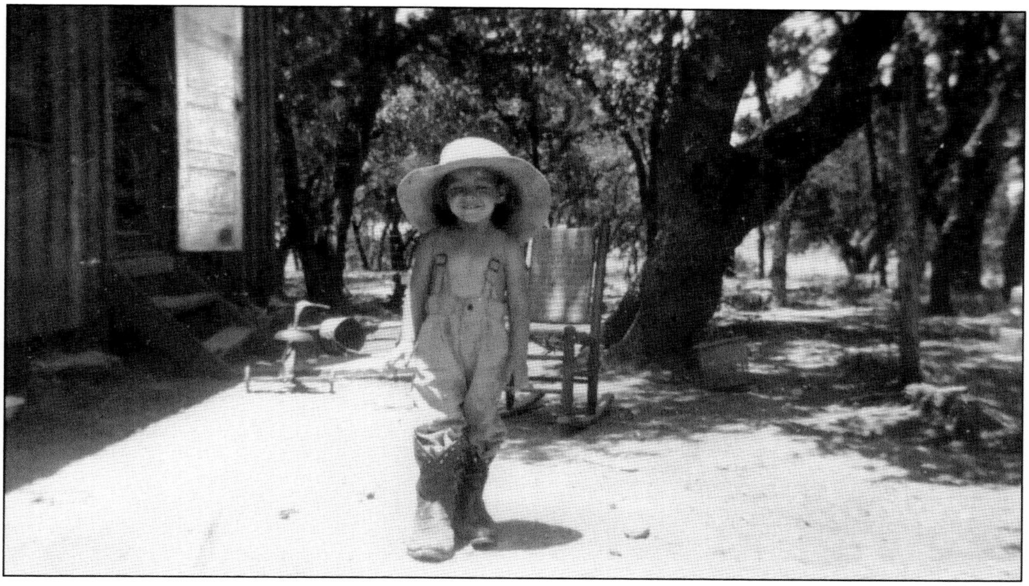

When the dam was completed, the lake stood dry for almost a year until the rains finally came in 1913. Despite the poor roads that led to the lake, it immediately became popular with fishermen, hunters, and tourists. Along with Diversion Lake, south of the dam, it was the only lake in south central Texas. In the 1920s, Edward Asa and Loy Ellen Davenport Johnson bought acreage along the Medina Lake from the Spettel family. It was near Mitchell Crossing, where Bladen Mitchell had his herding pins for cattle that were being driven to Bandera across the Medina River before the lake was built. The Johnsons opened their fishing camp, Goat Hill, which was continuously run by the family until 2007. Pictured above is Burgin Johnson. The men shown below are unidentified. (Both, courtesy of Burgin and Valli Johnson.)

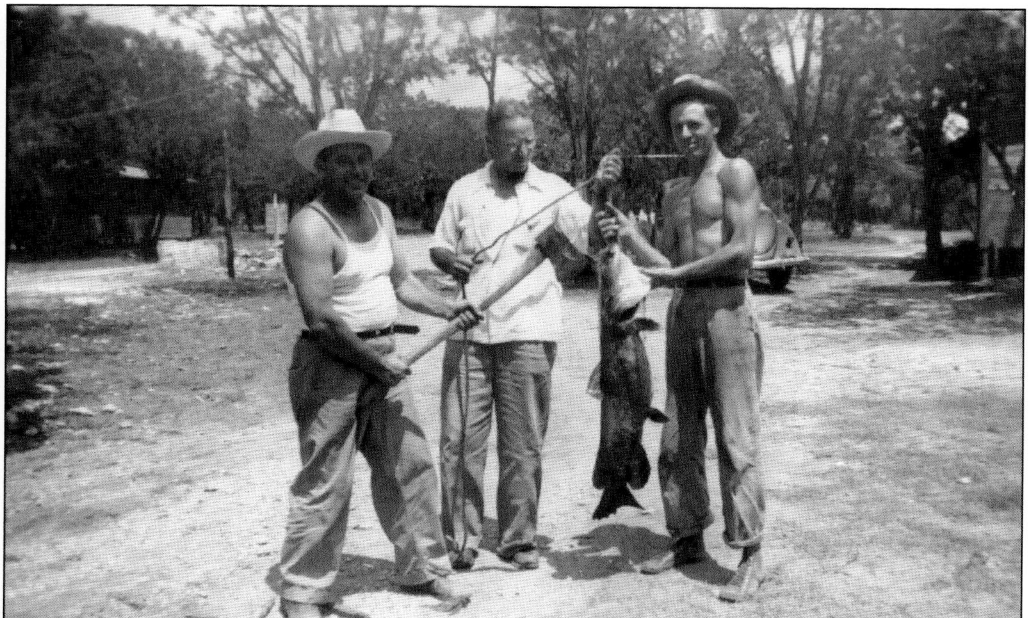

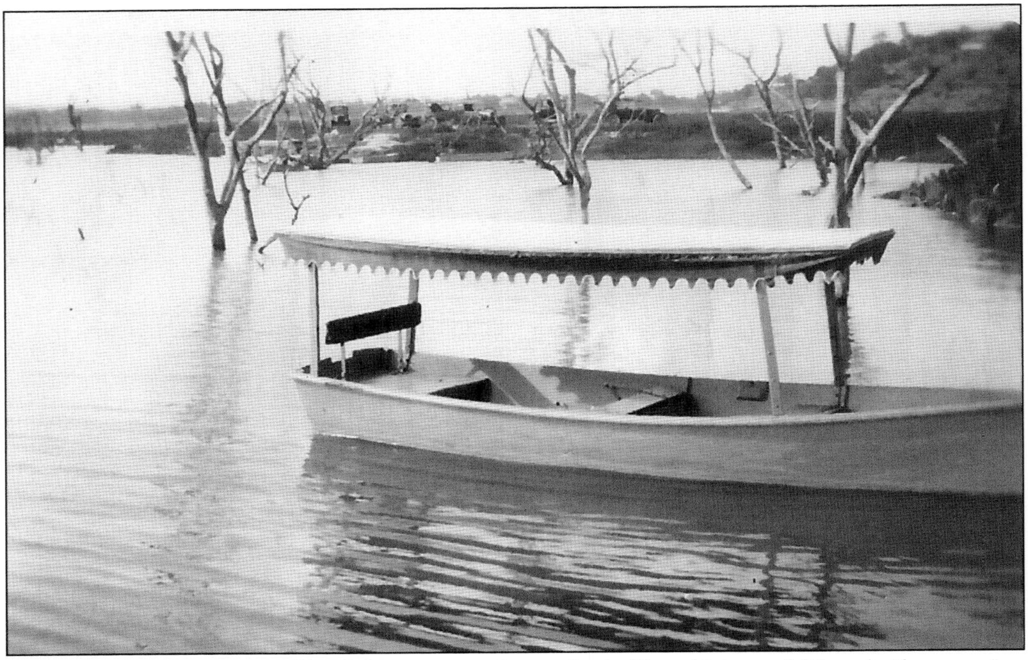

To add to the enjoyment of his fishing camp, Anton Leibold and his son Milton built excursion boats for vacationers to view the lake. Anton and Milton took tours to the dam about 15 miles down the lake. Tourists came from all over the state, and the camp was especially popular with military personnel from the nearby bases in San Antonio. (Courtesy of Marlene Leibold Grothues.)

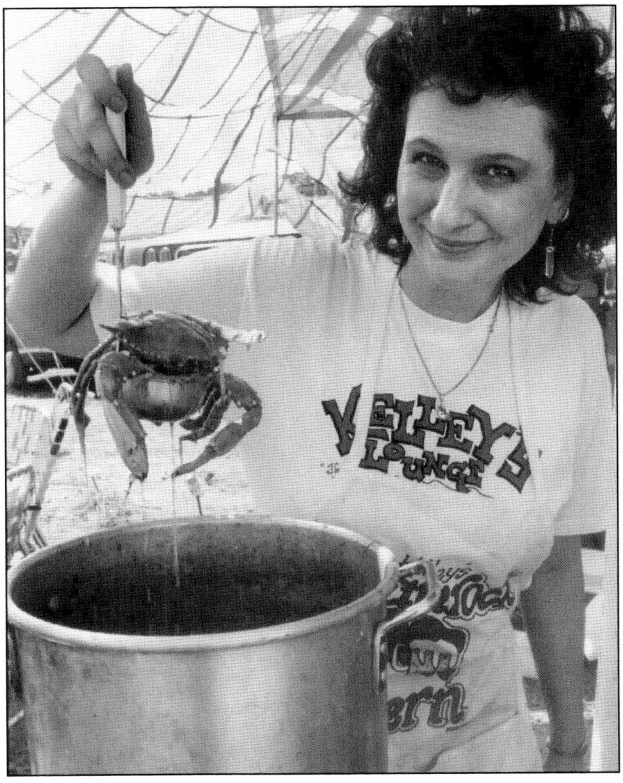

County road improvements that began in the 1930s stopped with the outbreak of World War II, which delayed development around the lake until the 1950s. The community known as Upper Medina Lake became Lakehills after a post office was established there in the early 1960s. Today the residents of Lakehills come together every year in September to celebrate their annual Cajun Festival. (Courtesy of the Bandera County Historical Commission.)

Five

NATURE'S FURY

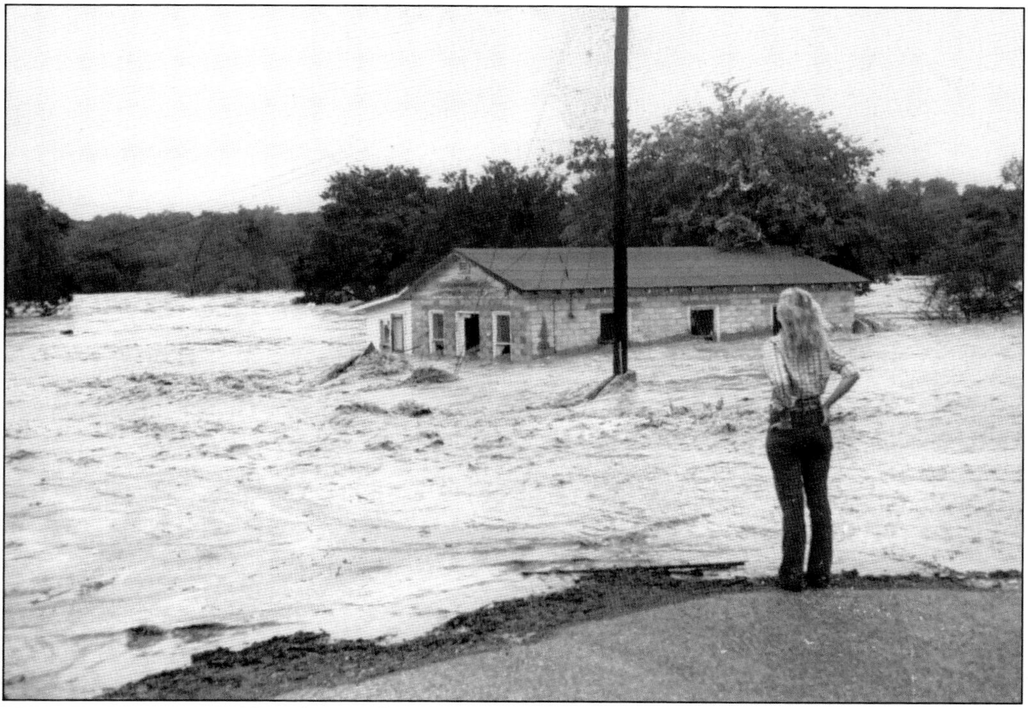

Native Americans told early Bandera settlers of floods that stretched from mountaintop to mountaintop. Such was the "Hundred Year Flood of 1978," which devastated Bandera County, leaving 15 people dead and caused the county to declare a national disaster area. The vastness of the flooding the Native Americans described is surely visible to this young woman as she views the surging floodwaters.

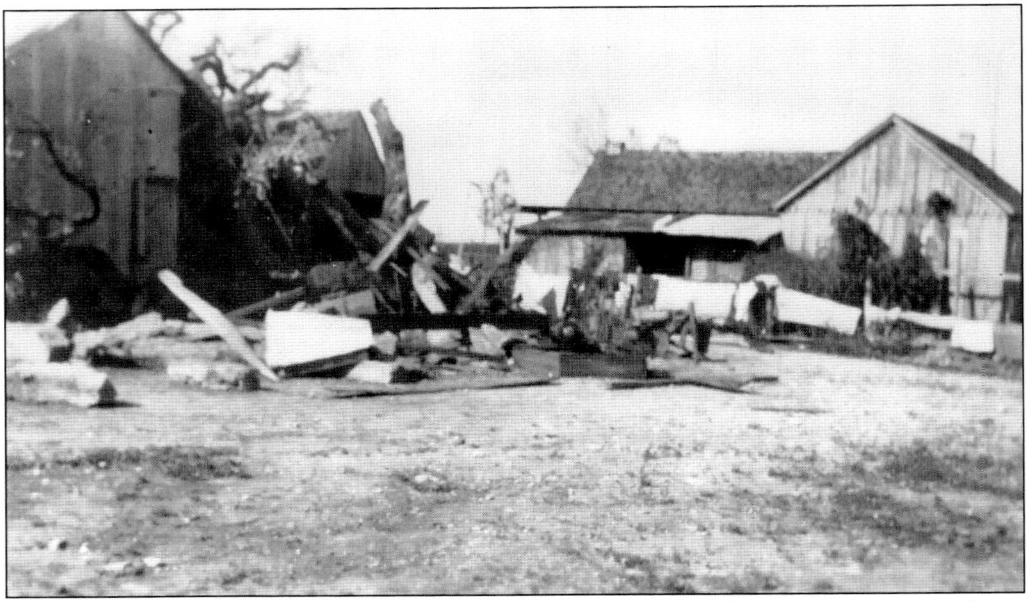

While Bandera County's temperate climate was often cited by town fathers to attract new residents, it has never been immune to weather extremes. The early 1900s witnessed a series of floods and even tornadoes. In the above photograph, ranchers John and Sarah Batto documented damage to their property by what they referred to as a "cyclone." The storm of April 13, 1927, tore through the area, leveling the town of Rocksprings and leaving damage estimated at $1 million. More than 50 people were killed. Damage to the Buster Bruce Ranch, near the Medina River Crossing, is shown below. In 1949, a similar storm hit the Pipe Creek area, leaving dozens injured and four dead. The *Bandera Bulletin* reported that several homes were swept away when the tornado struck without warning. (Above, courtesy of Theresa Helbert; below, courtesy of the Bandera County Historical Commission.)

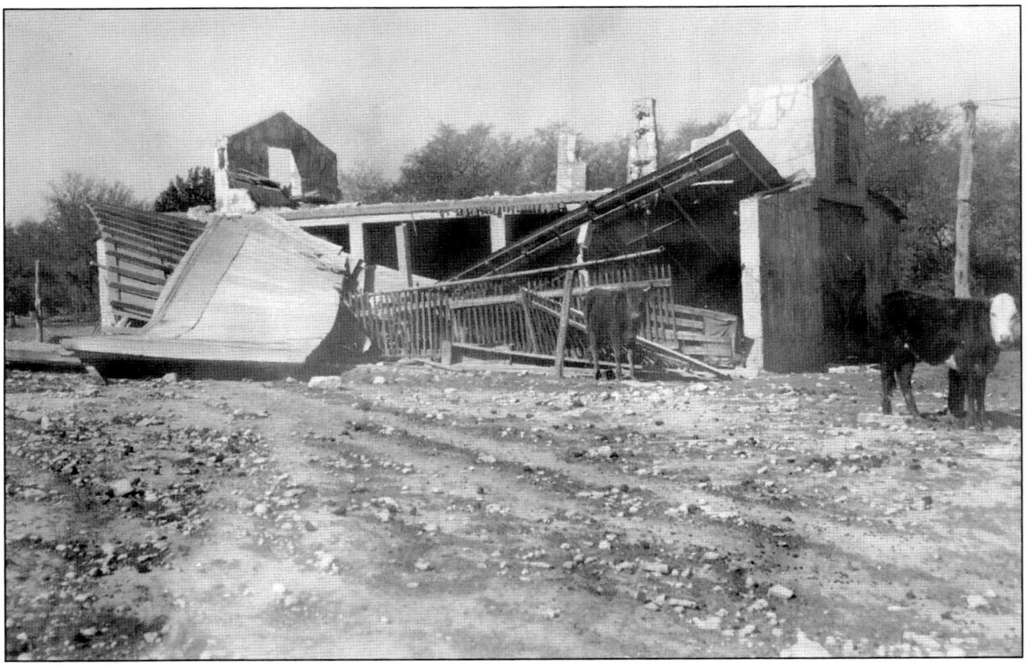

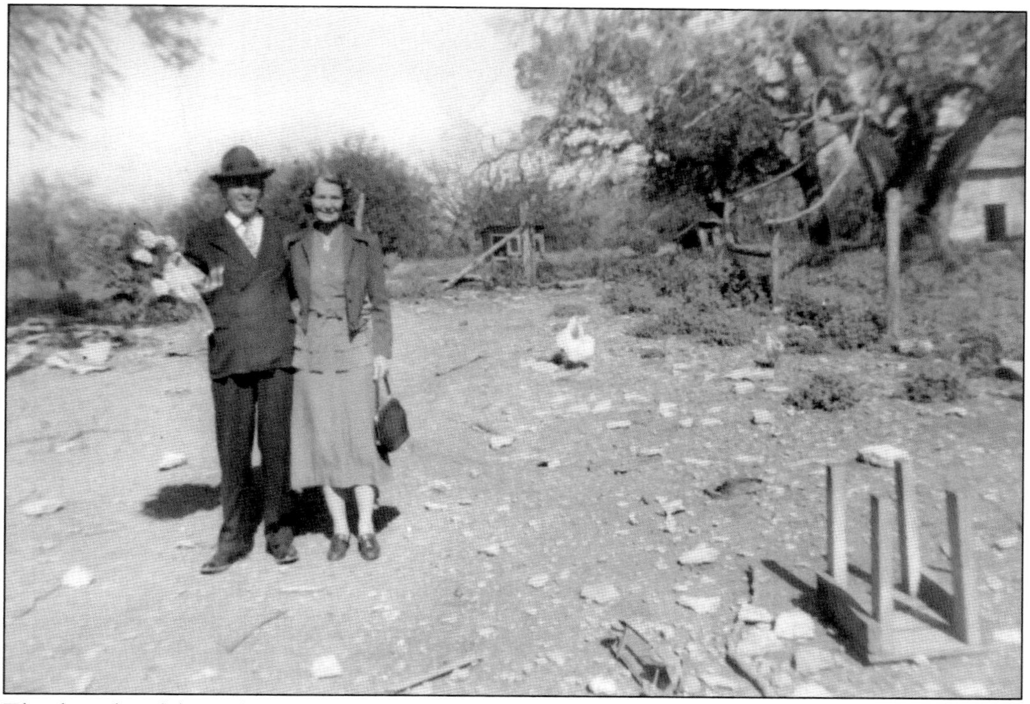

The drought of the 1950s was one of the most severe on record, characterized by both low rainfall and extremely high temperatures. Rainfall in Texas was below normal in 75 percent of the state, including Bandera County. Pictured above are ranchers James and Linda Shaw in the front yard of their home near Rangers Crossing. At least they did not have to worry about mowing! (Courtesy of Robin Shaw.)

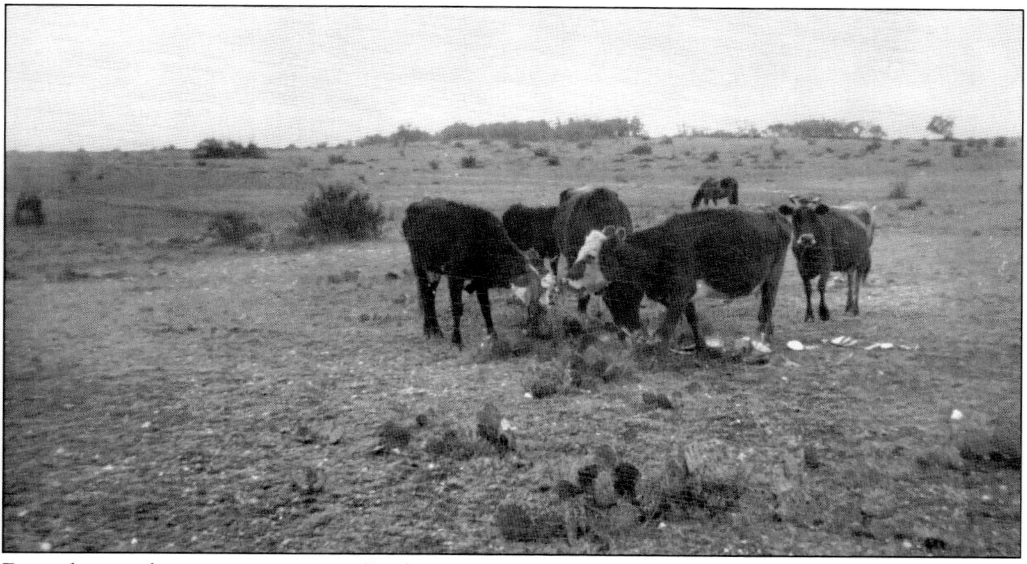

Drought conditions were especially damaging for local agriculture and ranching. Crop yields declined by as much as 50 percent in parts of the state. Because grazing livestock became impossible, along with the low hay crop yields, ranchers turned to what was left—cactus. "Pear burners" were used to burn the spines from cactus pads and prickly pears, giving cattle a source of moisture and food. (Courtesy of the Bandera County Historical Commission.)

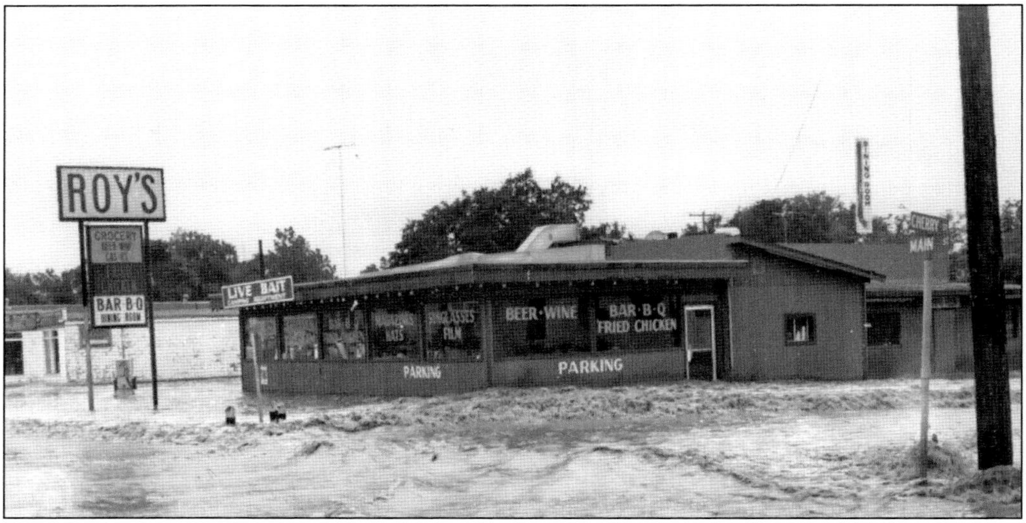

There is a saying in Texas that if it is not hot and dry, then it is flooding. Bandera County has certainly had its share of droughts and floods. In the early part of August 1978, the usually calm Medina River surged as a result of rainwater from Hurricane Amelia. Residents had spent several months suffering through a drought when the storm hit. As Hurricane Amelia crossed the Gulf of Mexico, the National Weather Service had predicted it would move in a northeasterly direction. Amelia had something else in mind and veered toward the Hill Country, where the storm stalled, dumping up to 20 inches of rain. Bandera's Main Street became a raging river at the height of the flood.

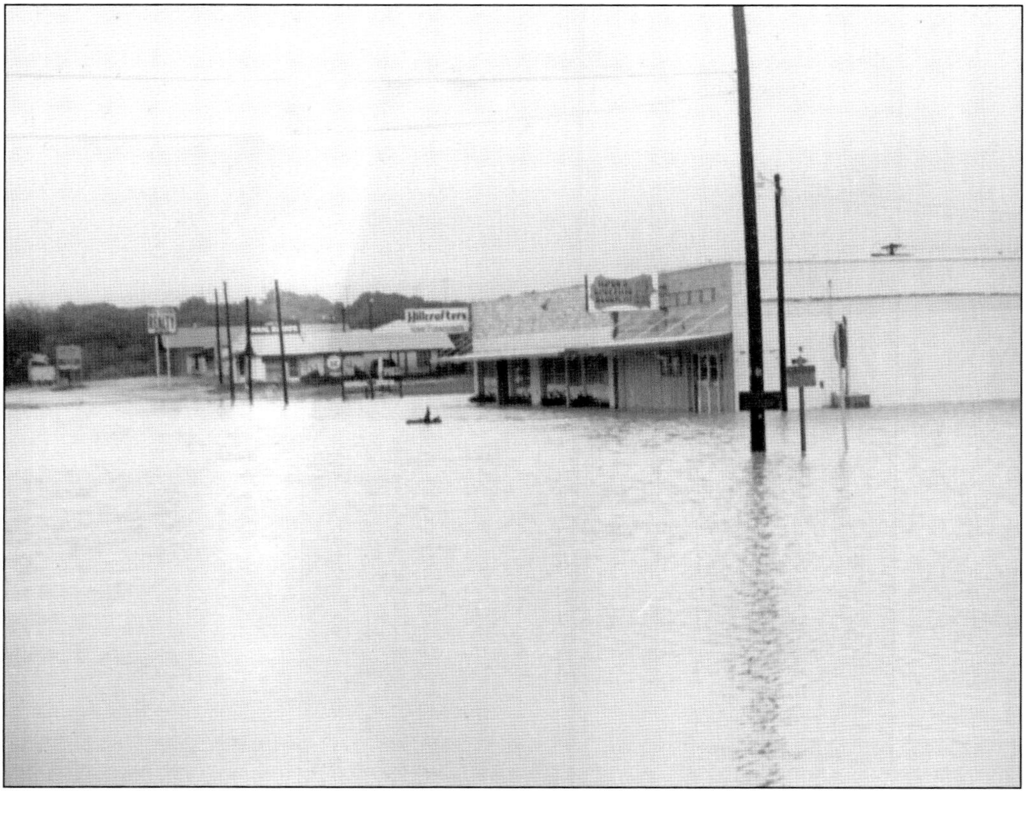

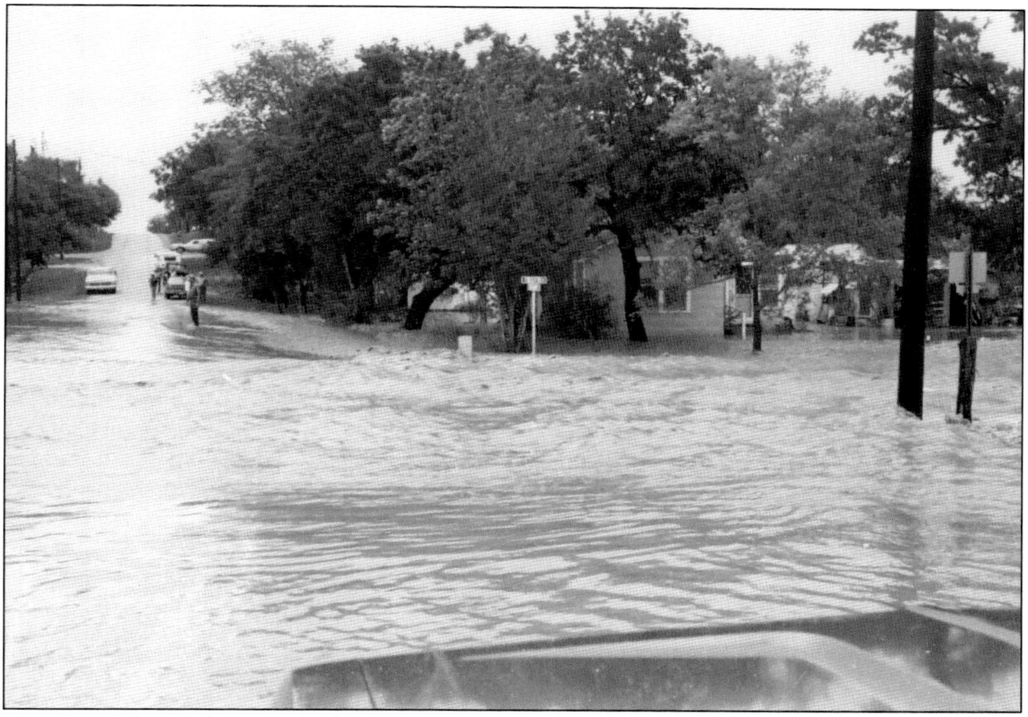

The rains affected the rivers and springs in the area. Pictured above is Joe Kalka's home on Twelfth Street, near the site of a spring that was once used by early residents as a source of drinking water. The flooding in this part of town did not come from the overflow of the Medina River but rather from the spring located near the Kalka home.

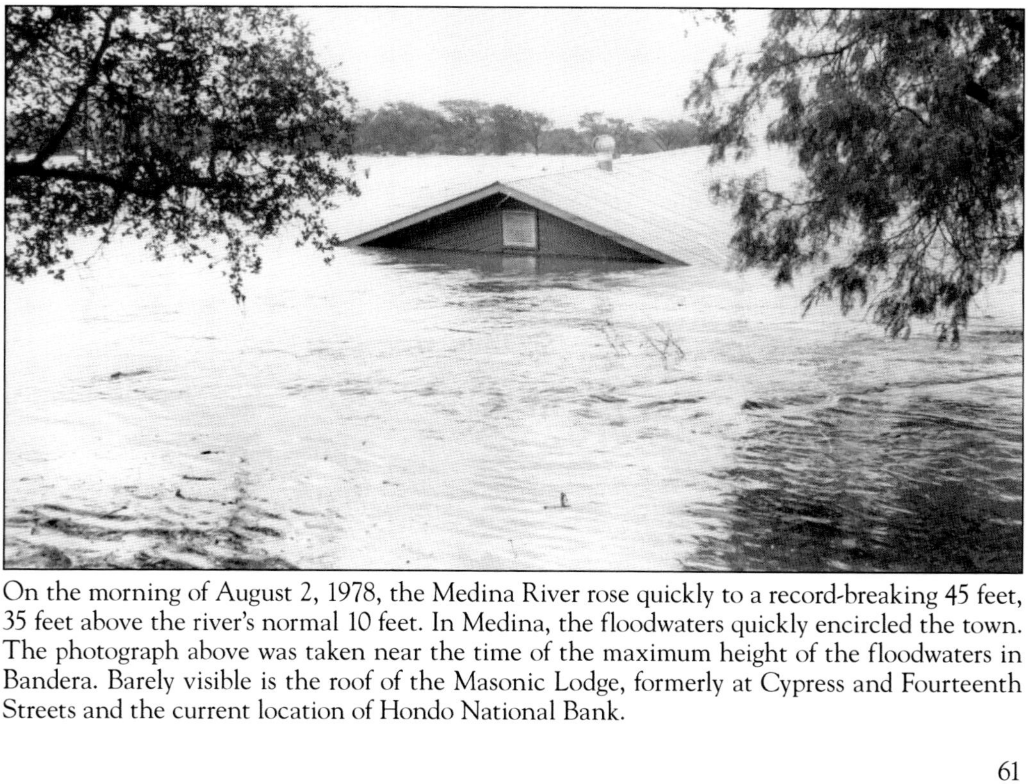

On the morning of August 2, 1978, the Medina River rose quickly to a record-breaking 45 feet, 35 feet above the river's normal 10 feet. In Medina, the floodwaters quickly encircled the town. The photograph above was taken near the time of the maximum height of the floodwaters in Bandera. Barely visible is the roof of the Masonic Lodge, formerly at Cypress and Fourteenth Streets and the current location of Hondo National Bank.

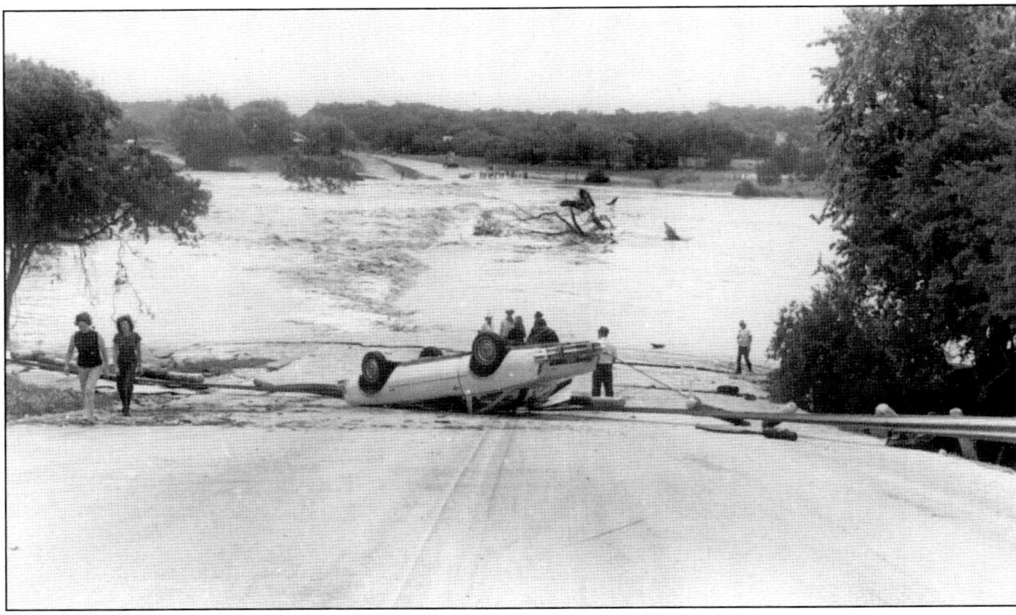

The quickly rising waters stranded residents, and many barely made it to safety. Staying at a motel near the river, the owner of this car chained the vehicle to a guardrail to keep from losing it. The power of the rushing water flipped the car over, but the chain held.

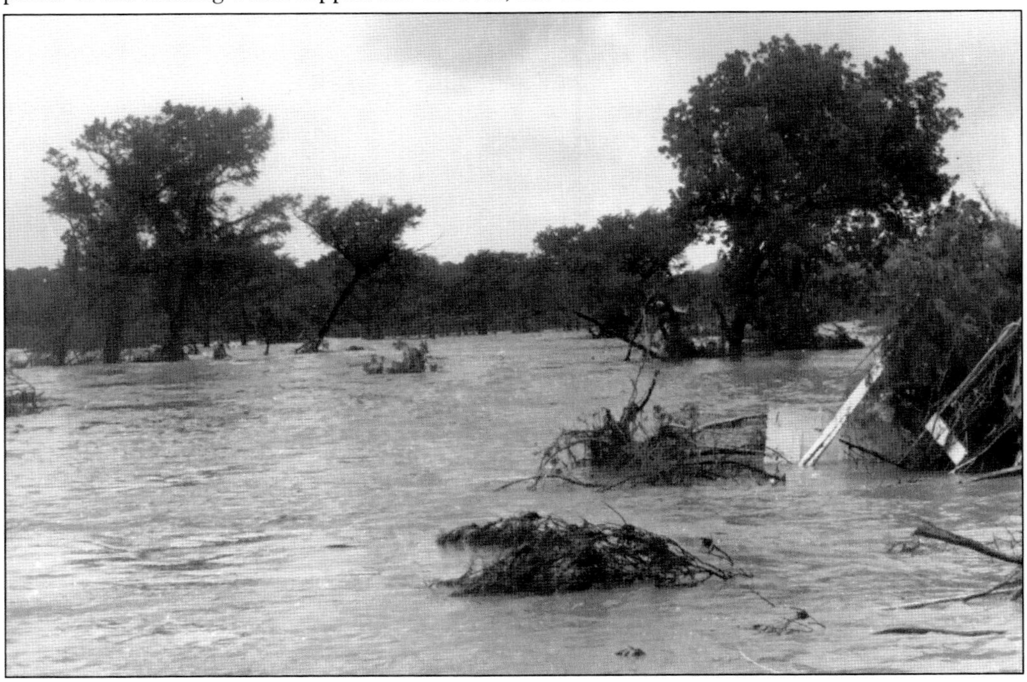

Many found themselves stranded in treetops. Kim Tomes, Miss USA of 1977, spent nine hours stranded in a tree. She could hear the moans of other victims and kept herself calm by practicing the national anthem. Steve Muller, now the owner of a Bandera guest ranch, found himself stranded near Tomes. He held her infant nephew the entire time after taking the baby from her sister. At the time, he said, "She had the tree reserved next to me." Today Tomes calls Muller a hero for keeping her nephew safe through the horrifying ordeal.

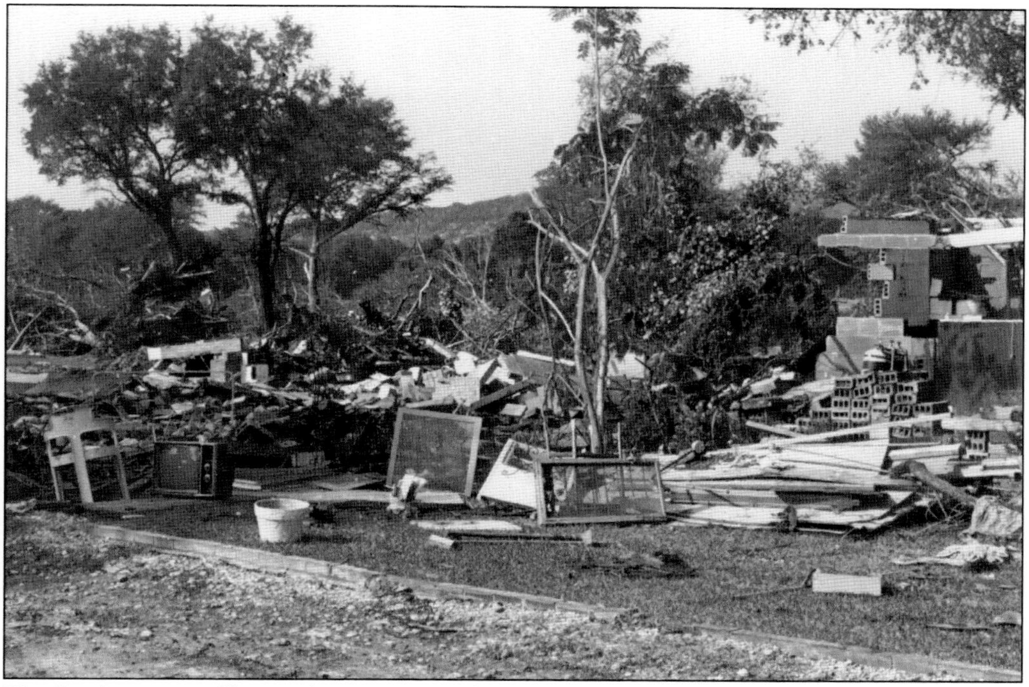

The flooding ravaged homes, businesses, ranches, and dude ranches. The devastation was described as the worst the area had seen since the flood of 1900. Residents told of floodwaters that rose so quickly, they only had time to climb on their roofs before the swift current quickly overtook their homes. While many rode the storm out on their rooftops, others watched as their homes were swept away. The powerful floodwaters washed away doors, windows, and even crashed through walls. In the aftermath of the flood, residents were given specific guidelines regarding claims to their homes and personal property: "If possible, estimate the replacement costs of this property. Do not throw away furniture or damaged personal property . . . Even worthless property should be retained. For further verification of your loss, take photos of the damaged property."

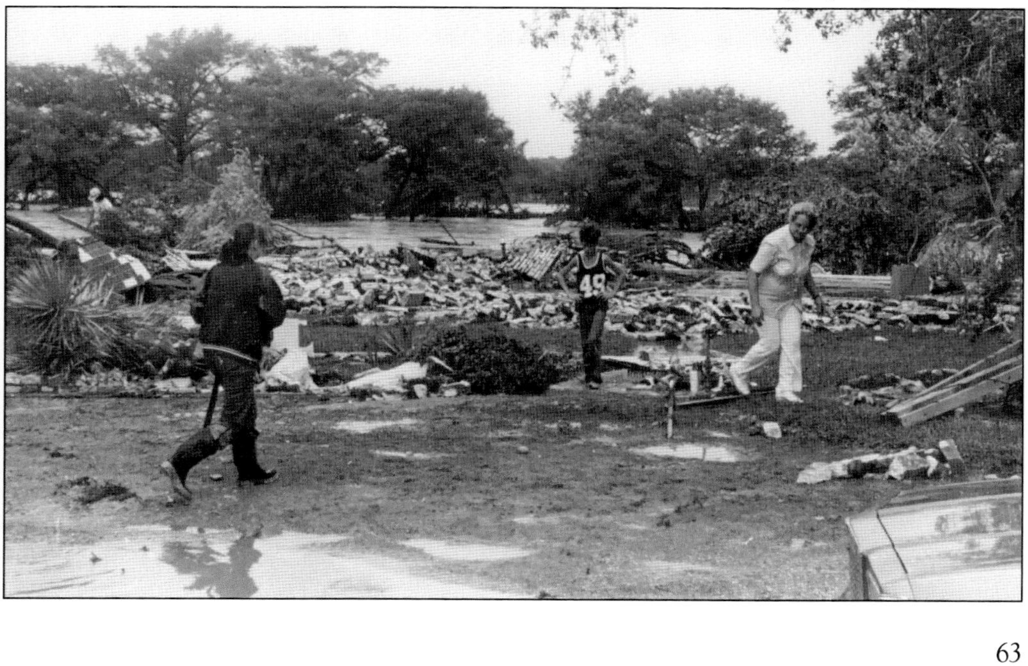

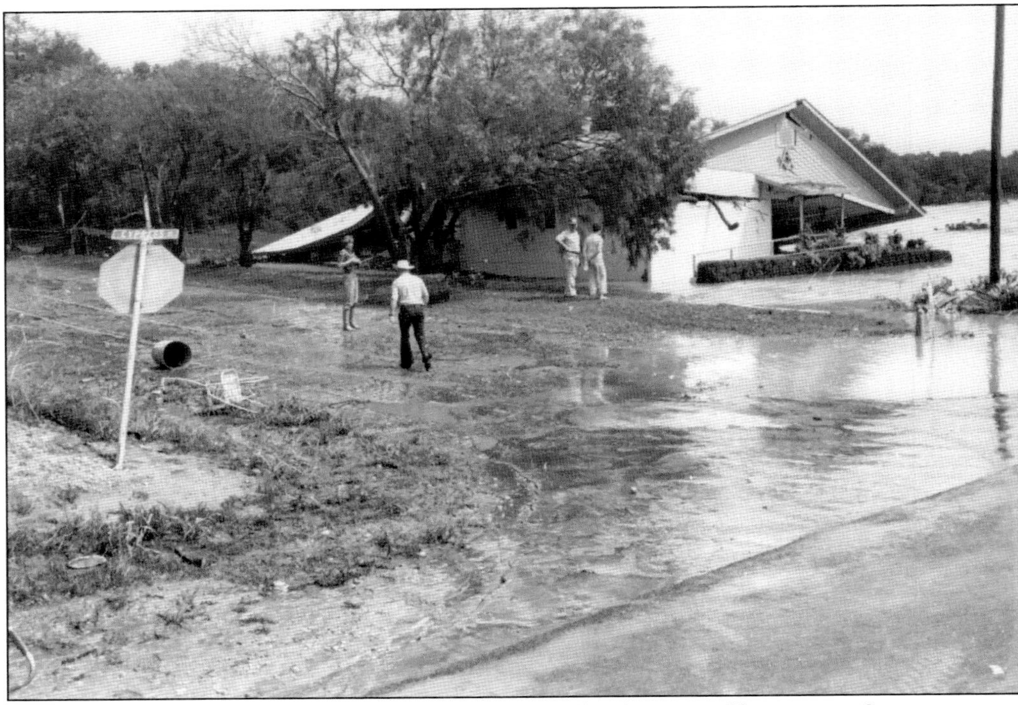

The flood damaged and destroyed infrastructure as well as homes and businesses. Cars were swept away and later found in odd places. Local schools and churches sheltered those who had lost everything. Many recounted terrifying ordeals as the water overtook them quickly and without warning. Claribel Lovelace told local newspapers that she had been trapped in her rock house as 8 feet of muddy river water came crashing through her home from the nearby Medina River. The 80-year-old woman found herself against the ceiling with her mouth opened toward the ceiling and her hair in the water. With only 6 inches of air to breath, she was able to hold on until rescuers found her. The flood claimed 15 lives throughout the devastated area.

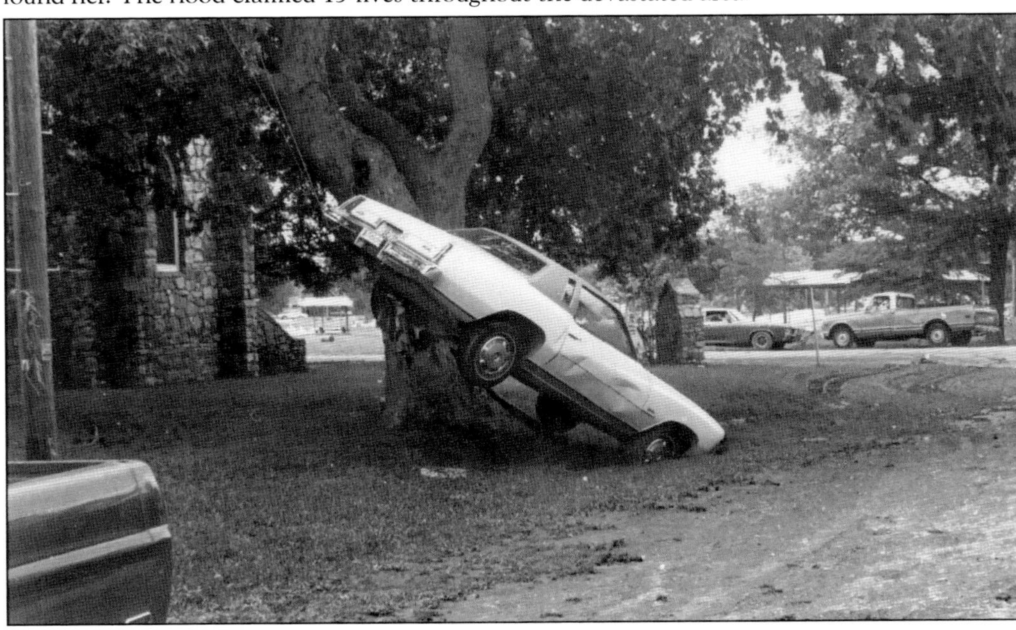

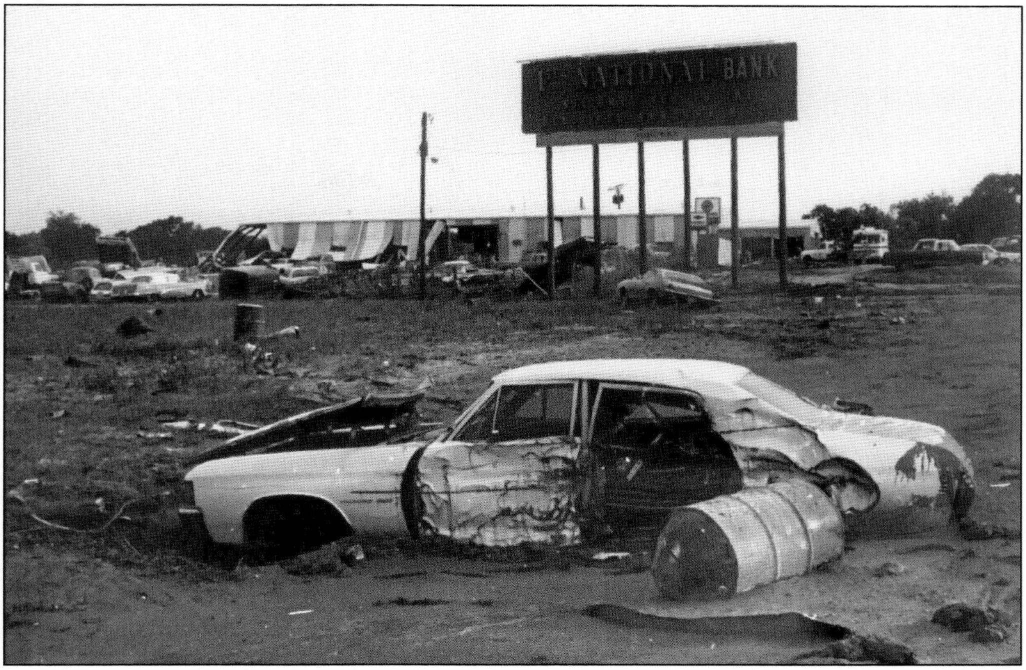

Local dealership Clint Dowell Chevrolet sustained a loss in excess of $1 million after dozens of new and used cars were swept away. Richard Evans, an employee at the time, told the *San Antonio Express News*, "We just had to stand there and watch the water wash everything away. I've lived here a long time and I've never seen the waters rise like this." The employees were amazed to find that all the new cars had been washed down the river, while the used cars were piled high across the street.

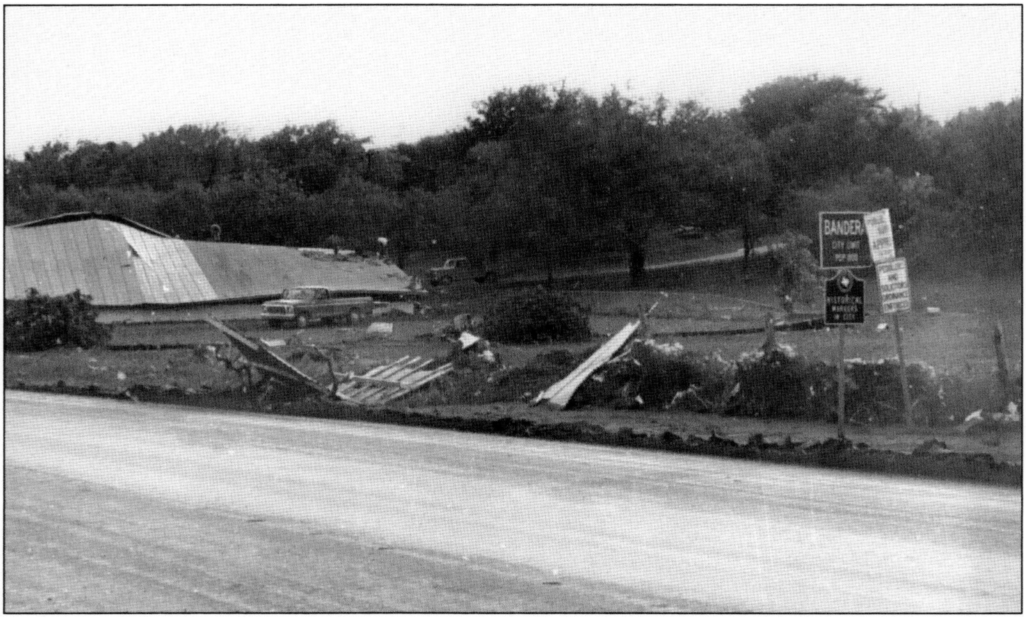

Bandera County had suffered three major floods, in 1900, in 1919, and in 1978, in the month of August. Residents know that floods are always a possibility, as floods came again in May 2002. While destructive, this latest flood was not as devastating as the 1978 flood.

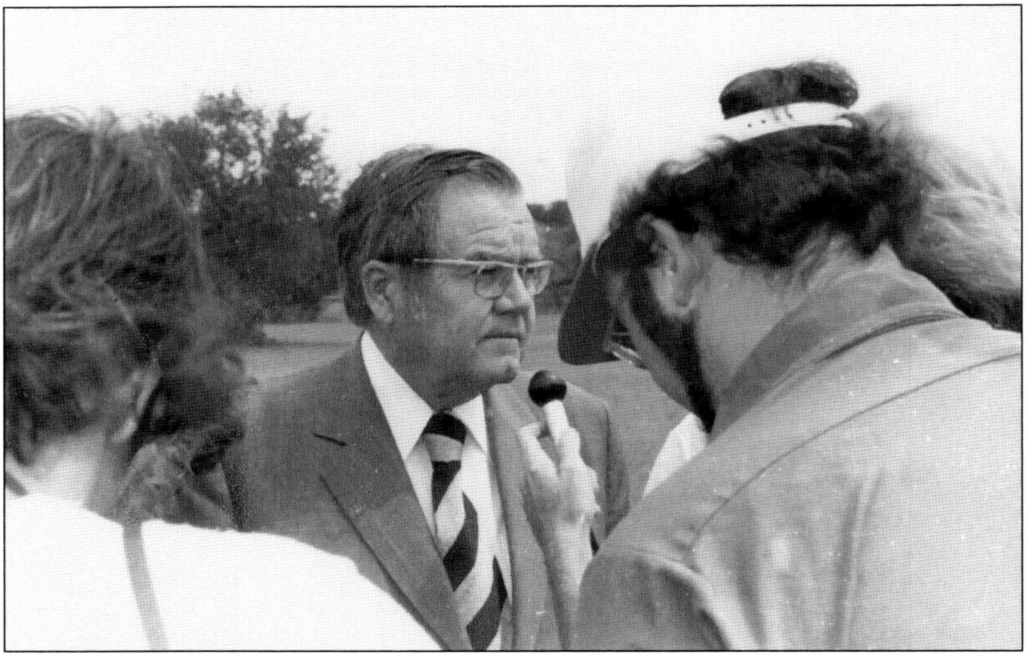

Texas governor Dolph Briscoe visited Bandera County on August 3, 1978, to survey the flood-stricken area. So struck by the devastation, he proclaimed that it was the worst flood Texas had ever seen and asked Pres. Jimmy Carter to declare it a natural disaster area. President Carter responded quickly and declared Bandera County a disaster area on August 4, 1978. Help arrived in the form of the National Guard and Military Assistance to Safety and Traffic (MAST).

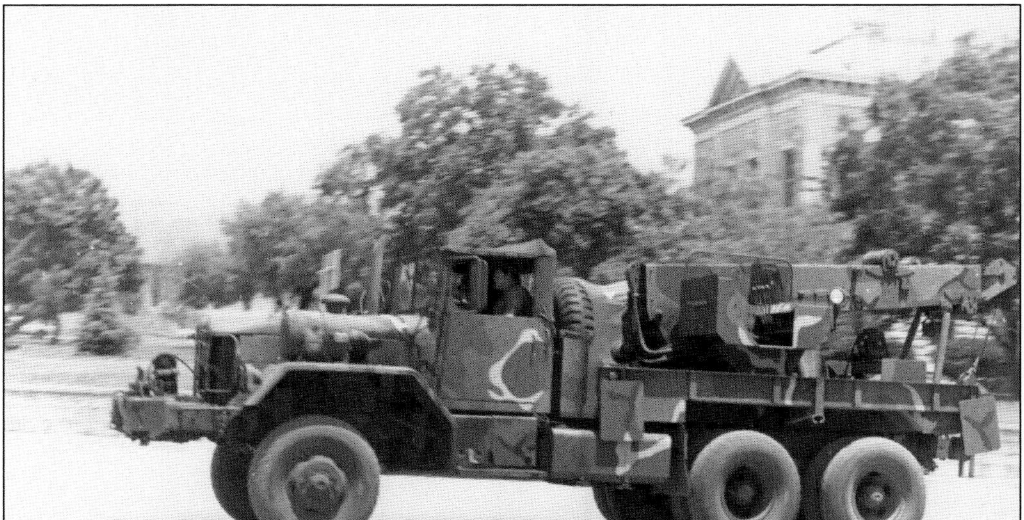

The National Guard troops were joined by helicopter rescue units from the 507th Medical Company at Fort Sam Houston in San Antonio. Guardsmen helped maintain order, and MAST helicopters were used to rescue residents in remote areas. The National Guard brought much needed supplies and water, but overworked rescue crews also had the grim task of searching for flood victims.

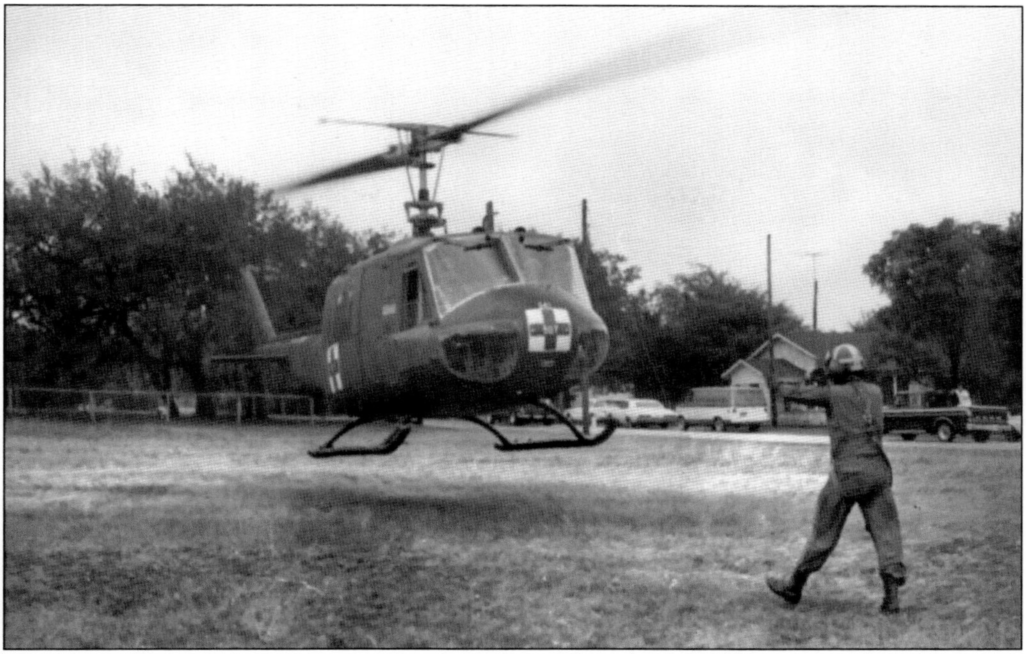

Helicopter crews had the task of finding stranded residents in trees and on rooftops. There were also numerous church and youth camps in the area, filled with summer campers. While most of the camps had suffered some flood damage, the biggest obstacles were the washed-out roads that connected them to civilization. As the helicopters landed at each camp, the crewmen delivered food and water, and checked if anyone needed medical attention.

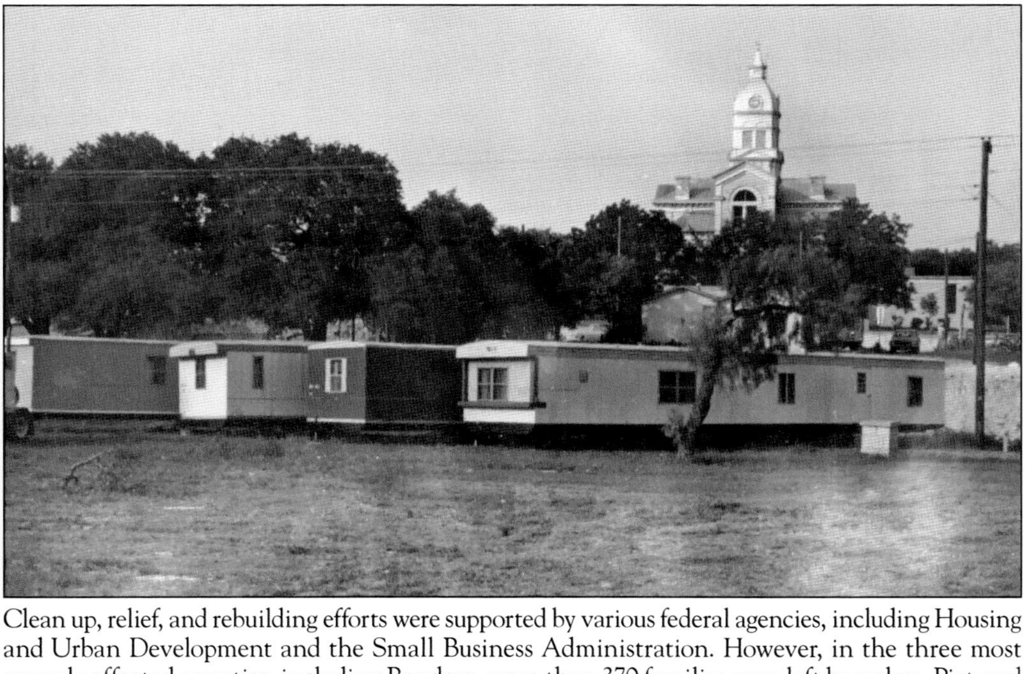

Clean up, relief, and rebuilding efforts were supported by various federal agencies, including Housing and Urban Development and the Small Business Administration. However, in the three most severely affected counties, including Bandera, more than 370 families were left homeless. Pictured above are four of the mobile homes moved in to provide temporary housing. Months later, the cleanup continued, as tons of debris continued to be removed from around the county.

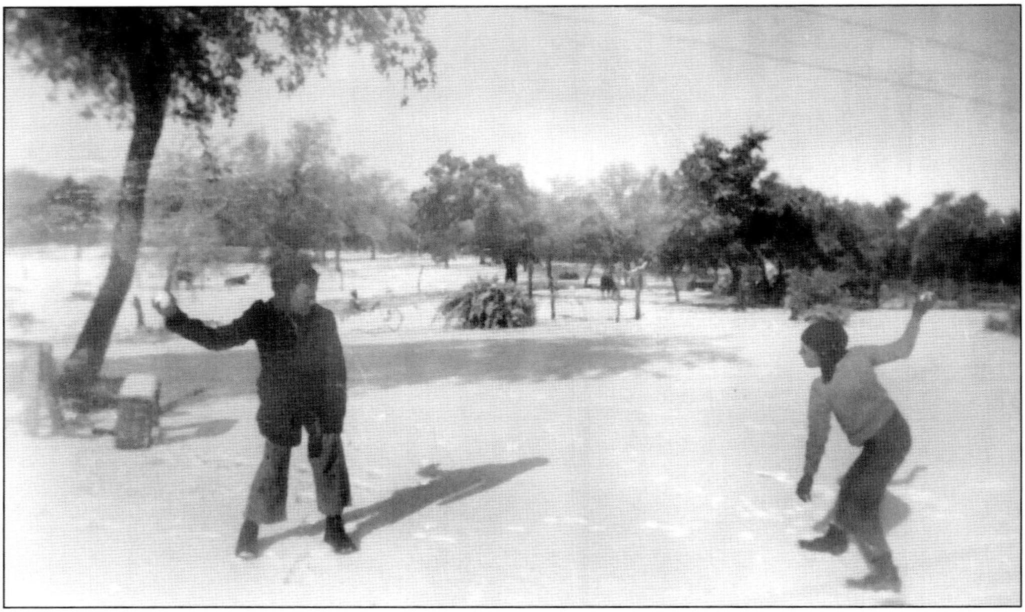

Not all weather extremes are destructive. Mother Nature can be just as nice, bringing joy and fun in the way of an occasional snowstorm. For those who live in South Texas, snow brings forth a winter wonderland, a playground for both young and old. Life comes to a standstill as businesses and schools close. For a brief time, one can breathe deeply the crisp cold air and take precious time off to enjoy a rare event. The last significant snowstorm occurred in 1985, when more than 18 inches of snow fell on Bandera County in a matter of days. (Above, courtesy of Theresa Helbert; below, courtesy of Betty Laskowski D'Spain.)

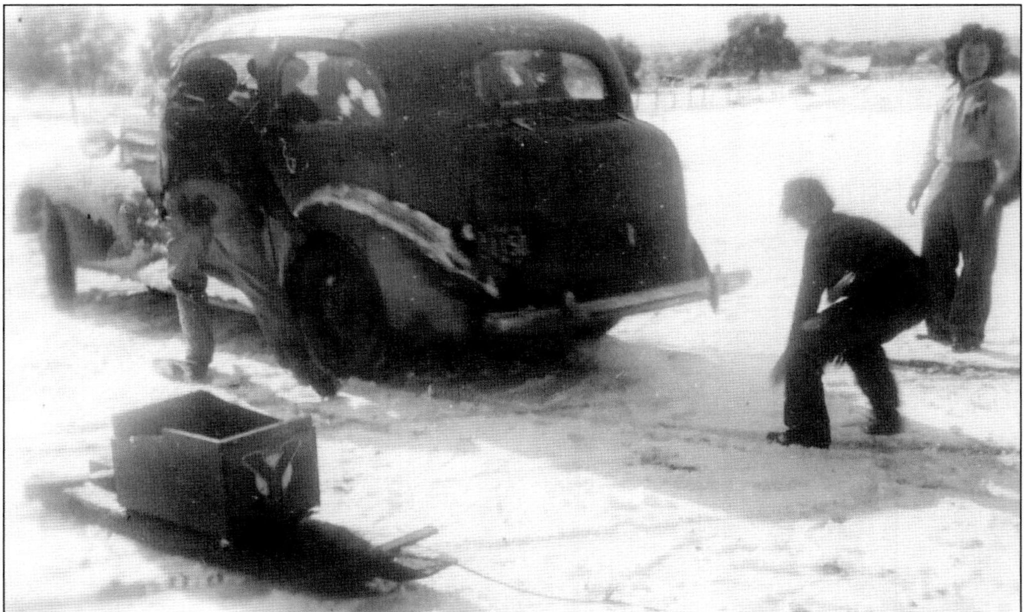

Six

Rodeos and Roundups

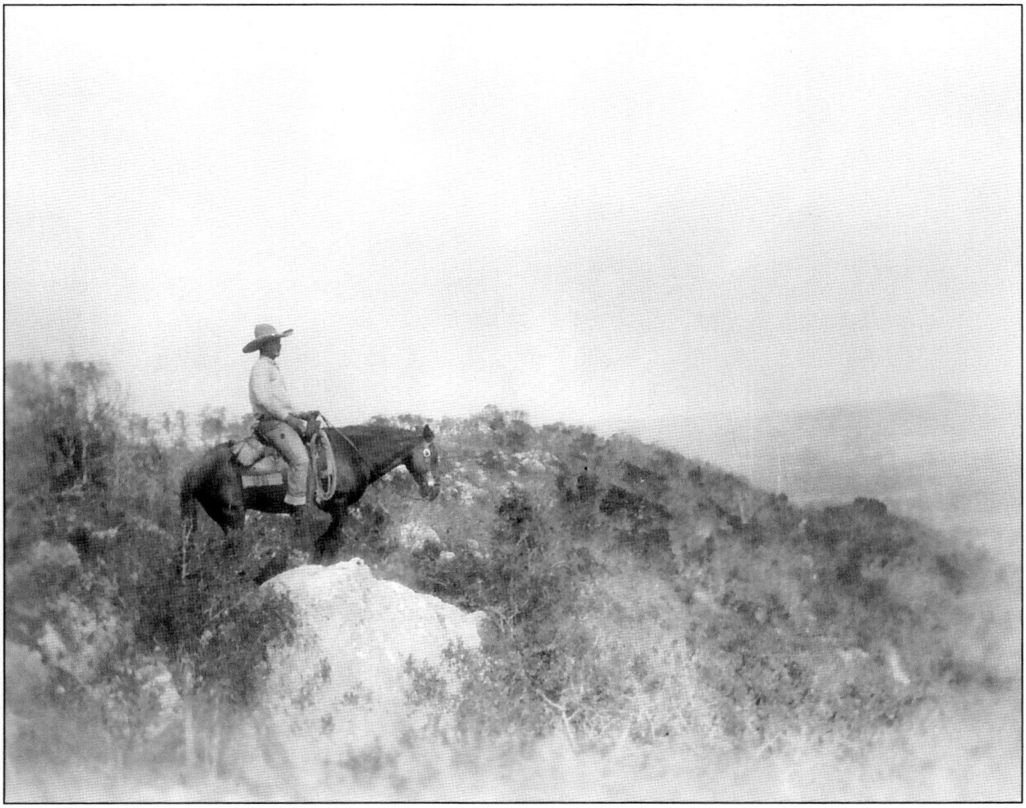

By the 1870s, the Western Trail was the principal thoroughfare for Texas cattle bound for northern markets. Cattle from South Texas were driven across the Medina River and through Bandera County on their way to Bandera Pass and the trail leading north. The cattle drives were finished by the early 1890s, but the legacy of the Texas cowboy has endured. (Courtesy of the Bandera County Historical Commission.)

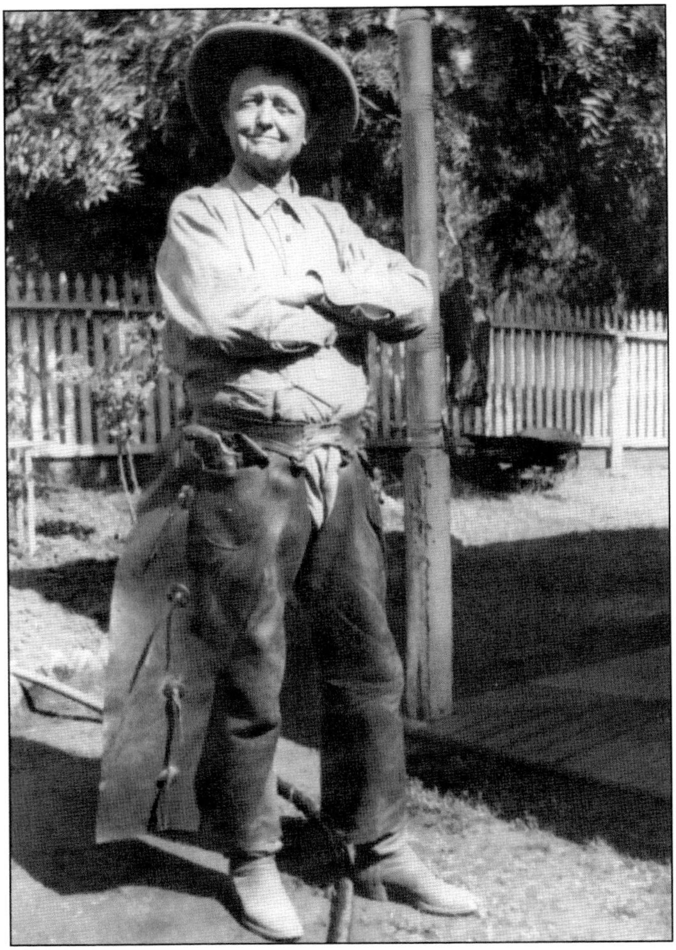

The myth of the Hollywood cowboy can overshadow the actual hardships of living on the trail or working a ranch. Born on a cattle ranch in 1857, Lewis Strickland (shown at left) settled on Mason Creek near Bandera, where he successfully ran cattle for 30 years. He had a colorful life and enjoyed telling stories, like the time when Native American raids forced him to turn back while attempting to drive cattle from Bandera to Kansas. Edward Asa Johnson (pictured below) was a different type of cowboy. Coming to Texas from Oklahoma with his family in a wagon, he settled around Medina Lake in 1916. He ranched on various parcels of land throughout the county by leasing the land he needed to raise sheep, goats, and cattle, moving his herd as a new lease would arise. (Left, courtesy of Frontier Times Museum Collection; below, courtesy of Burgin and Valli Johnson.)

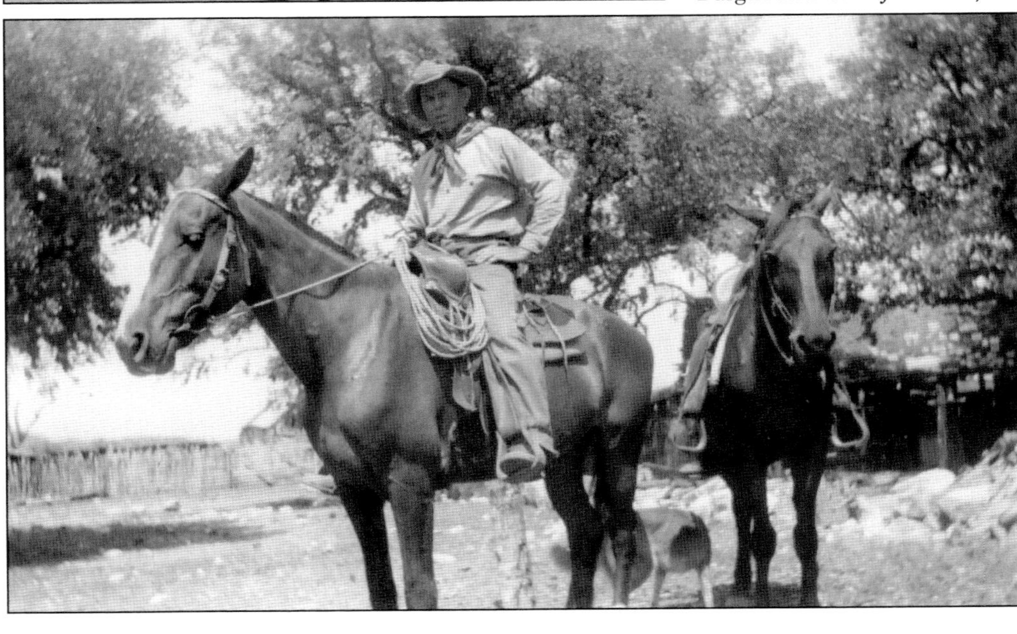

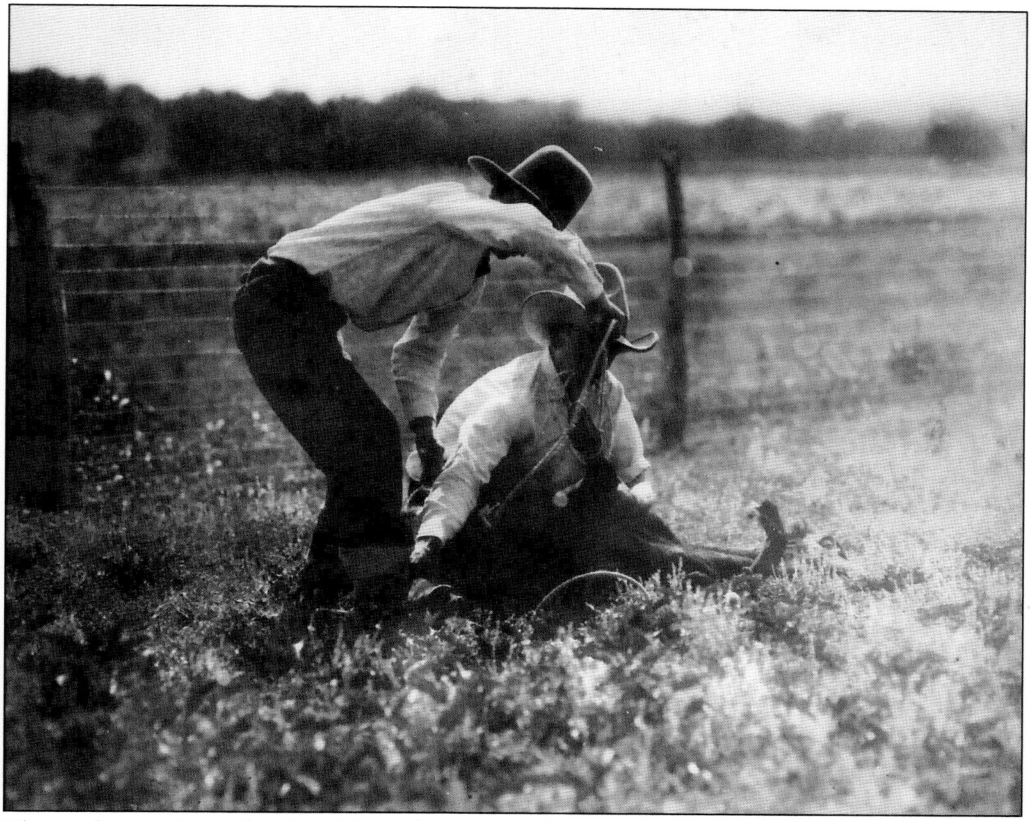

The cowboy tradition developed from the *vaquero*, the Mexican herdsmen of South Texas, whose roots were in the Spanish Colonial era. Anglo cowboys learned many of their techniques of handling cattle from the vaqueros, and by the time of the cattle drive, the cowboy had adopted the vaquero's saddle, chaps, bandana, wide-brim hat, lasso, and spurs. The style of dress and the skills learned on the ranch that were adapted to work cattle became the conventional image of the Texan cowboy. Early rodeos began when cowboys began competing against each other in the tasks they performed every day on the ranch, such as cattle roping. The rodeos were more like social gatherings for ranch families and would last all day and through the night. (Above, courtesy of the Bandera County Historical Association; below, courtesy of Scooter Fries.)

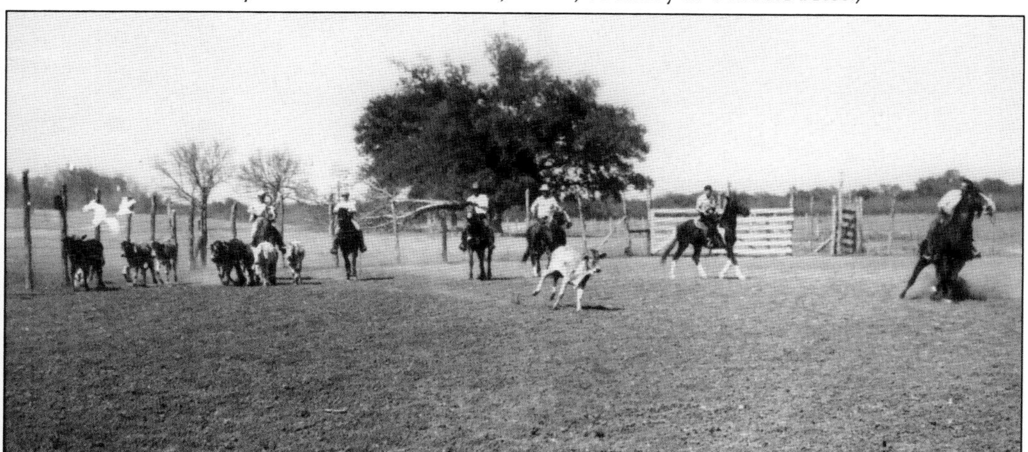

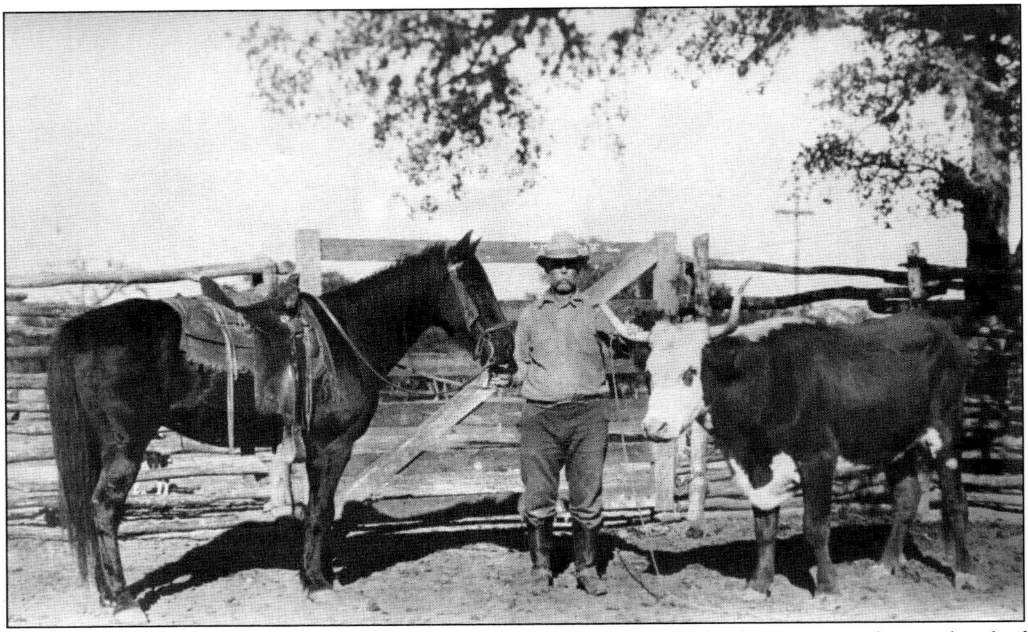

Ed Mansfield, affectionately called "Uncle Ed," believed he was the last man to drive a herd of cattle through downtown Kerrville in 1892. The day after he drove 1,600 head of cattle through knee-deep mud, a sign was posted that it was illegal to drive more than 15 head of cattle through town. He was a well-loved and respected rancher who served as the first president of the Bandera County Ranchmen and Farmers Association. (Courtesy of Luella Vandeveer.)

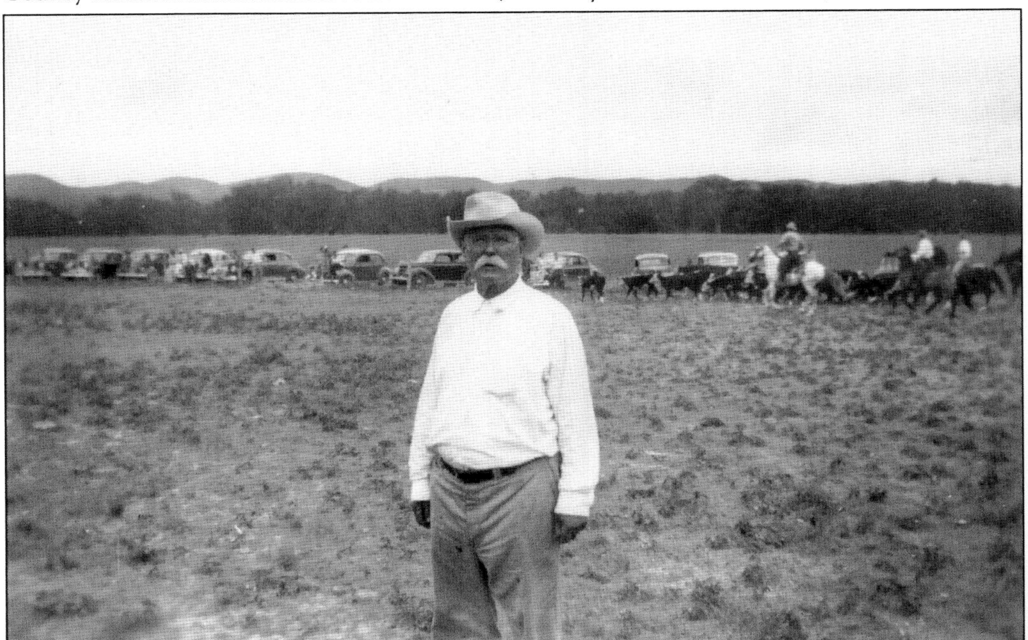

Mansfield donated the land from his ranch for Mansfield Park and began holding rodeos there in 1924. These early rodeos were instrumental in the development of Bandera County's champion ropers, who performed and honed their skills at the park. Mansfield himself was a skilled roper and continued to rope well into his 70s. (Courtesy of the Bandera County Historical Commission.)

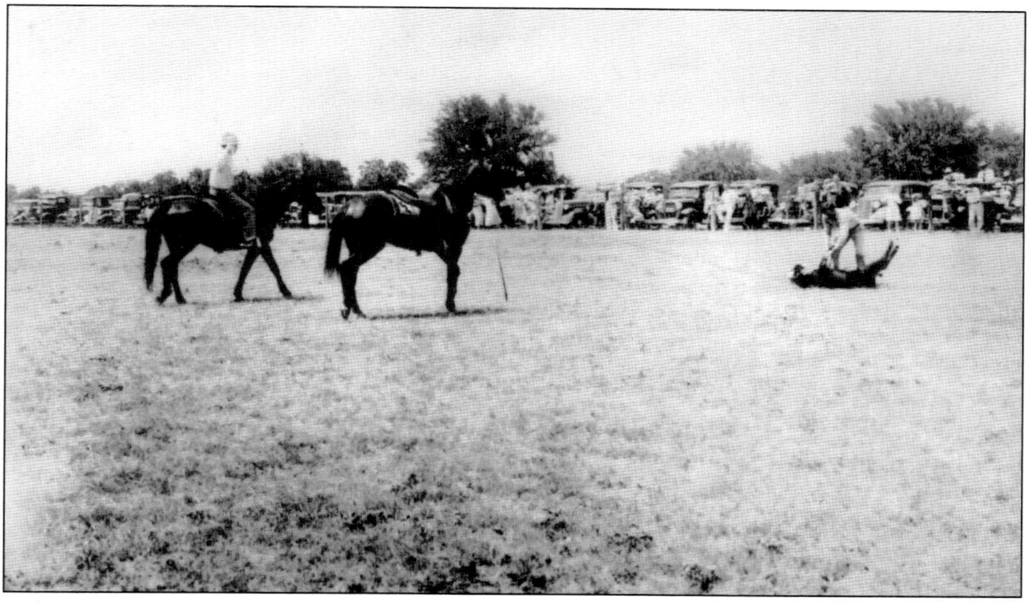

Before the grandstand was built, guests would drive up to the fairground in their cars, park, and watch the cowboys compete in calf roping, bull riding, bulldogging, and other competitive events. Once the cowboys would complete one event, the cattle were then driven to the other side of the fairground to continue the competitions. Mansfield Park was the training ground for seven world, national, and state roping champions—Toots Mansfield, Ray Wharton, Buddy Groff, Scooter Fries, Clay Billings, Todd Whitewood, and Jimmy Adams. Bandera honors these champions, along with the latest addition, Clint Singleton, with a bronze and native stone monument on the courthouse square, which was dedicated in 1982. (Above, courtesy of Christopher Baumle; below, courtesy of the Bandera County Historical Commission.)

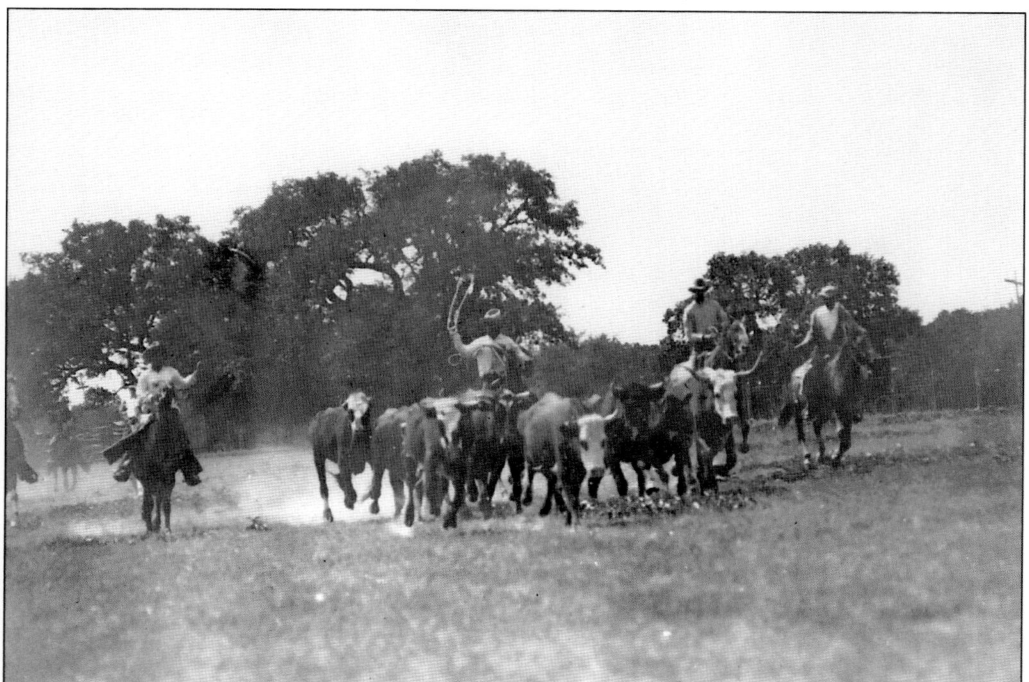

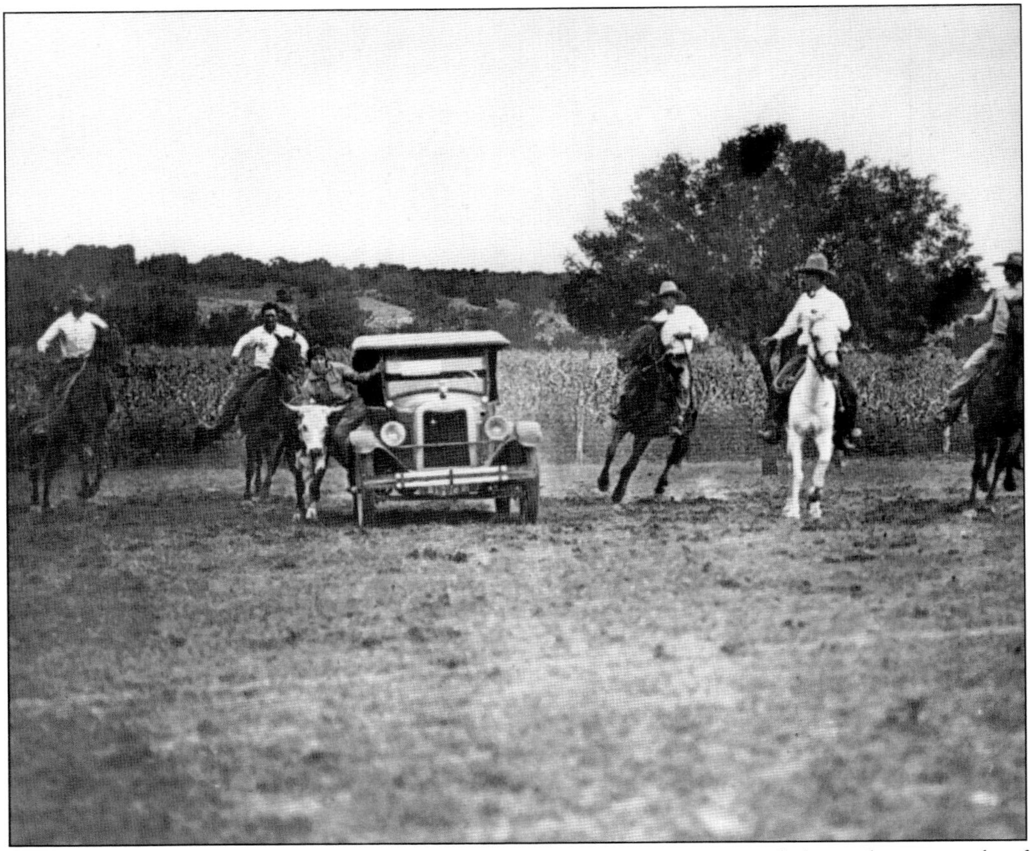

Ed Mansfield, with his dry sense of humor and friendly ways, opened the rodeo grounds of Mansfield Park to anyone who wanted to try their hand at roping and bulldogging. In 1926, son Frank Mansfield drove the car for a Miss Snow of Oklahoma as she bulldogged five steers that day from the car, leading one to wonder if this was a rodeo event that never caught on. (Courtesy of Frontier Times Museum Collection.)

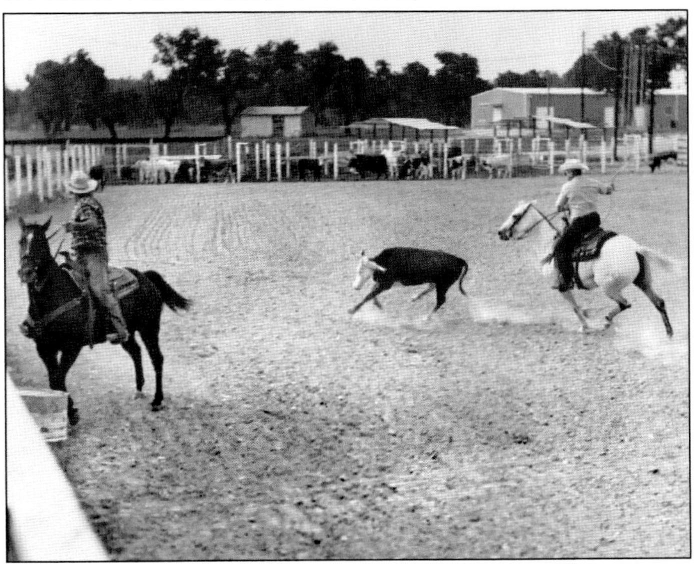

Mansfield Park continues to be used today for rodeos and special events. The Frontier Times Museum sponsors the National Day of the Cowboy the last weekend of every July by holding a competitive ranch rodeo at the arena. The rodeo showcases the ability to accomplish ranch tasks as a team, just as it is done on the ranch. Both local ranch hands and national competitors compete in the event. (Courtesy of the Bandera County Historical Commission.)

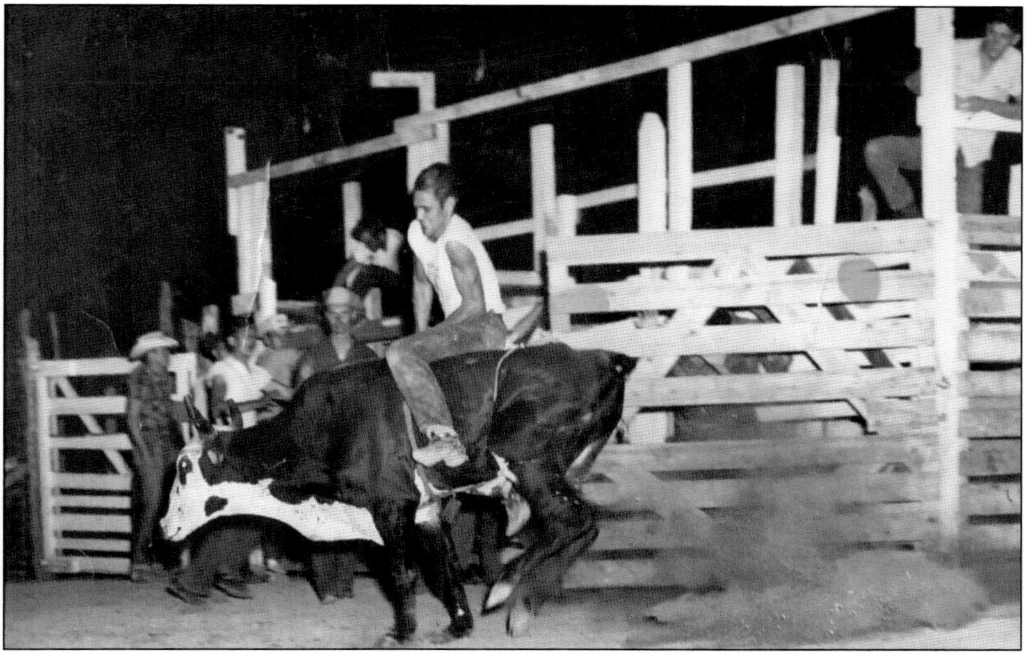

True grit, strength, commitment to practice, athletic ability, and a determination to win make a rodeo champion. By the early 1900s, early rodeos had moved beyond social gatherings to be more competitive, as cowboys competed for titles and prizes. The rodeo competitor is always pushing himself, oftentimes to injury, but it is the love of the challenge that keeps him going. (Courtesy of Scooter Fries.)

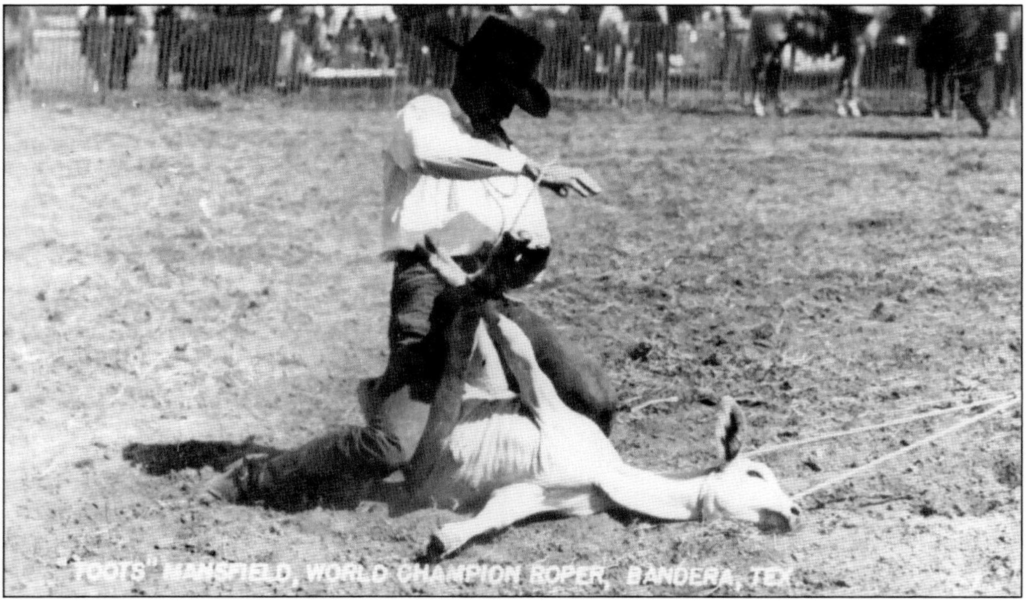

Long ago on a South Texas ranch, rancher Juan Salinas watched a ranch hand repeatedly miss the calf in a calf-roping event. He felt the young man would never get it right. The young cowboy, Toots Mansfield, proved him wrong and went on to win World Champion Calf Roper seven times from 1939 to 1950. Toots, nephew of Ed Mansfield, became a national celebrity and was inducted into the Cowboy Hall of Fame in 1981. (Courtesy of Luella Vanderveer.)

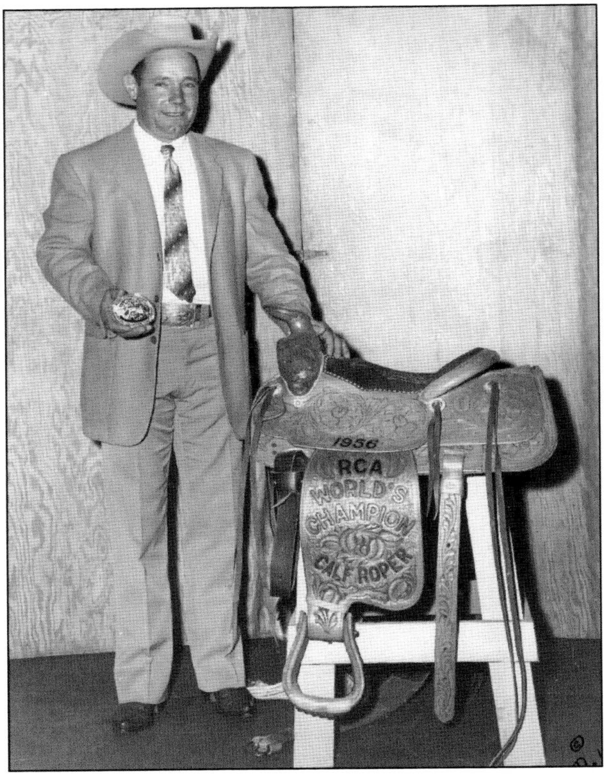

Known as the "Mighty Mite," Ray Wharton became the 1956 Rodeo Cowboy Association World Calf-Roping Champion. He began roping as a toddler, when he slung a loop over anything that moved on his family ranch. A bad fall later resulted in a crippling bone disease in his arm, but through determination, he regained the use of his arm and went back to practicing roping. He won his first big rodeo in 1944, and since then, he has won or placed at every major rodeo he has entered. He credits his horses, Bones, Rusty, Cindy, and his favorite, Brownie, with his winning runs. He has shared his talent and knowledge with many young ropers, including champions Clay Billing and Todd Whitewood, and African American cowboy Cleo Hearn. Wharton trained Hearn during a time when African American cowboys faced much discrimination. (Both, courtesy of Ray Wharton.)

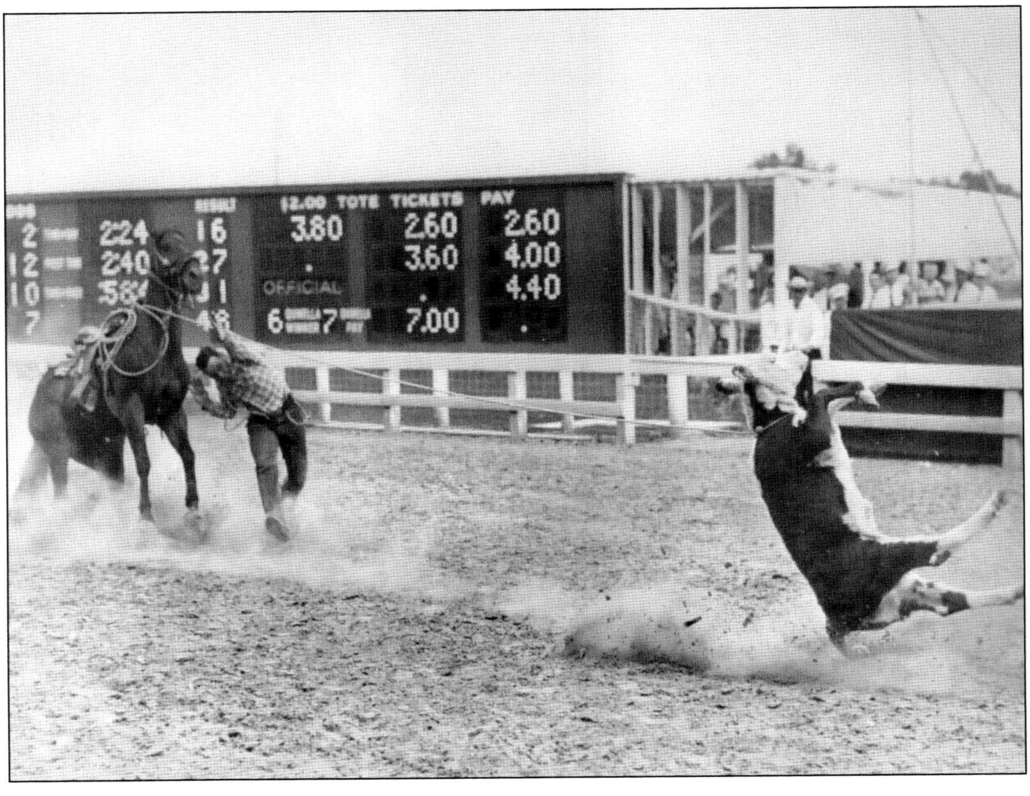

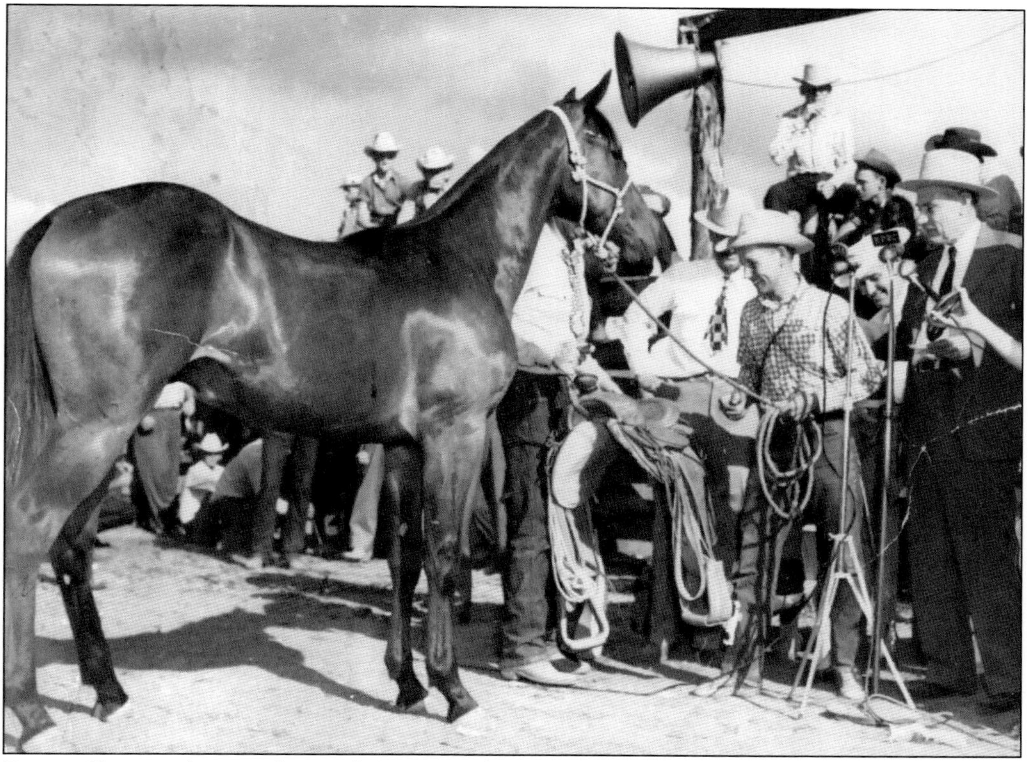

Scooter Fries was born on his uncle Bennie Adamietz's U-Bar Guest Ranch and was given his first pony when he was three. By eight years old, he was performing roping exhibitions at Mansfield Park and around South Texas. Inspired by Toots Mansfield, he practiced daily at Mansfield Park, which Ed Mansfield made available to him. He was already a veteran roper when he won the Texas Junior State Roping Champion of 1948. The photograph above shows Gov. Coke Stevenson as he presented Scooter with a horse and saddle. In 1950, he won another state championship in steer wrestling and went on to win the national championship. In 1951, he won his third state championship in tie-down roping and also won the national reserve championship. It was Ray Wharton and Buddy Groff who brought him to the Rodeo Cowboys Association circuit. (Both, courtesy of Scooter Fries.)

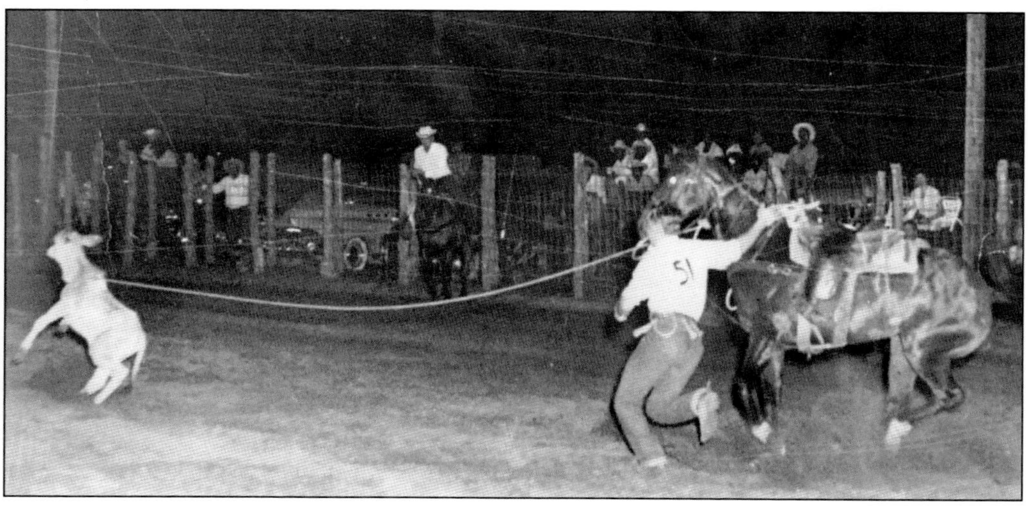

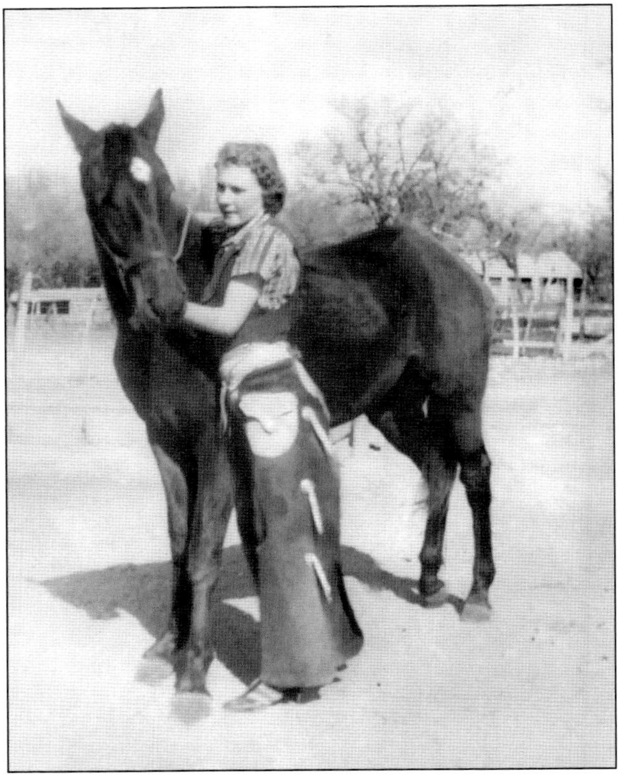

Growing up in Tarpley, Clay Billings (pictured below) learned roping from his father, Felix, who started to rodeo and ranch after finishing ninth grade. His mother, Lorene (left), was a barrel racer, and his brother Howard won several awards and married Mary Kay Anderwald Billing, a champion barrel racer. As a teenager, Clay was trained by Ray Wharton, who sold him a 4-year-old gelding called Strek. With Strek, Clay went on to win the tie-down championship at the Medina Future Farmers of America and, a month later, became the state high school calf-roping champion. That same year, 1975, he won the national championship. During his career, he won five saddles and numerous silver belt buckles. His name is etched on the rodeo champion monument on Bandera's courthouse square. (Both, courtesy of Linda Billings.)

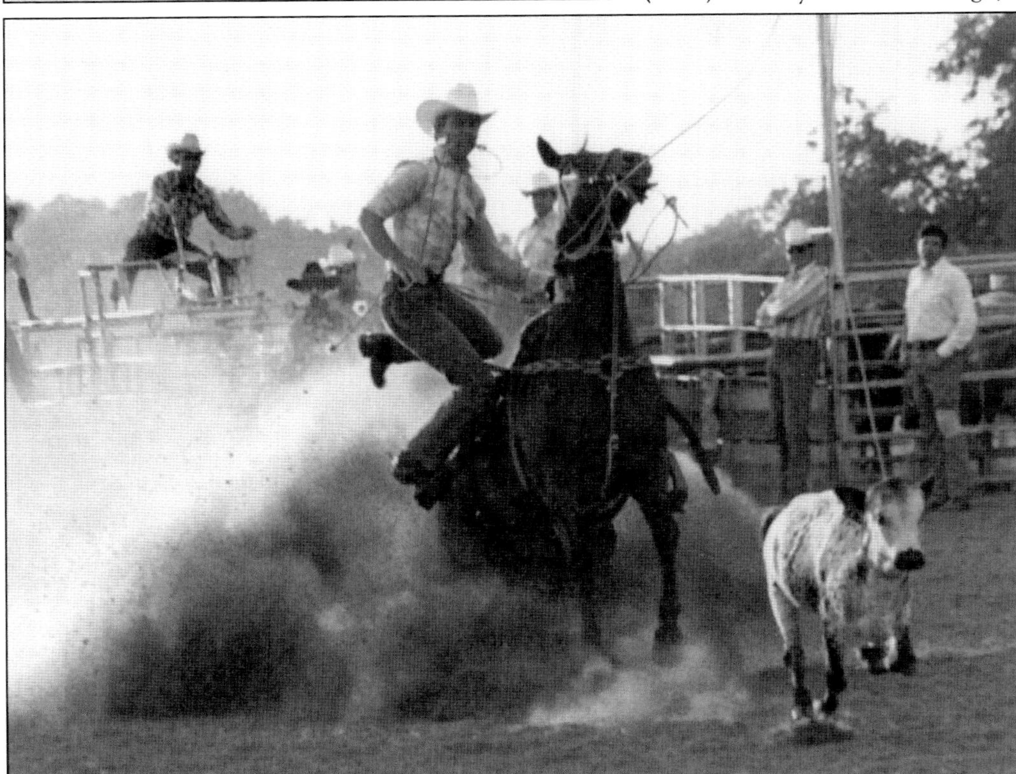

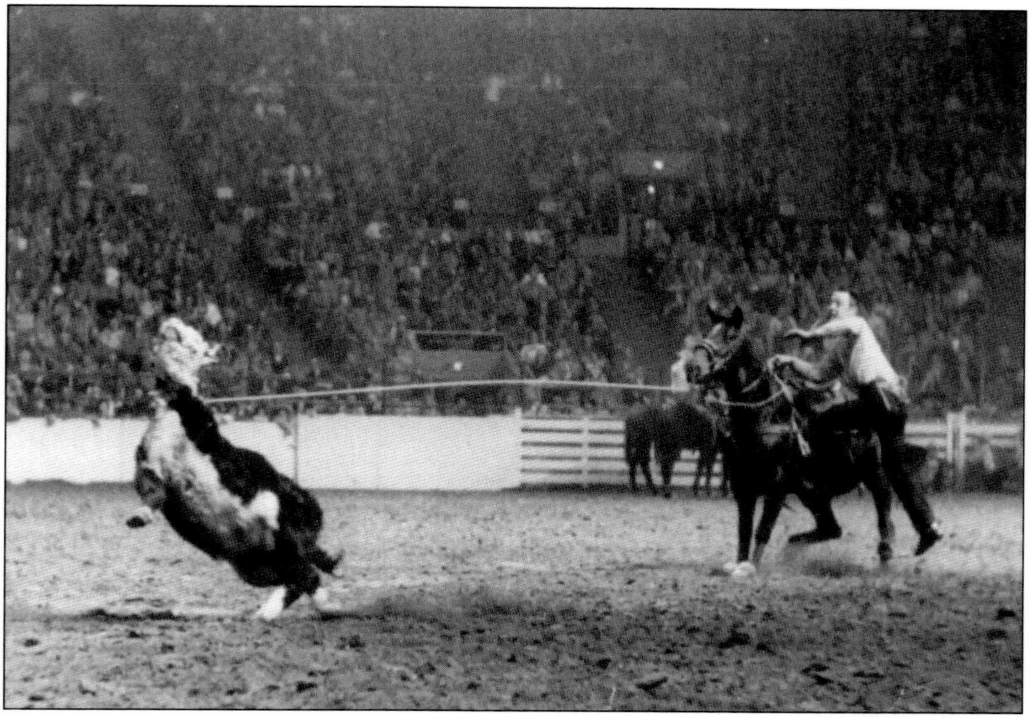

Moving across from Mansfield Park in 1946 was fortunate for Buddy Groff. Ed Mansfield allowed Groff to use the arena, and it was here that Groff learned how to rope. He traveled the Rodeo Cowboy Association's circuit, where it was necessary to compete against masters such as Toots Mansfield and Ray Wharton. He was Reserve World Champion in 1954 and repeated that in 1956, finishing behind his friend Wharton. (Courtesy of Linda Billings.)

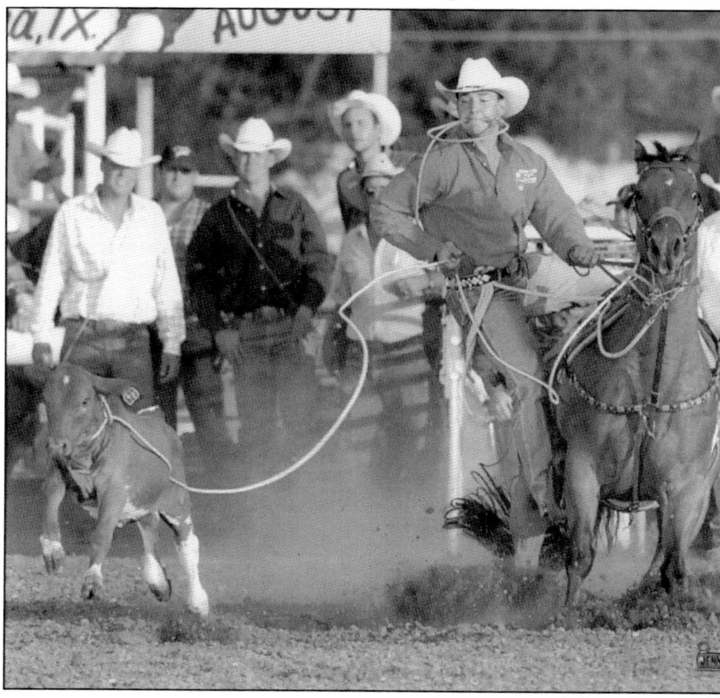

The newest rodeo champion on Bandera's cowboy roll of honor, Clint Singleton was only 19 when he was crowned junior world champion of calf roping. A Medina High School football star, Singleton began riding in the rodeo at an early age. He was trained by rodeo champion Todd Whitewood, who was trained by Ray Wharton. Whitewood (far left) watches his protégé in this photograph, taken of Singleton in action. (Photograph by Jennings Photography; courtesy of Clint Singleton.)

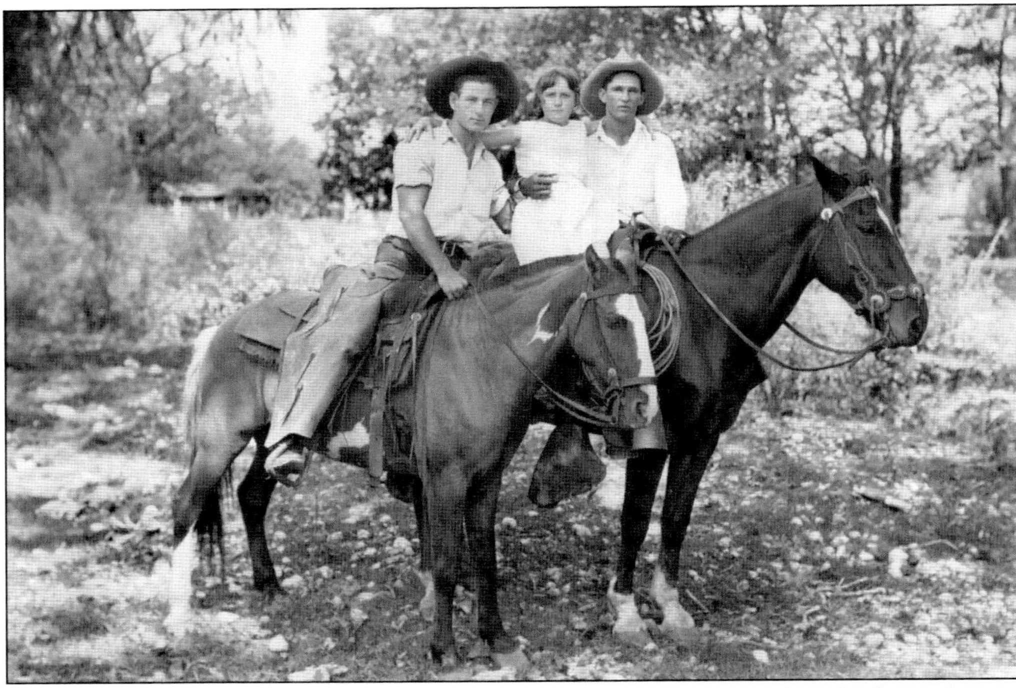

Many cowboys found work not only on ranches or competing in rodeos, but also by performing in expositions throughout South Texas. In 1925, Ed Mansfield took his rodeo on the road to San Antonio's Woodlawn Lake, where Hayden Mansfield (right) performed with little Edith Kelly (center) and this unidentified cowboy. Reminiscent of early Wild West shows, their skits required precision riding skills. (Courtesy of Luella Vanderveer.)

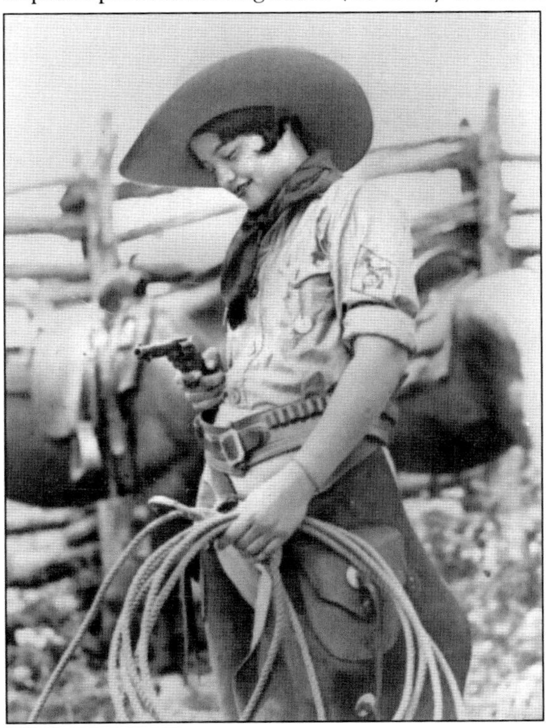

From the early days of rodeo, ladies wanted to be part of the action. Women had always worked the ranches and developed their horsemanship skills alongside cowboys. Hollywood loved the idea of the pretty girl on a horse, and early on, women were featured in Western films. Thelma Surber Davenport, a Bandera beauty, tried her hand in Hollywood before returning home to marry a bank president. (Courtesy of the Bandera County Historical Commission.)

Bennie Adamietz was known as one of Bandera's most colorful cowboys, and obviously from this photograph, he was a cowboy that was admired by the ladies. His family turned their working ranch into a dude ranch, Bennie's U-Bar Guest Ranch. As a dude wrangler, he taught riding and ranching skills, and performed for his guests. Along with his nephew Scooter Fries, he also managed a roping school for aspiring rodeo champions. (Courtesy of Bobby and Mary Stein.)

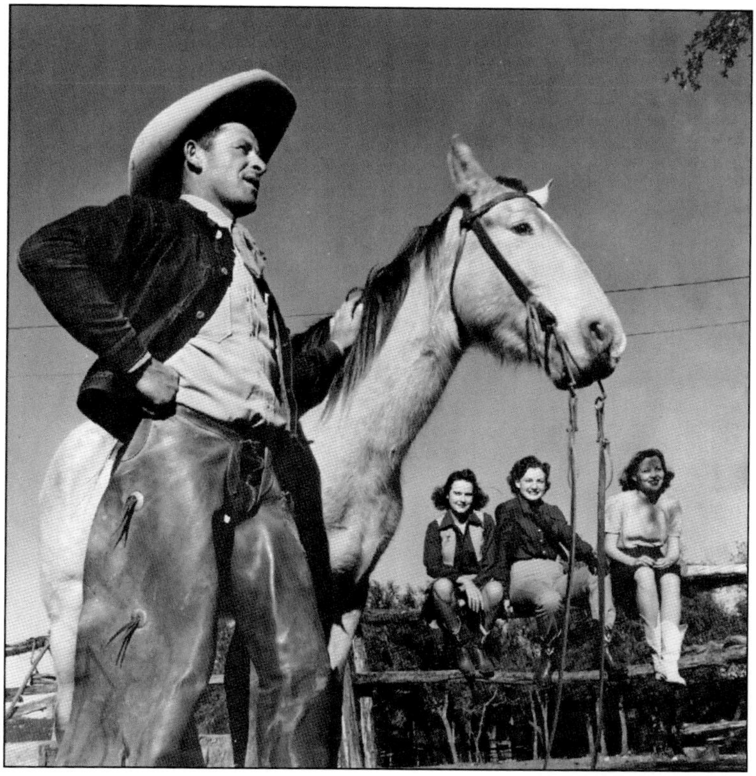

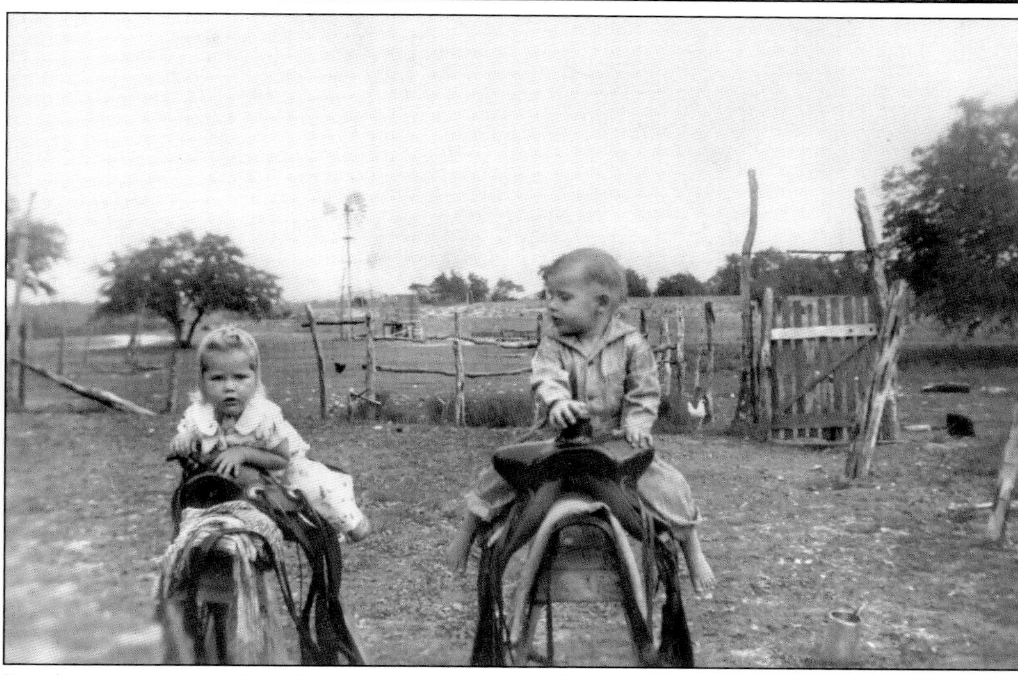

Bandera youngsters often dream of growing up to be cowgirls and cowboys. Here Bobby and Mary Anne Stein "ride the saddles" at Uncle Fabian's ranch. Children can compete in rodeos in their own events, such as the calf scramble or the rough-and-tumble mutton busting. (Courtesy of Bobby and Mary Stein.)

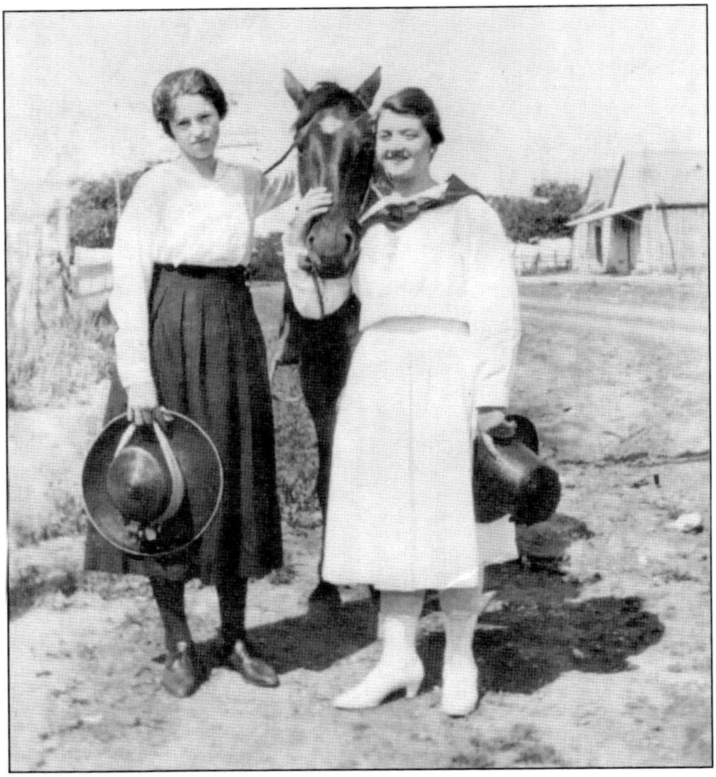

Living and working a ranch may be hard work, but these women show that it can be done with style and class. (Courtesy of Betty Laskowski D'Spain.)

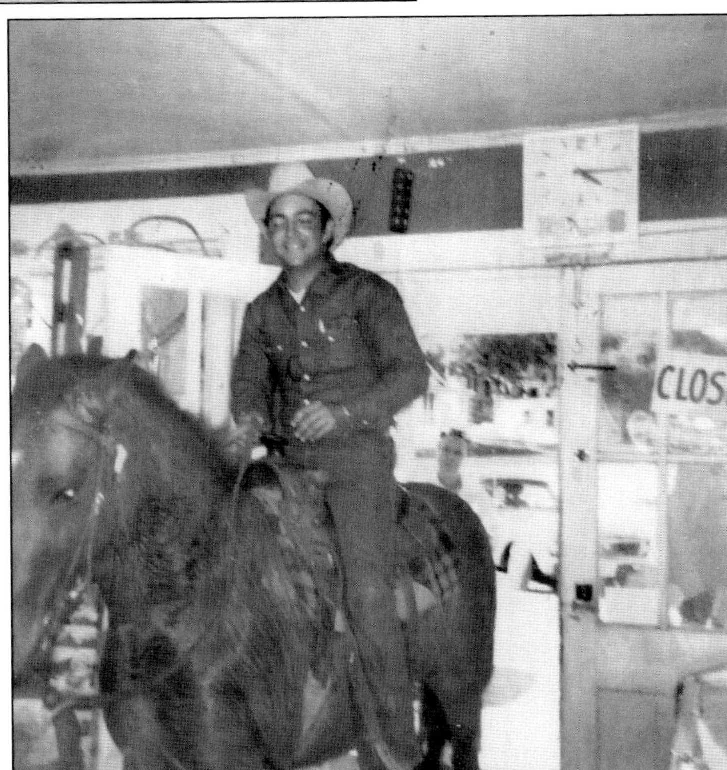

One's horse was one's work partner, or at the very least a treasured companion to take wherever the road may lead. Burgin Johnson visits Turk's General Store on Medina Lake with his favorite ride. (Courtesy of Burgin and Valli Johnson.)

Seven

Dudes, Dances, and Delights

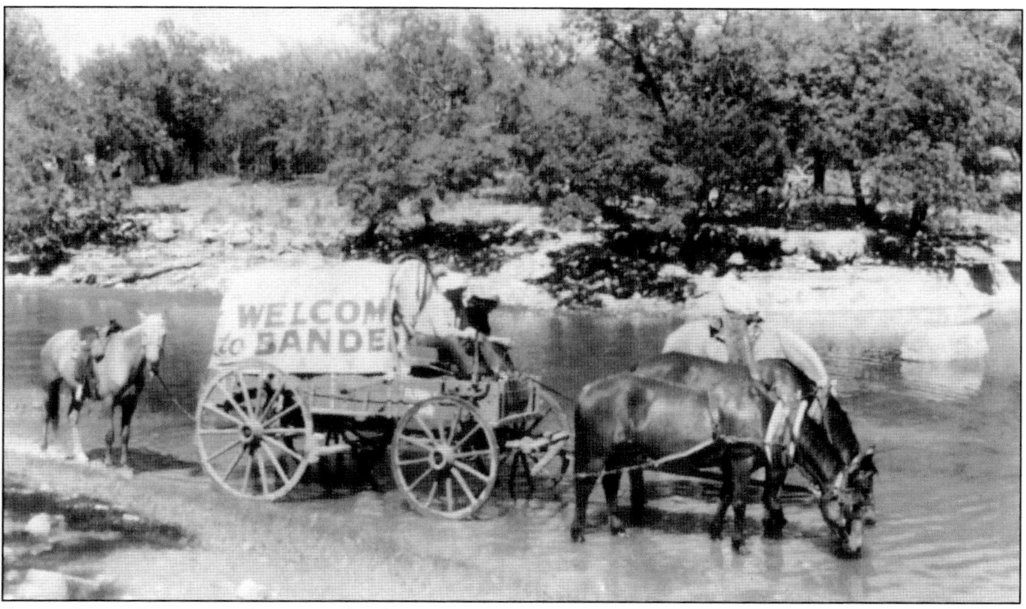

As early as the 1880s, business leaders were touting Bandera County as a healthful respite for "many invalids." The pure atmosphere, temperate climate, and splendid water supply were beneficial for a wide variety of maladies, from consumption to gout. By the 1920s, tourists came to stay on authentic ranches, and dude ranches opened throughout the county. Along with honky-tonks and dancing, Bandera became known for a Western-style good time. (Courtesy of Clay Conoly.)

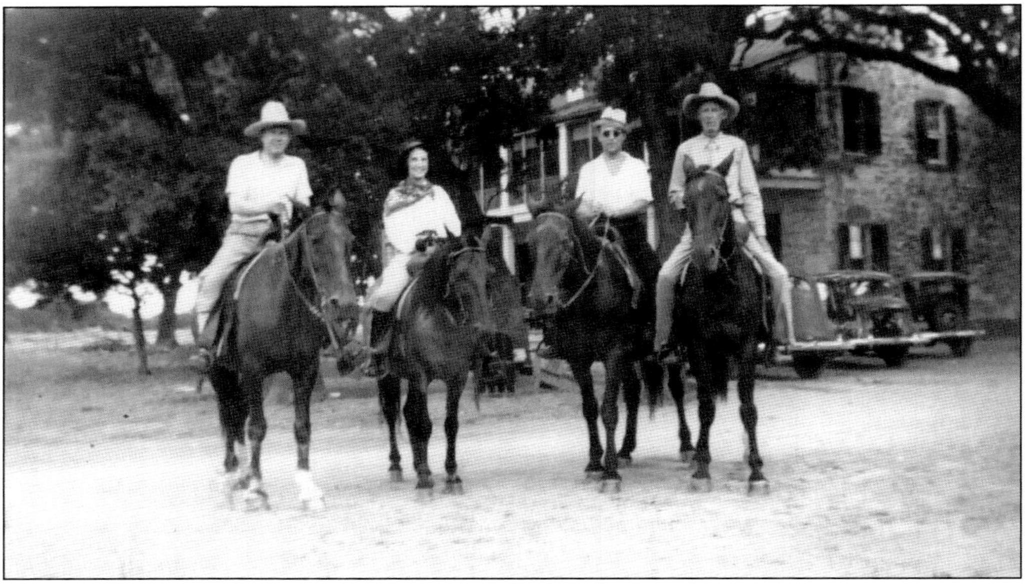

In Texas, the dude ranch industry began when Eb and Kate Buck began taking summer boarders at their ranch on Julian Creek in 1920 to supplement their income. Eb's brother Frank (left), the ranch's dude wrangler, was quoted in 1937, "Twenty-seven years ago I came here to stay around a few days until I made up my mind what I wanted to do. I haven't made up my mind yet, so I'm still here." (Courtesy of the Frontier Times Museum Collection.)

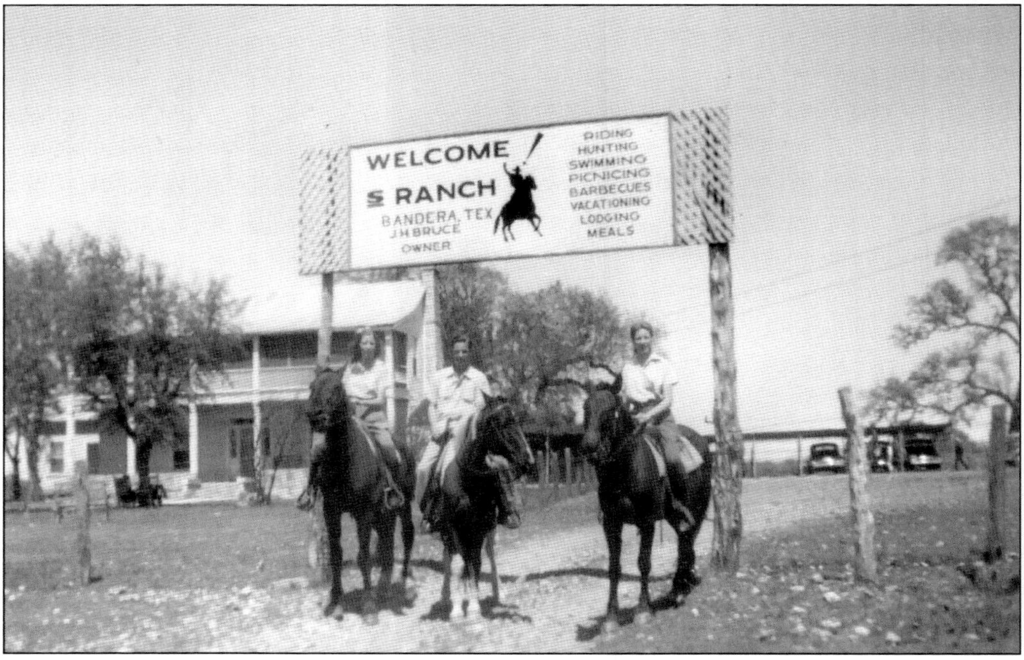

The Bruce family opened their S-Bar Ranch to accommodate the Buck Ranch's overflow of visitors. Guests stayed in the original ranch house, built in 1879. By the time the highway to San Antonio was completed in 1936, Bandera was a well-known tourist destination. (Courtesy of the Frontier Times Museum Collection.)

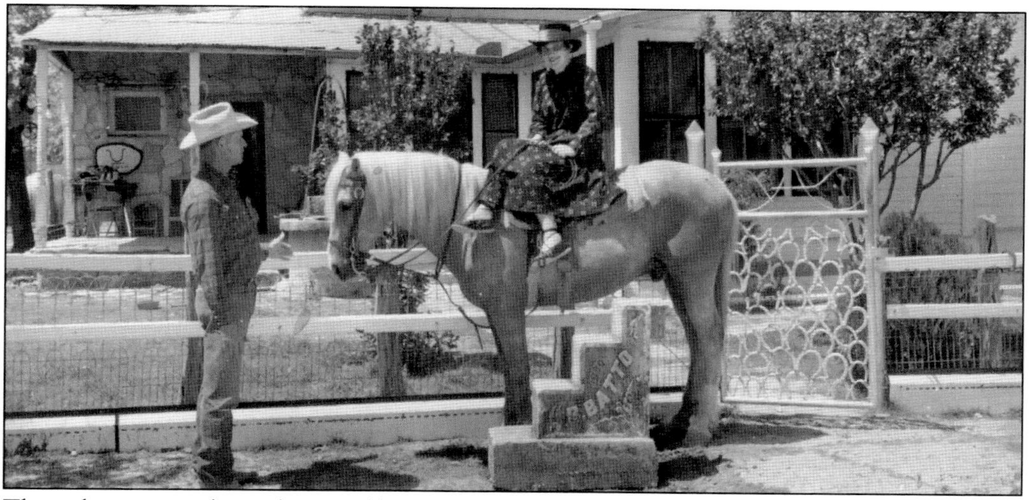

This rider is assisted onto her steed by an old-fashioned mounting block at Bennie's U-Bar Guest Ranch. Notice the Batto name on the block. By 1948, there were 17 dude ranches, and the 1940s and 1950s became known as the golden age of dude ranches. Each ranch would publish a glossy brochure to entice potential guests with the joys that were awaiting them. (Courtesy of Scooter Fries.)

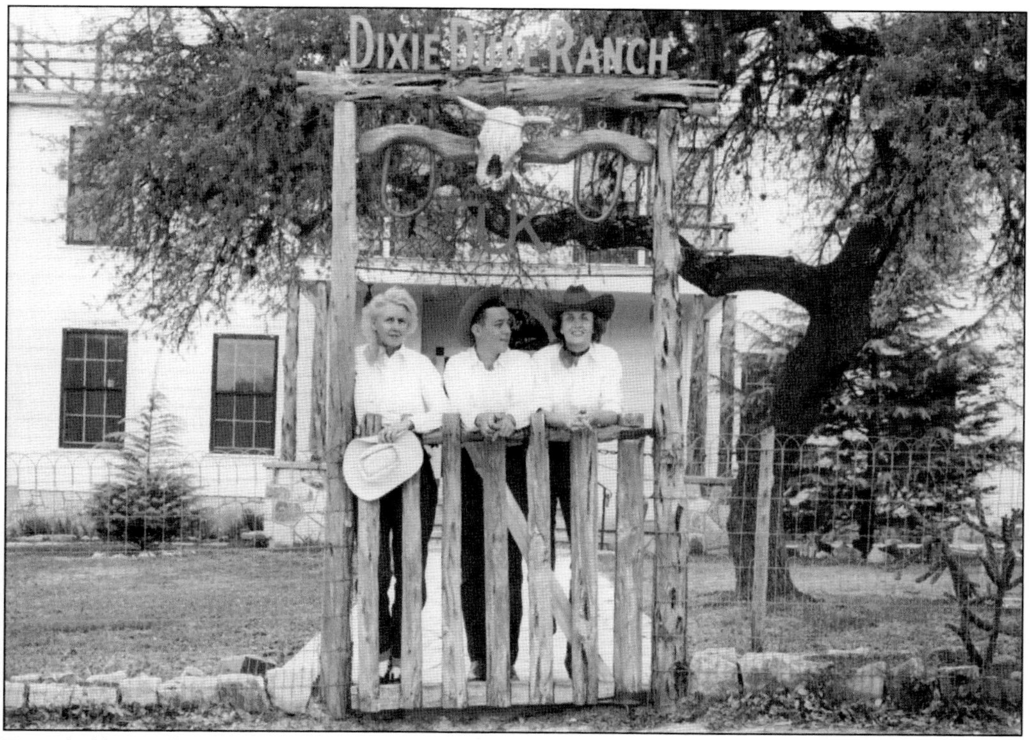

Founded by William Wallace Whitney in 1901, the Dixie Dude Ranch began welcoming guests in 1937, while remaining a working ranch. The owner, Billie Crowell (left), seen here with Clay and Darlene Conoly (right), was the editor of the *Dude Wrangler*, a publication devoted to the dude ranch business. In 2005, the ranch received recognition as a Texas Historic Ranch by the Family Land Heritage Program of the Texas Department of Agriculture for continuous operation by the same family for more than a century. (Courtesy of Clay Conoly.)

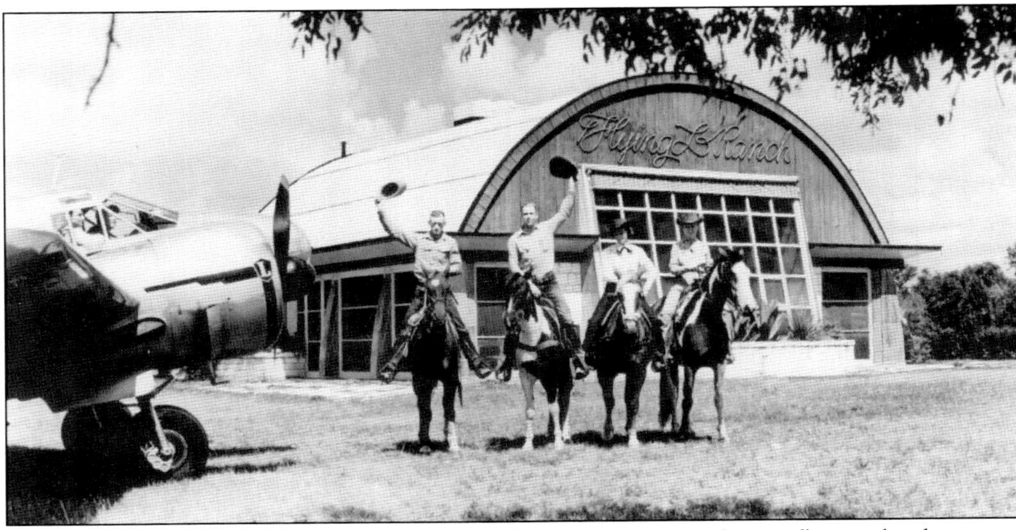

The Flying L Ranch was conceived by Col. Jack Lapham, a retired army flyer, polo player, and sportsman pilot. Lapham boasted that he would bring a modern airport to Bandera and opened the Flying L in 1946. The Flying L had an airstrip and a hanger with a restaurant and lounge. His brochures catered to those who wanted to fly their private airplanes to the ranch. (Courtesy of Judy Hicks.)

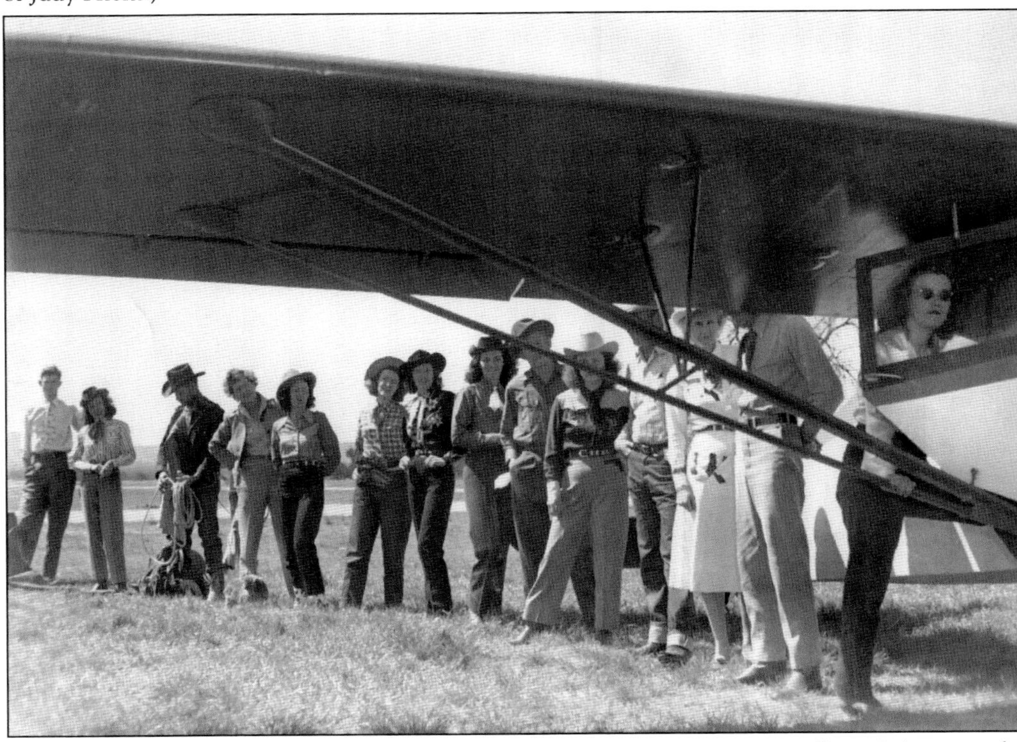

More dude ranches added landing strips to their property for guests to "fly in." Arriving by private airplane was the ultimate modern luxury. The Circle R Guest Ranch in Medina assured all visitors arriving by airplane that they would be met by the Circle R buckboard for the trip to ranch headquarters. The Mayan Ranch and Lost Valley also had their own landing strips to accommodate chartered airplanes. (Courtesy of Scooter Fries.)

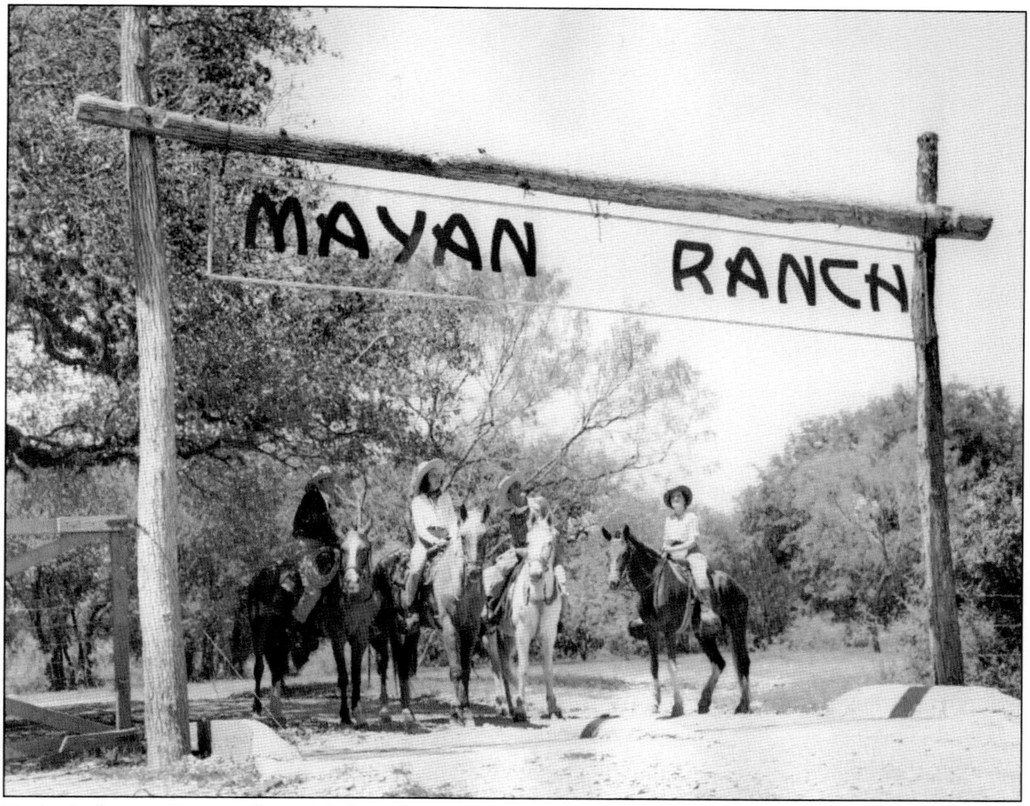

Early dude ranches emphasized that they were working ranches where guests could participate or observe ranch life. The Reeder Ranch let their guests know in their brochure what they were expected to do. Guests could join running cattle, sheep, and goats, and during the farming season, there were cows to milk, chickens to feed, hay to cut, a garden to tend, and fresh vegetables to be picked. Energetic guests were told they could share the work—without paying extra for the privilege. By the 1930s, dude ranches began offering more activities for their guests beyond ranching chores. The Hicks family has been welcoming guests since 1951 to the Mayan Ranch. Not expected to milk the cows, guests at the Mayan were treated to an abundance of activities, from saloon girl dances to Hawaiian luaus. At right, owner Don Hicks welcomes guests with a Texas-sized hello. (Both, courtesy of Judy Hicks.)

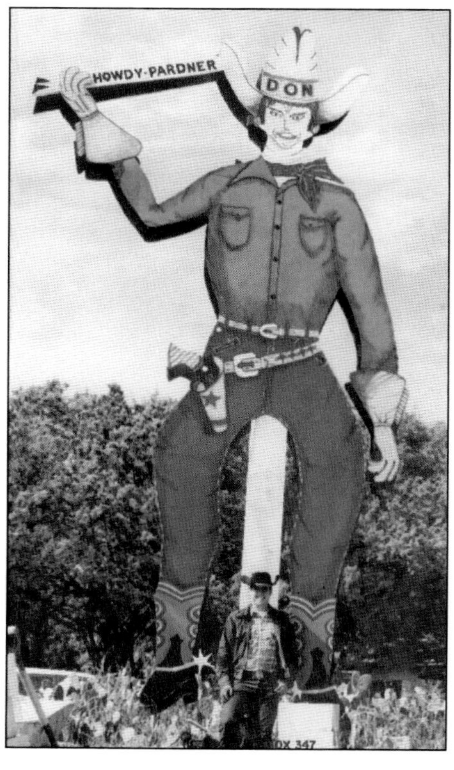

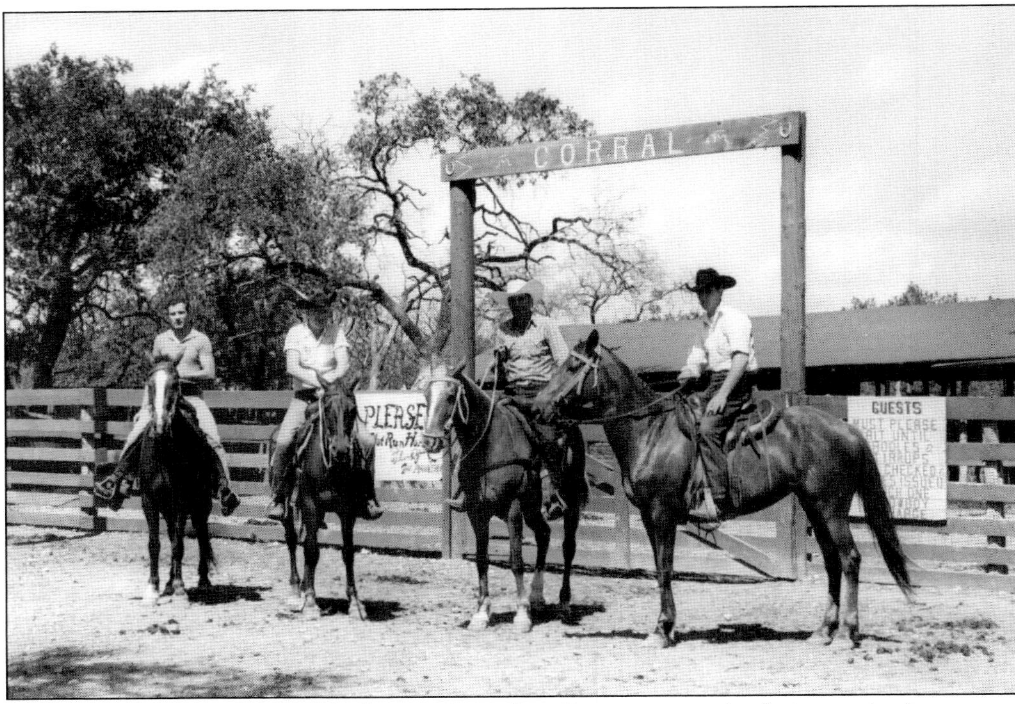

The original "dude" was a "tenderfoot" or "greenhorn" unaccustomed to being out in the country. A dude wrangler was the cowboy on a ranch who "wrangled" the visiting dudes. A main attraction to the dude ranches was the horse rides, and the dude wrangler was responsible for teaching guests how to ride. Billie Crowell of the Dixie Dude told the *Bandera Bulletin* that trail rides were not always part of the visit. Guests would ride horses into town, but the Dixie Dude was the first to let their guests ride just for the fun of it. Later ranches bragged on their trail rides, "Saddling up in the big corral is a thrilling spectacle. Saddle trails over the picturesque mountains into the town of Bandera are replete with scenic, rustic beauty." (Both, courtesy of Judy Hicks.)

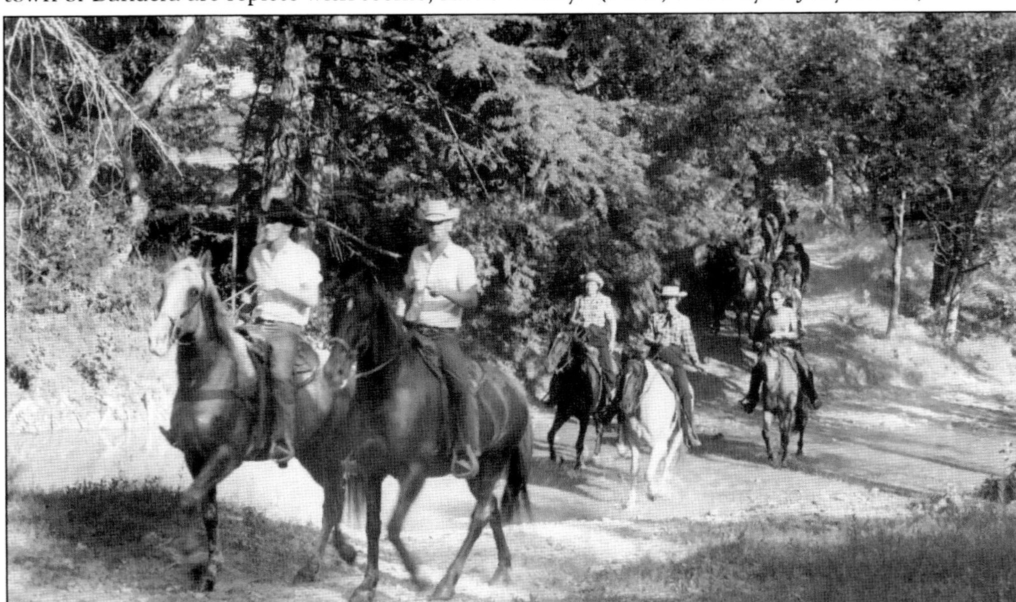

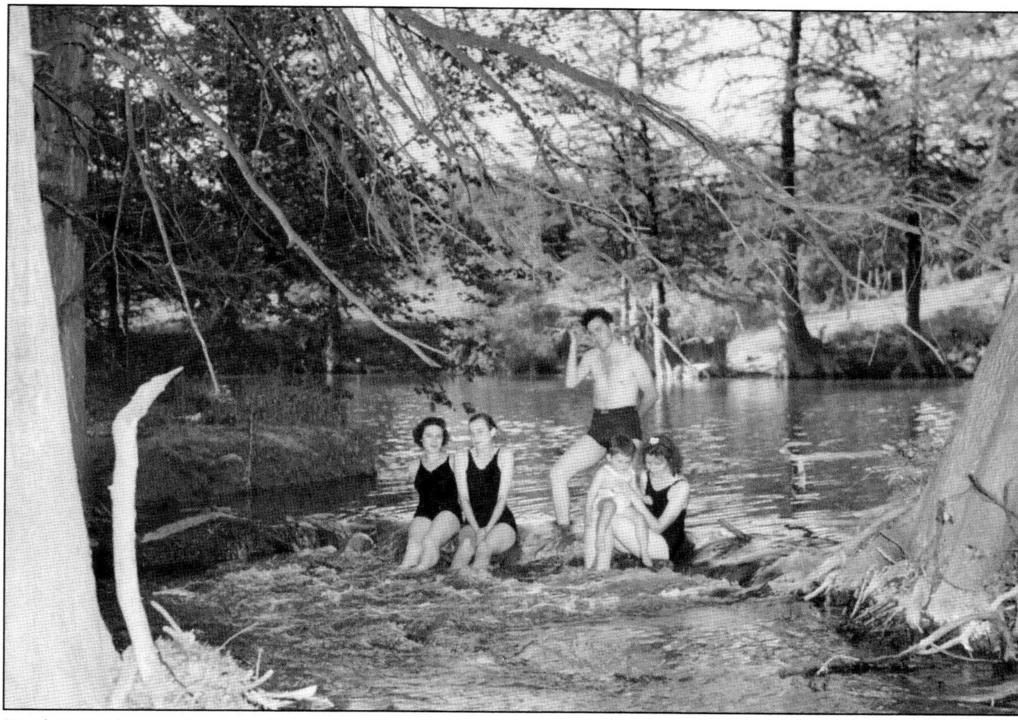

Dude ranches strived to keep their guests happy and busy, if one preferred to "live in the vivid, thrilling action of real ranch activity." They also emphasized that guests could enjoy complete rest and quiet relaxation sitting on the porch. Riding in the roundups and participating in rodeos was offered, along with colorful cowboy and cowgirl dances, nightly sing-alongs, chuck wagon trail dinners, fishing, and swimming. Guests were reminded to pack a bathing suit, to dress casually in jeans or khakis, and not to overlook gay shirts and ten-gallon hats. Those missing Western-appropriate clothes in their closets at home need not worry, as many ranches had their own style shops available for shopping. (Above, courtesy of Judy Hicks; below, courtesy of Scooter Fries.)

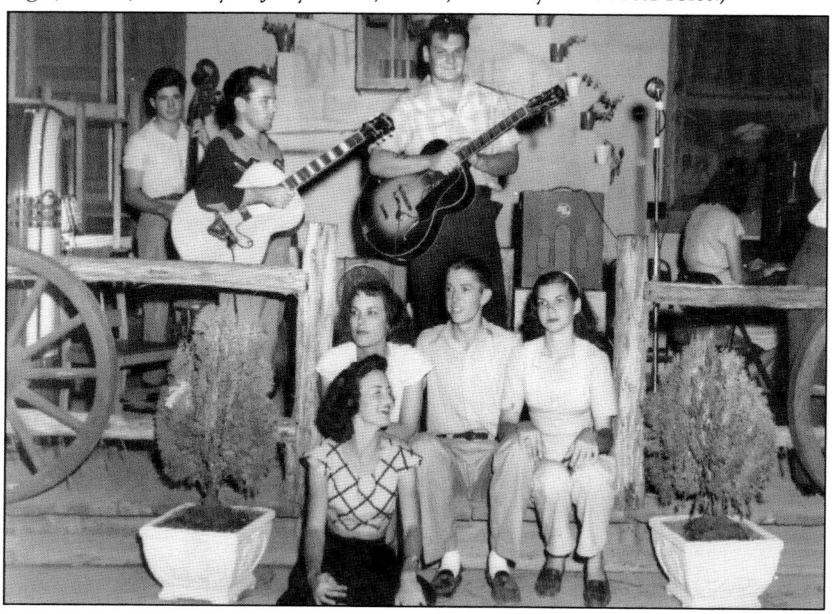

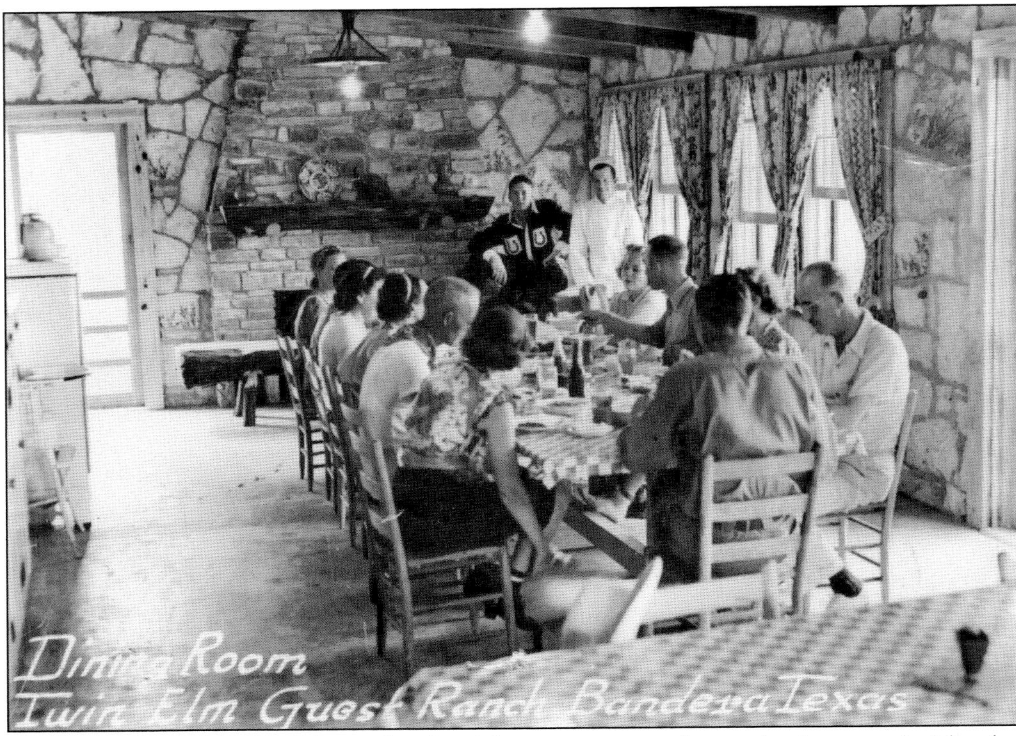

Chuck wagon dinners, eating a cowboy breakfast over an open fire, or sharing a meal with other guests in the dining room were all part of the package. The ranches took great pride in advertising excellent food served family-style, with homemade preserves, hot biscuits, plenty of milk, cream, butter, and eggs produced on the ranch, fresh meat and chicken grown on the ranch, and goat milk for those who wished it. During World War II, guests were told to bring their ration cards if they were planning on staying a week or longer, since guests were on their own expense if visiting neighboring towns. Shown above is the dining room at the Twin Elms, and below is a campfire cooking at the Mayan Ranch. (Above, courtesy of Frontier Times Museum Collection; below, courtesy of Judy Hicks.)

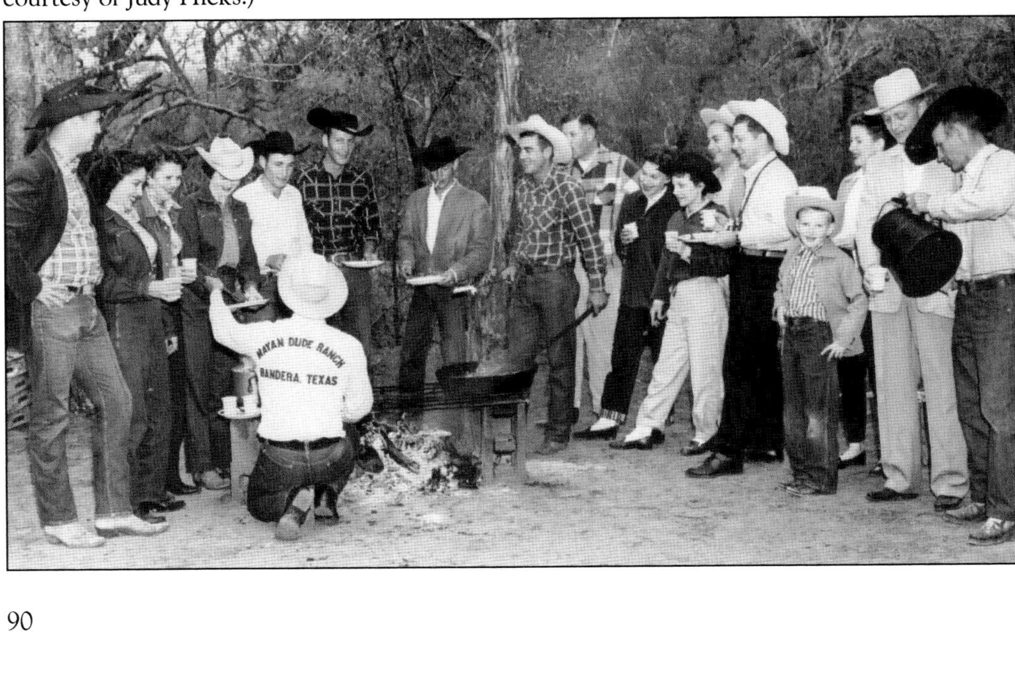

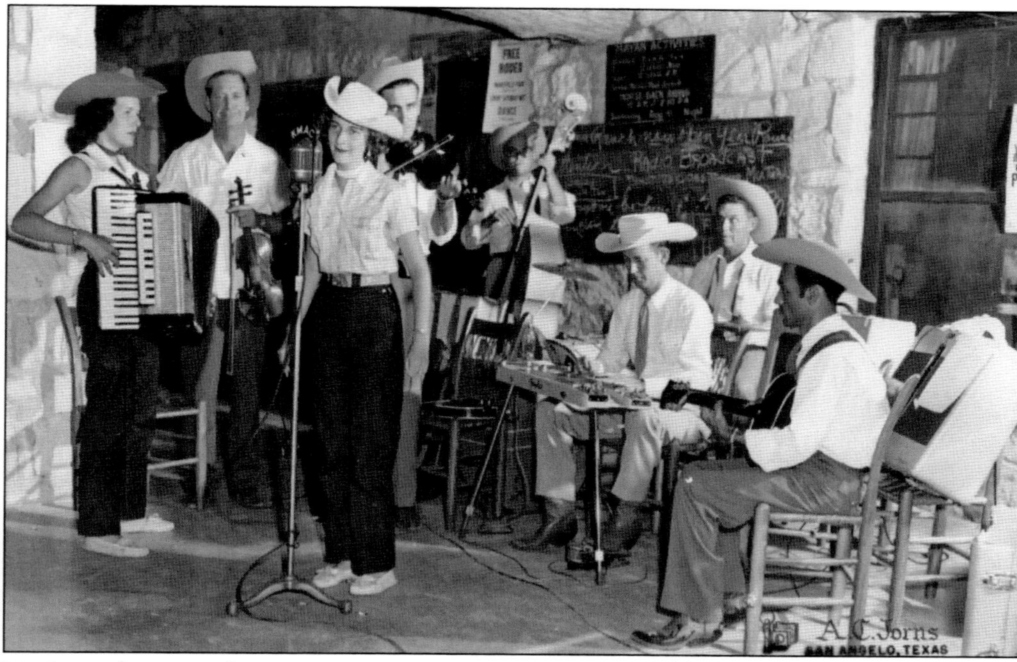

Music set the atmosphere, transporting guests to a romantic Old West. Dances were held at the ranch, and local bands were brought in to provide the entertainment. Members of the Smiley Whitley and the Texans and the Texas Tomboys, an all-girl Western swing band, perform at the Mayan Ranch. (Courtesy of Judy Hicks.)

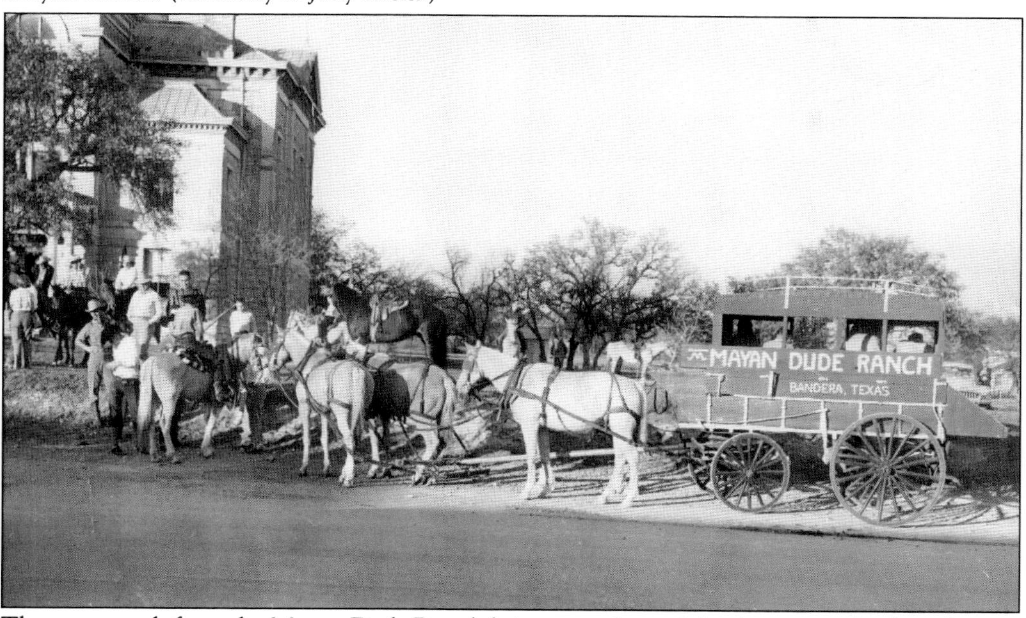

The stagecoach from the Mayan Dude Ranch brings members of the American Geology Society convention to downtown Bandera for a night on the town. Dude ranches played host to family reunions, conventions, and members of the armed forces. During World War II, cadets from Randolph Field, Kelly Field, and Fort Sam Houston streamed to Bandera on the weekends and would sleep in their cars when the ranches ran out of room. (Courtesy of the Frontier Times Museum Collection.)

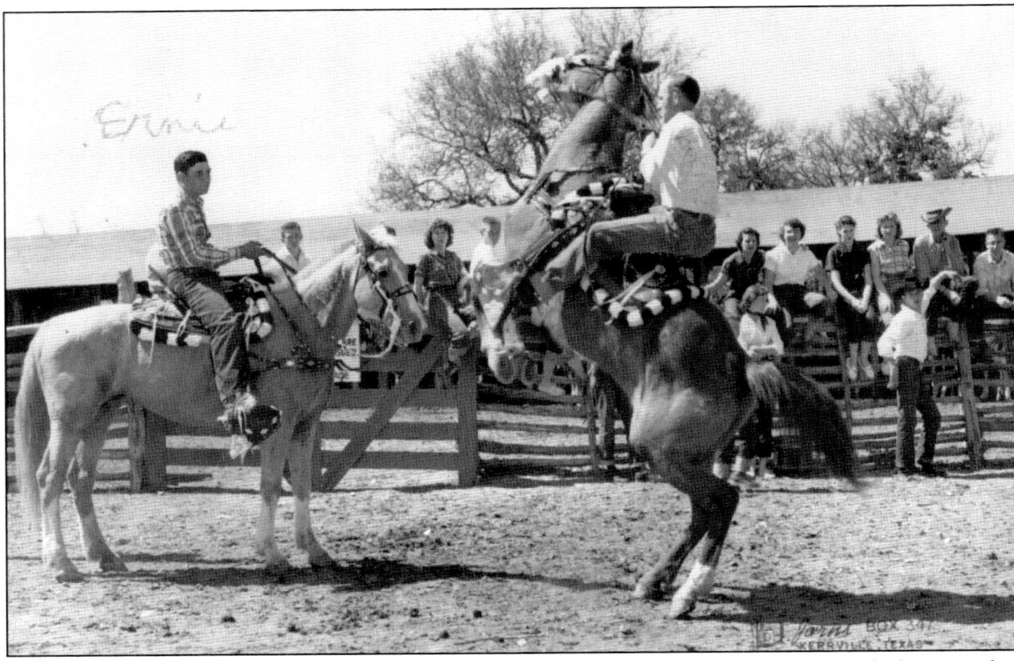

Rodeos were an important and thrilling part of the dude ranch experience. The dude wranglers that took you on a trail ride earlier in the day would perform traditional rodeo events, such as calf roping, bulldogging, and bronco busting. Horse tricks and rope tricks added to the awe and excitement of watching cowboys perform. (Courtesy of Judy Hicks.)

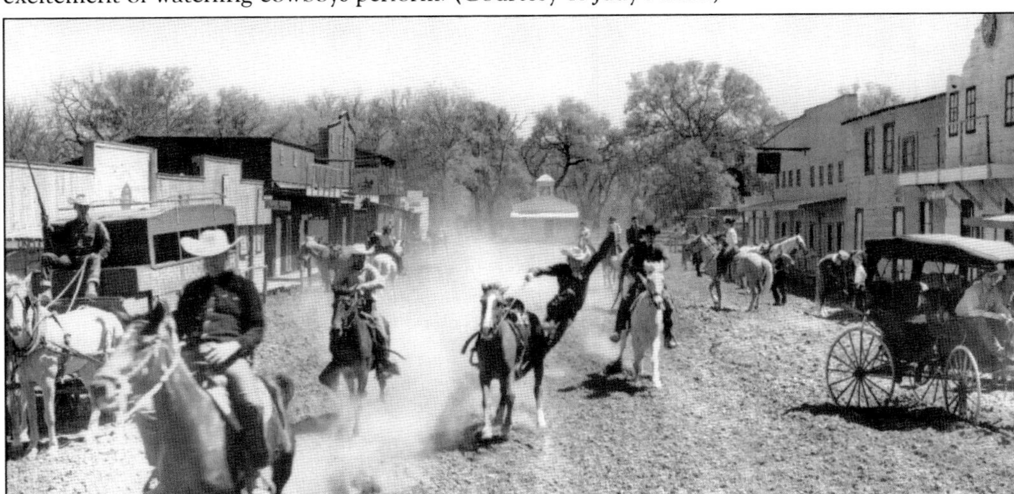

The Mayan Ranch and Lost Valley built elaborate frontier towns where gunfights erupted on the streets and runaway stagecoaches whipped through the town, adding to the frenzied excitement of an Old West town. One might find dance hall girls lounging in front of the saloon or cowboys riding into town looking for trouble. Lost Valley's town also led to an amusement park, with carnival attractions and a Ferris wheel. (Courtesy of Judy Hicks.)

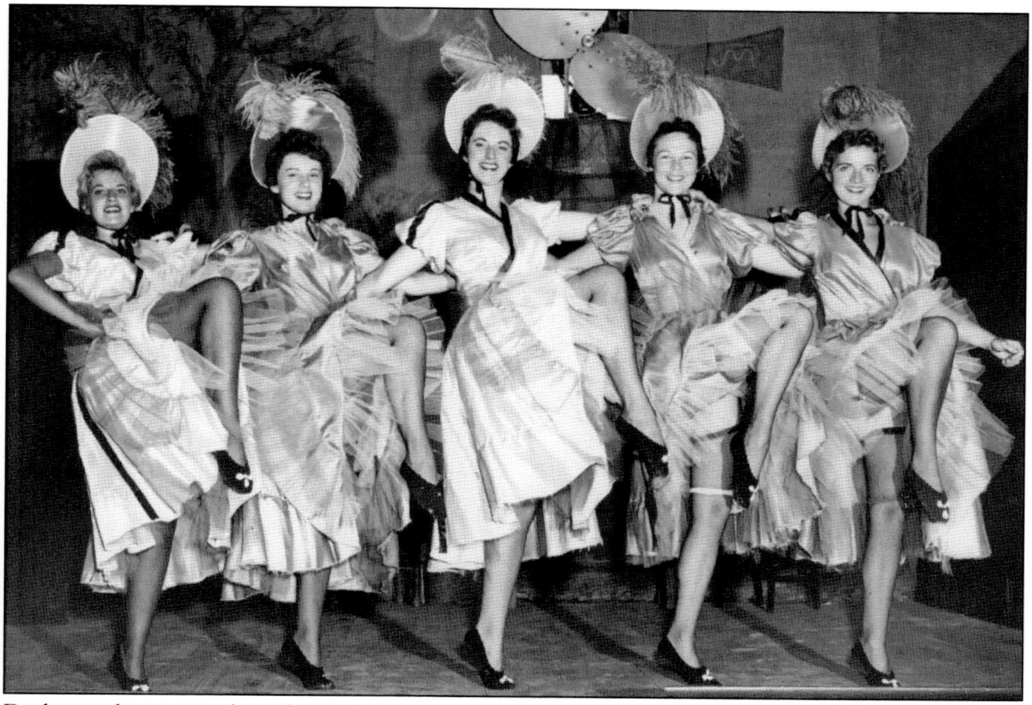

Dude ranches were often about theatrics and performances, creating an experience for guests to feel as though they were in the Old West, if only for a little while. Even Hollywood came to the dude ranches. The Mayan Ranch and its frontier town have been used for movie sets, and John Wayne was a popular guest at the Flying L. Saloon girls dance at the Mayan Ranch. (Courtesy of Judy Hicks.)

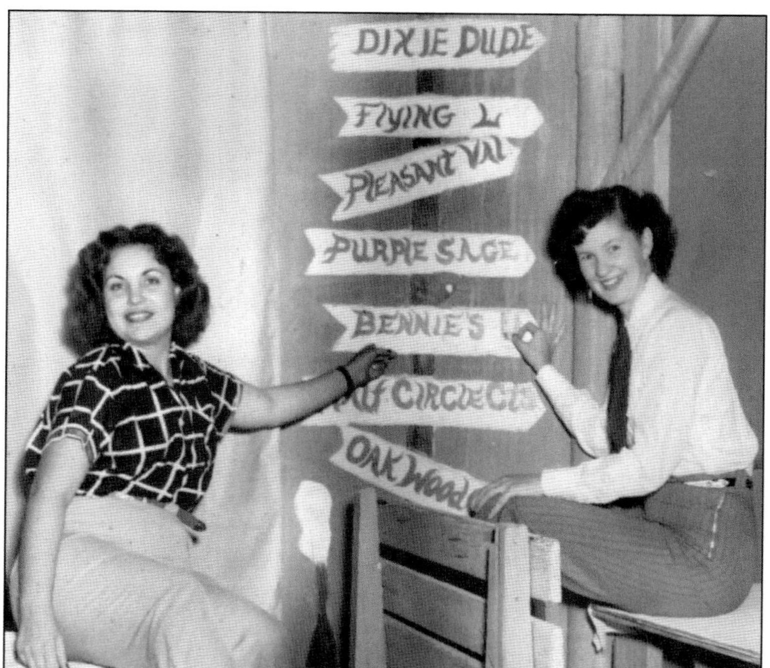

The majority of the dude ranches in Texas today are operating in Bandera County. Ranches such as the BR Lightning Ranch and Twin Elms still hold rodeos. While the landing strip has closed, the Flying L still strives to offer the unusual, having added a water park and an 18-hole golf course. The ranches continue to draw tourists and are a strong economic resource for Bandera County. (Courtesy of Scooter Fries.)

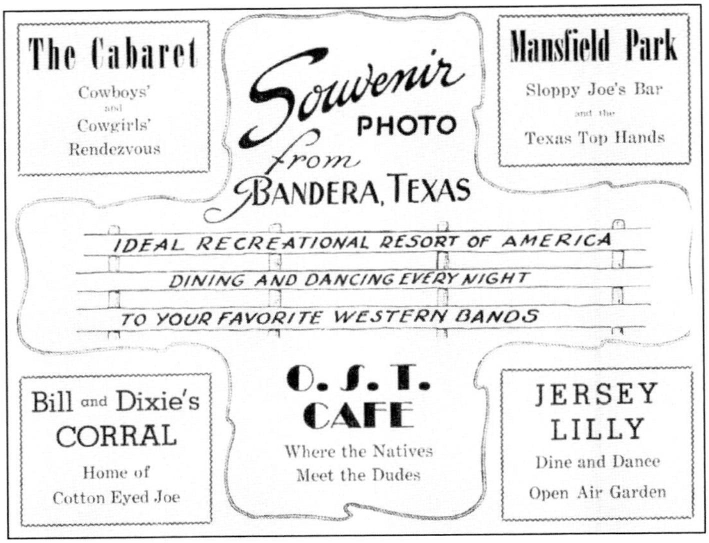

If guests became bored on the ranch, there was always something to do downtown. Joining guests from the other ranches was a great way to enjoy Bandera's dance and refreshment places. A popular place to gather then, and to gather today, was the Old Spanish Trail Cafe, better known as the "OST," where locals and revelers enjoyed enchiladas and danced to the jukebox. (Courtesy of the Frontier Times Museum Collection.)

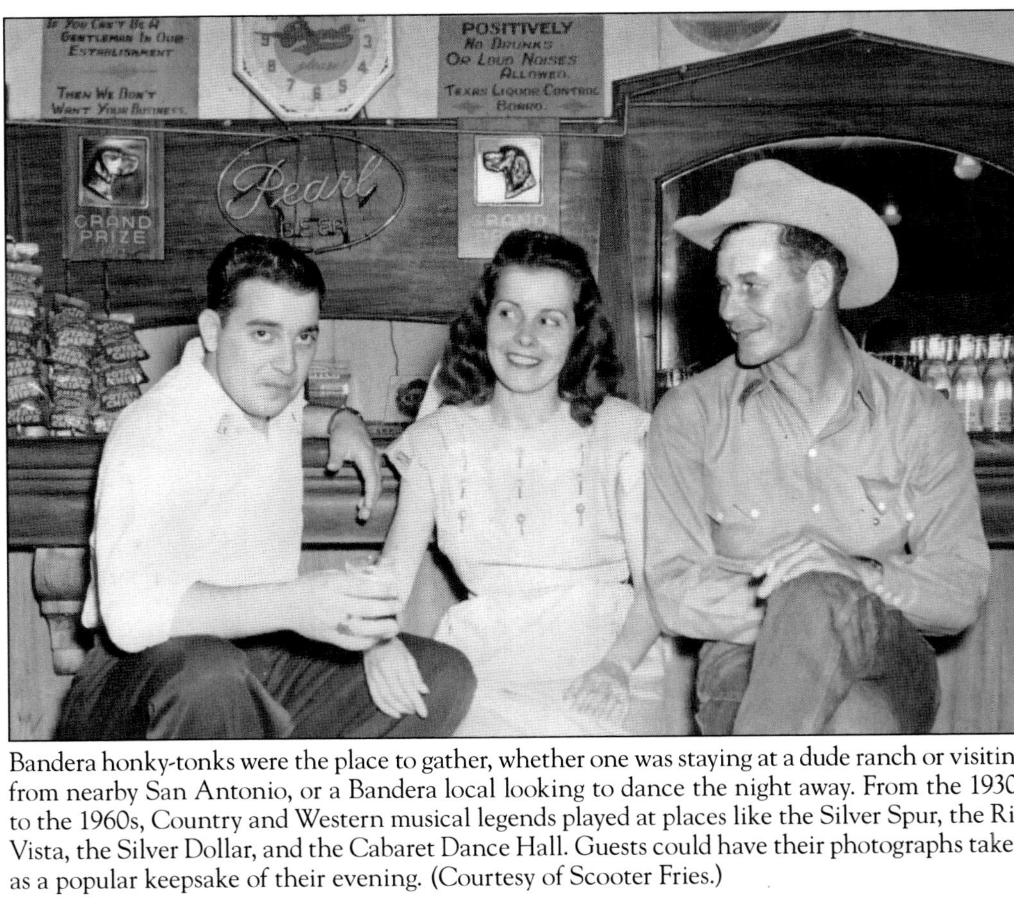

Bandera honky-tonks were the place to gather, whether one was staying at a dude ranch or visiting from nearby San Antonio, or a Bandera local looking to dance the night away. From the 1930s to the 1960s, Country and Western musical legends played at places like the Silver Spur, the Rio Vista, the Silver Dollar, and the Cabaret Dance Hall. Guests could have their photographs taken as a popular keepsake of their evening. (Courtesy of Scooter Fries.)

Dudes and dudettes were encouraged to learn the dance steps to the fiddler Adolph Hofner's "Cotton Eye Joe" and other pioneer dances like "Put Your Little Foot" so they could join the "native" folks in the downtown honky-tonks. Many took dance lessons in the comfort of the ranch before venturing out to dance among the natives. Benny Adamietz twirls a lovely lady around the dance floor. (Courtesy of Scooter Fries.)

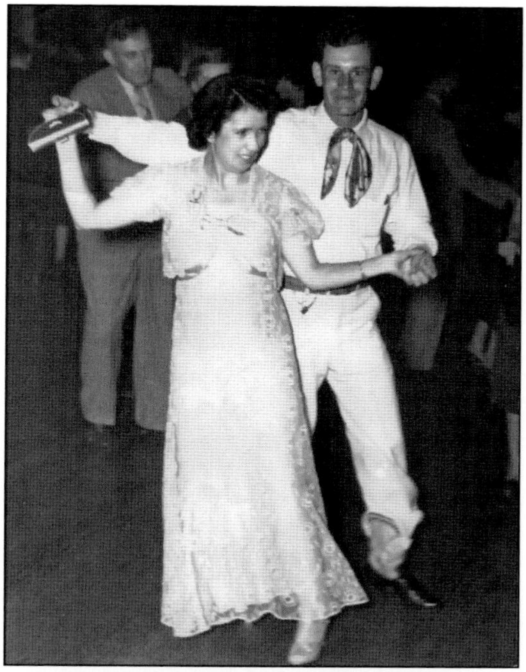

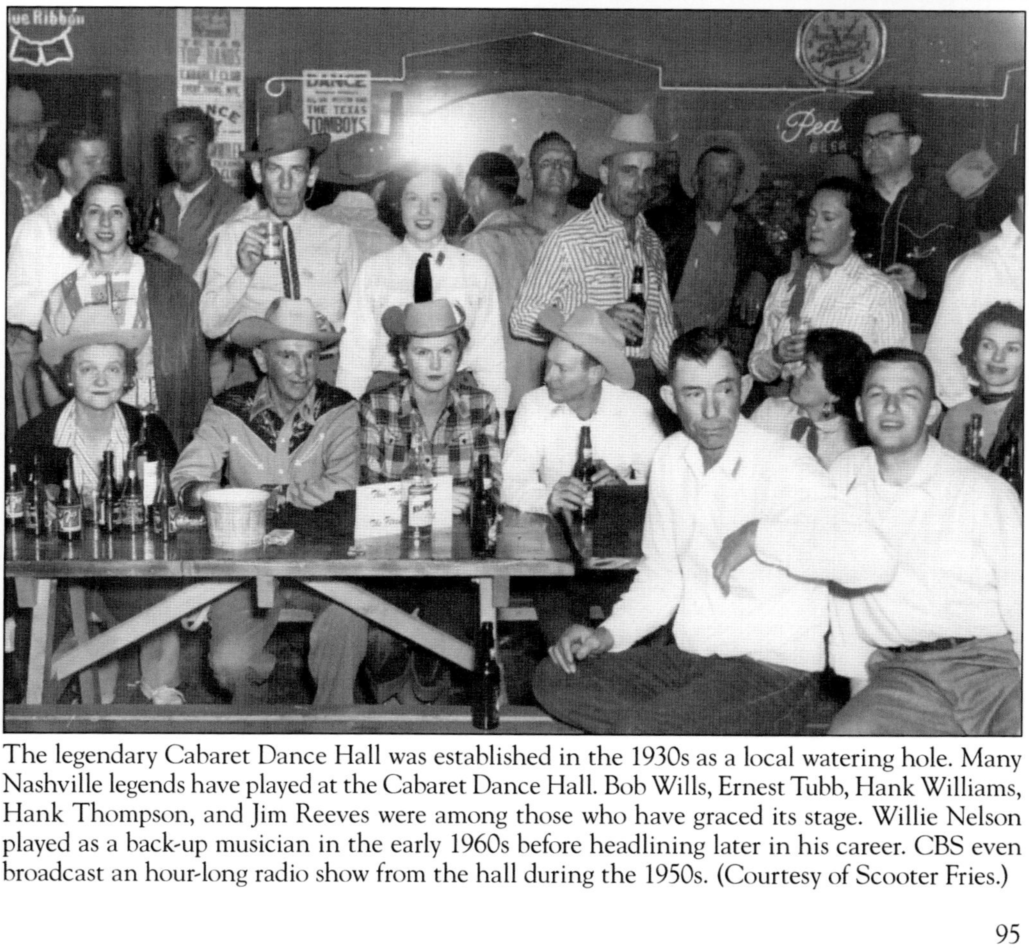

The legendary Cabaret Dance Hall was established in the 1930s as a local watering hole. Many Nashville legends have played at the Cabaret Dance Hall. Bob Wills, Ernest Tubb, Hank Williams, Hank Thompson, and Jim Reeves were among those who have graced its stage. Willie Nelson played as a back-up musician in the early 1960s before headlining later in his career. CBS even broadcast an hour-long radio show from the hall during the 1950s. (Courtesy of Scooter Fries.)

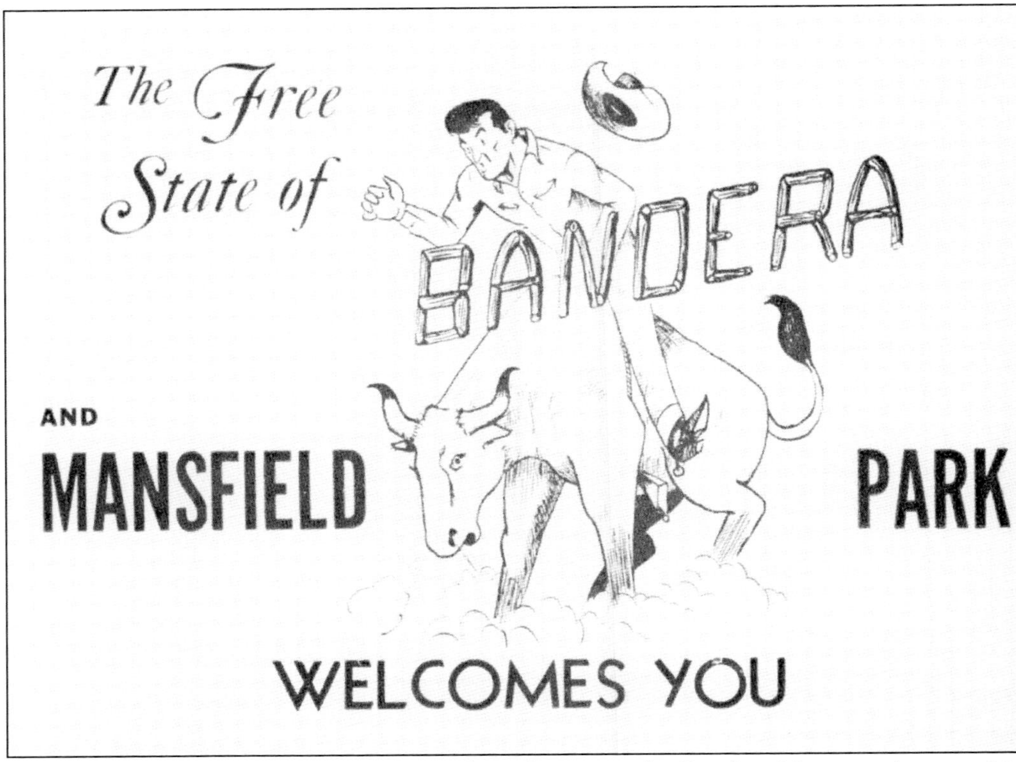

Public relations expert Samuel Montague (no relations to the Bandera Montagues) stopped in Bandera on his way to Mexico and was so impressed that he felt the town needed something special to promote it. With the support and enthusiasm of the chamber of commerce, he decided that Bandera was "going to stompede out of the country . . . we're going to set up our own Free State of Bandera." (Courtesy of Judy Hicks.)

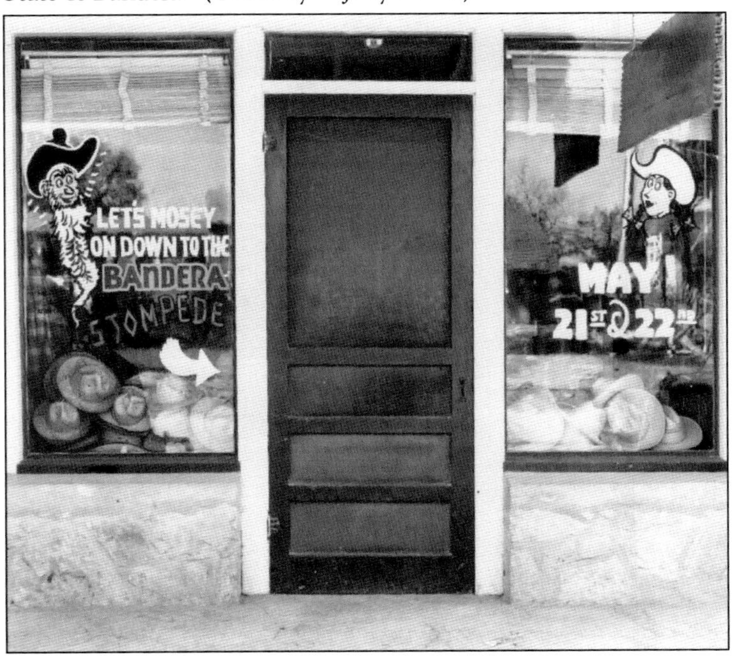

Montague sent a written ultimatum to President Truman signed by a fictitious cowboy named Zeke demanding a day for cowboys. The president was given 48 hours to agree. When Truman didn't respond, Zeke informed the president that Bandera had "stampeded" and was no longer part of the country. Though they never heard back from Truman, vice-president John Nance Garner thought the idea was a hoot. (Courtesy of the Bandera County Historical Commission.)

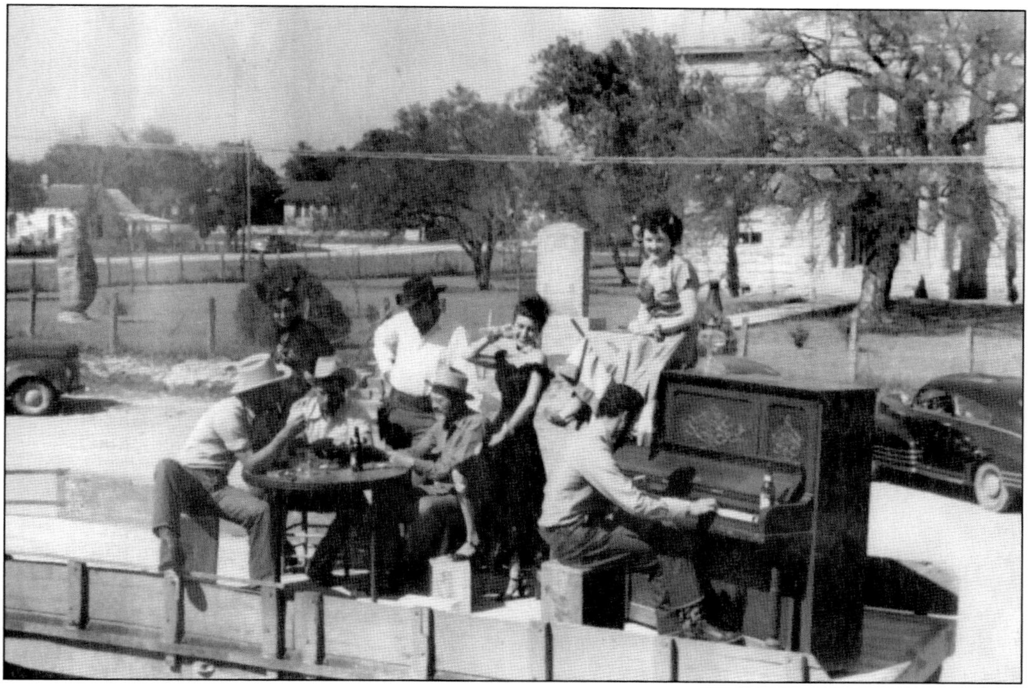

The first "Stompede" was held in May 1948 and attracted 10,000 people for the two-day event. Festivities included a street dance, tall-tale contests, rodeos, shooting and dancing exhibitions, armadillo races, dance hall music, fiddling contests, and a beard contest. To celebrate the occasion, the Allee Company sent wingless chickens to Stein's Clothiers. The glass box containing the two hapless creatures created a sensation as hundreds of visitors looked in vain to find those wings. The highlight of the celebration was a Western parade down Main Street. Floats included this dance hall scene from 1948 (above) and a station wagon of cub scouts from 1953 with crepe paper decorating their "float" (below). By the early 1950s, the crowds had grown to up to 20,000. (Above, courtesy of Clay Conoly; below, courtesy of Betty Laskowski D'Spain.)

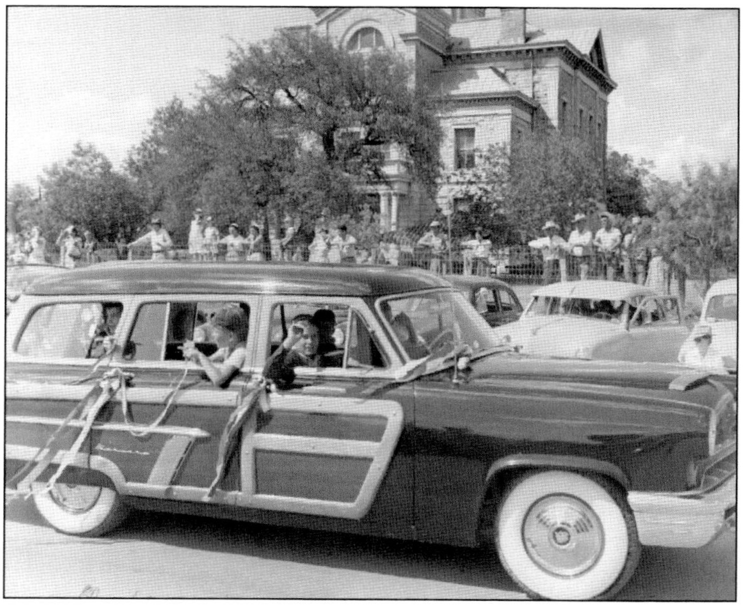

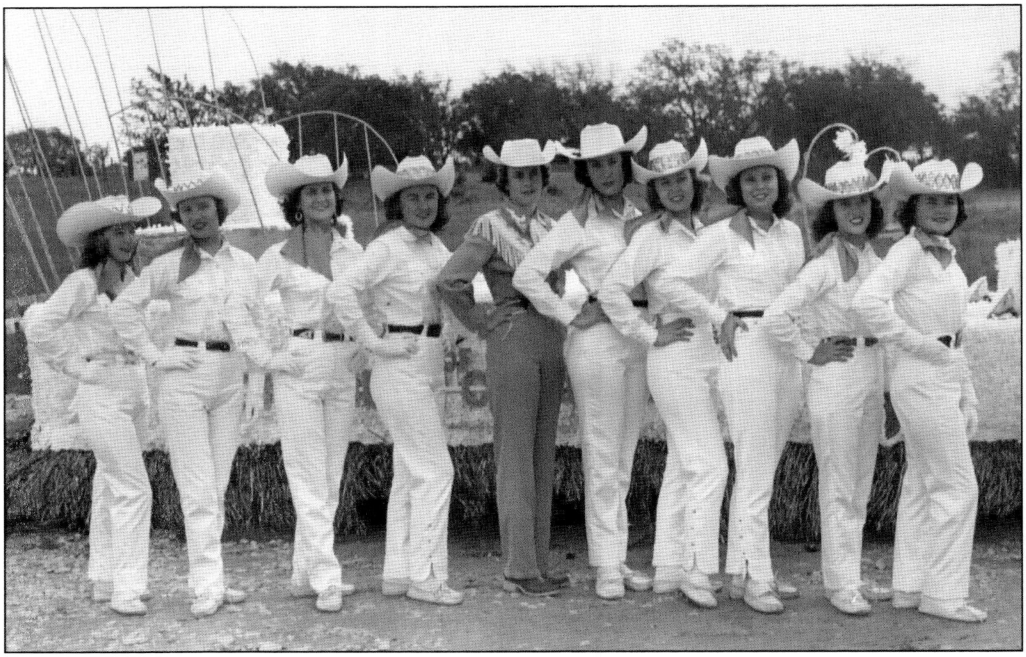

Young women competed to become a Stompede Cowbell and serve as ambassadors for the county. In the early years, the whole town was in on the joke of the "Free State" and looked upon Stompede as a celebration of Bandera's Western heritage. Unfortunately, the nature of the celebration began to change. Headlines touting the 1955 Stompede read, "Bandera's Thundering Stompede Starts Today." This hinted at the celebration's increasing rowdiness. (Courtesy of the Bandera County Historical Commission.)

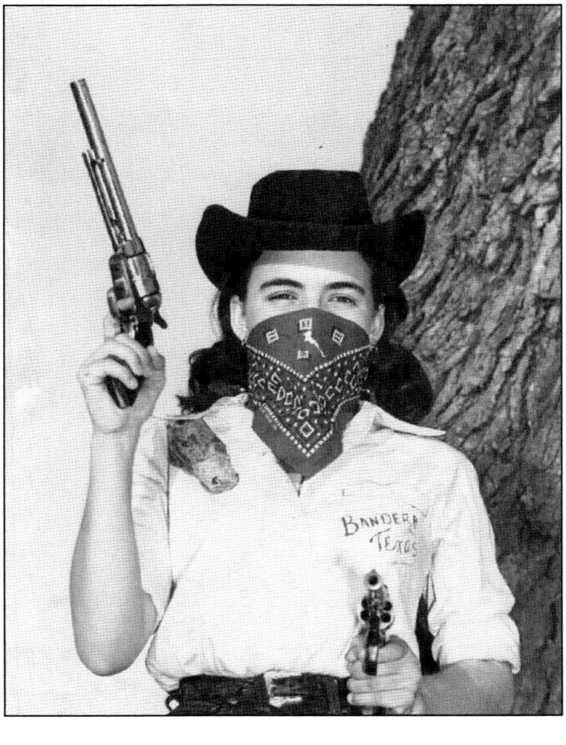

Riding into town and shooting it up was the opening of the Stompede through 1952. The event began to acquire a reputation for unruly behavior, as out-of-town revelers took the "Free State of Bandera" to heart, doing things in the "Free State" that would have landed them in jail back home. To avoid some of the rowdiness, trail drivers arrived in the morning but refrained from shooting up the town. (Courtesy of Judy Hicks.)

Many Bandera residents began to leave town during Stompede and were conflicted about whether to continue the event or not. Merchants were torn between their loyalty to their regular customers and the added income the celebration brought with it. The town was so divided that it became a central issue in the sheriff's race. The incumbent sheriff lost to R. B. Miller, who campaigned to shut the Stompede down.

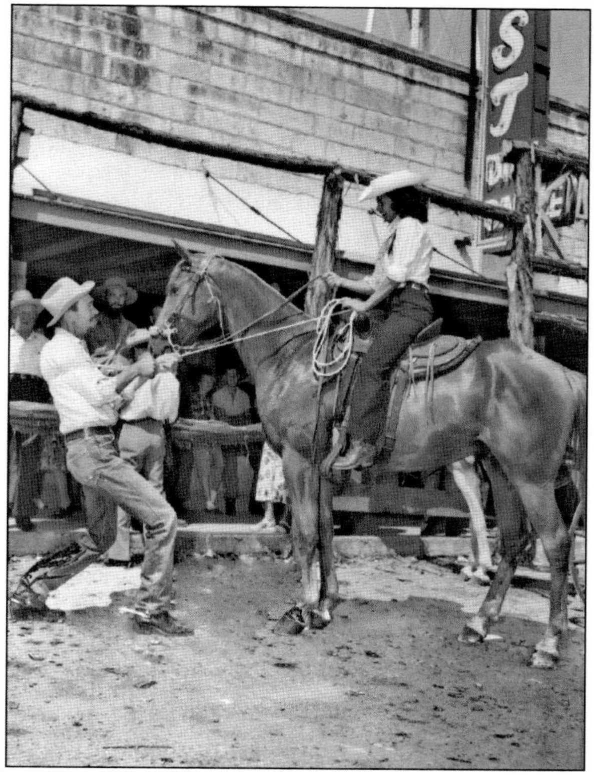

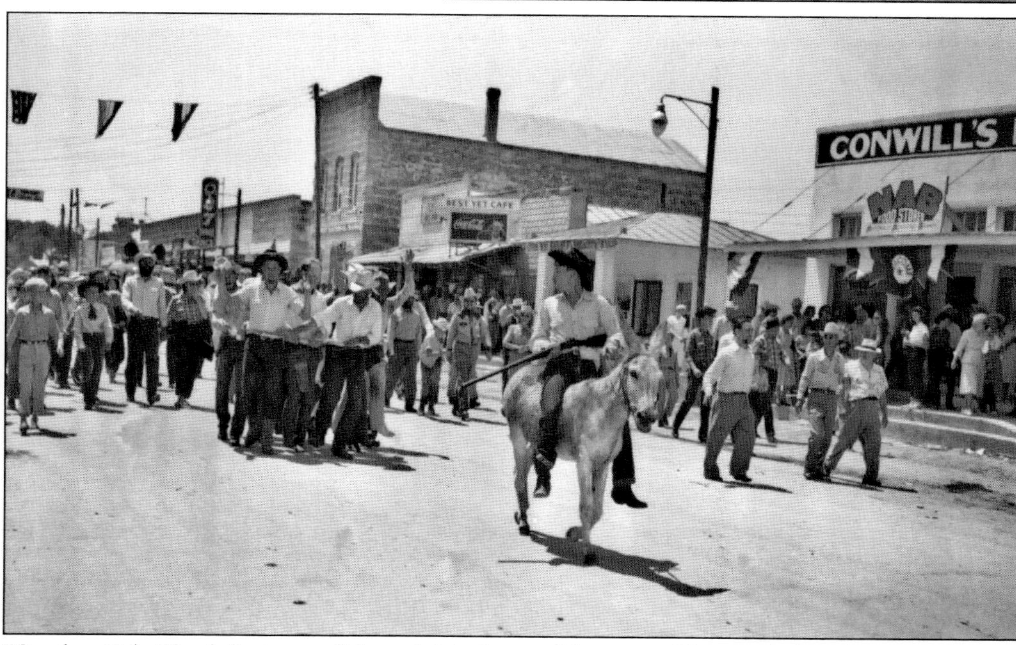

"Cowboy Zeke" leads "prisoners" down Main Street. The constable rounded up the cowboys after they "shot up" the town and had a shoot out on the street. In reality, the Texas Rangers and Department of Public Safety were brought in to help with crowd control in 1957. The celebration that began as a tongue-in-cheek joke to promote the town was now turning into a raucous free-for-all.

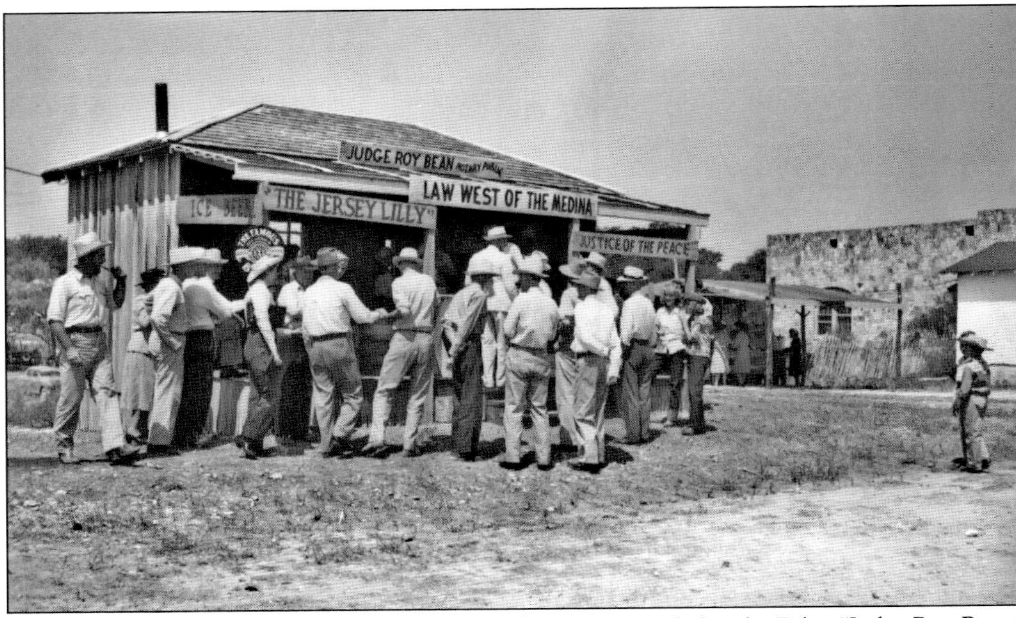

The crowd awaits the "verdict" on the cowboys that were rounded up by Zeke. "Judge Roy Bean" presided at the Jersey Lily, Bandera's replica of this famous building, and passed sentence on the appropriate punishment. After the trial, the accused may be condemned to a "hanging" on Main Street. While many remember the Stompede as a wild time, others remember it as a heck of a good time.

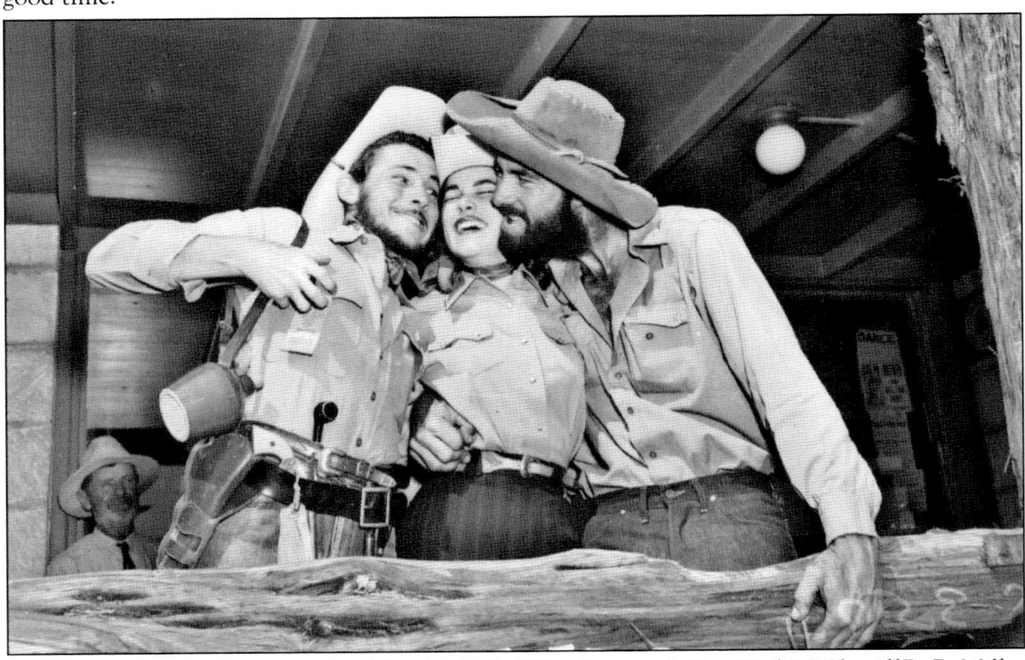

The *San Antonio Light* reported in May 16, 1961, "The Stompede Has Had It." Sheriff R. B. Miller told the press, "There will be no more Stompedes as long as I am sheriff . . . If I have to, I will fight every man in the chamber of commerce to keep from having such a disgraceful celebration in our town." Reminders of the party remain years after the last Stompede in the way of Zeke's hamburger stand and images of Cowboy Zeke found throughout town.

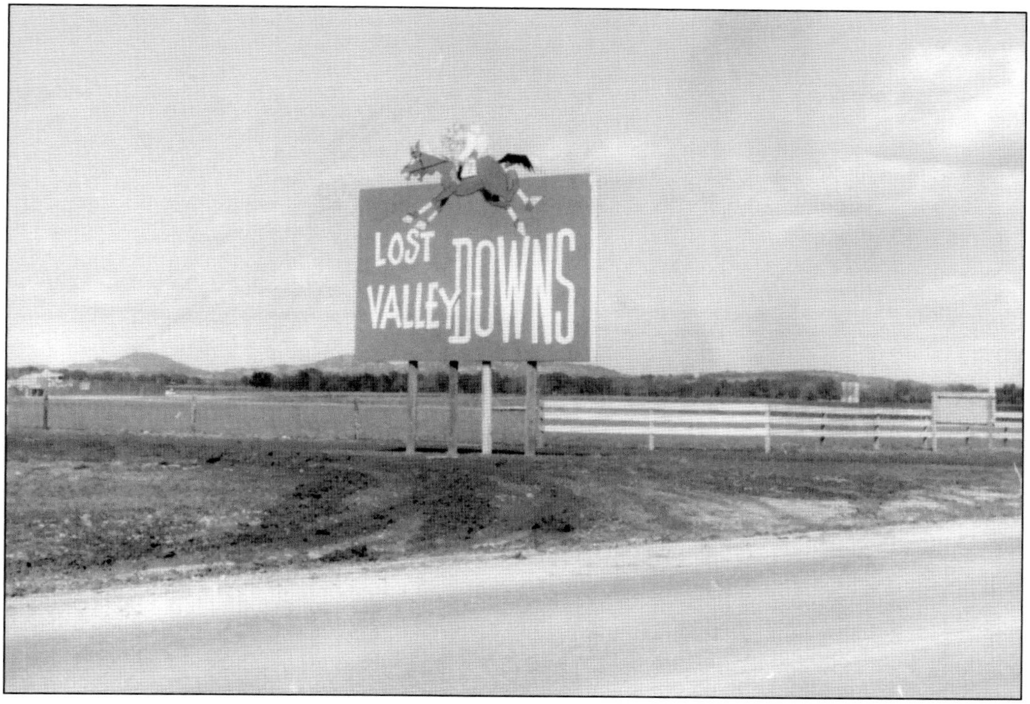

Horse racing has a long history in Bandera, when ranchers gathered informally in the 1800s to race their prize steeds. Bennie's U-Bar dude ranch offered its guests a well-equipped racetrack where "fine race horses from Bandera ranches and neighboring towns compete for generous purses every Saturday night." Lost Valley Downs operated during the 1960s and was a popular attraction even though pari-mutuel betting was not legal in Texas at that time. Without pari-mutuel betting, the track was more for horsemen to run their best horses rather than for public gambling. The last track to operate was Bandera Downs, which opened in 1984. At seven-eighths of a mile, the track was the longest in Texas at that time. When pari-mutuel betting was legalized, Lost Valley Downs became even more popular, until its closure in 1995. (Both, courtesy of the Bandera County Historical Commission.)

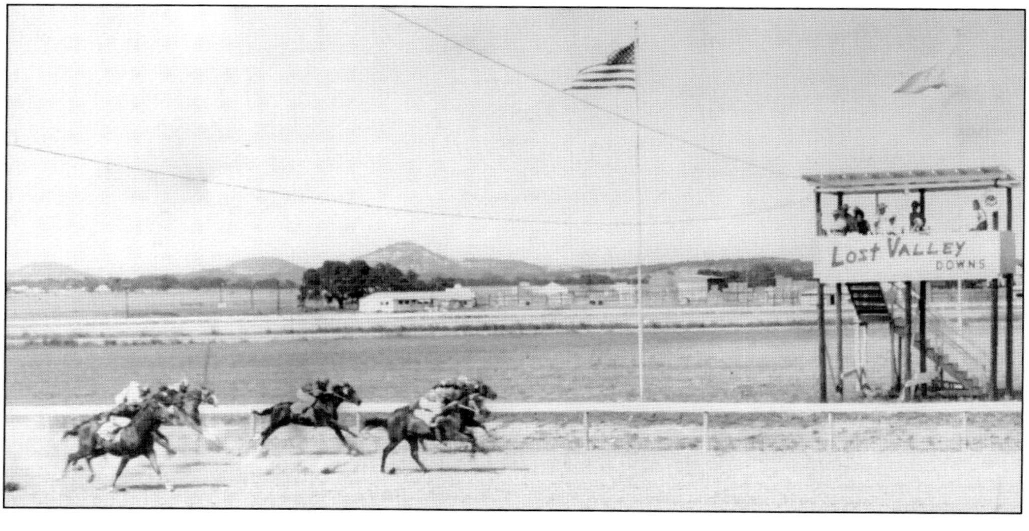

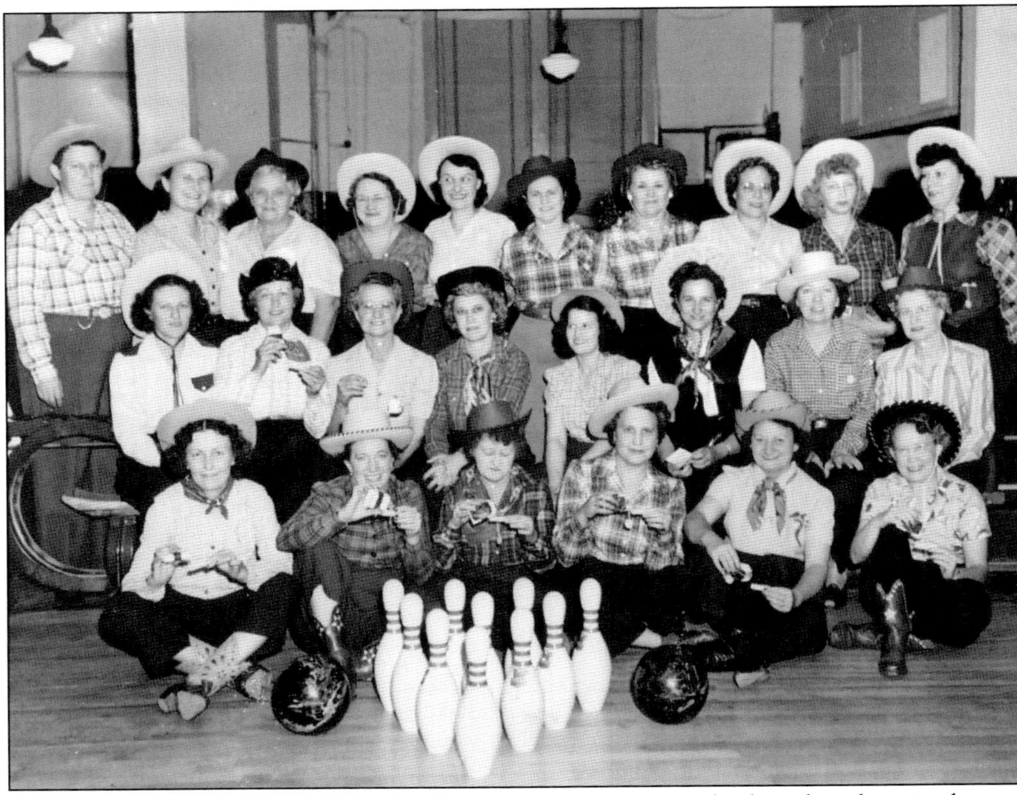

Maybe it is the distance from the next big town or just a natural talent, but there is always a happening or party to attend. Whether it is dancing at the Eleventh Street Bar, drinking beer at Arkey Blue's Silver Dollar Saloon, or bowling in Kerrville with friends, Bandera natives can always make a good time even better. (Courtesy of Scooter Fries.)

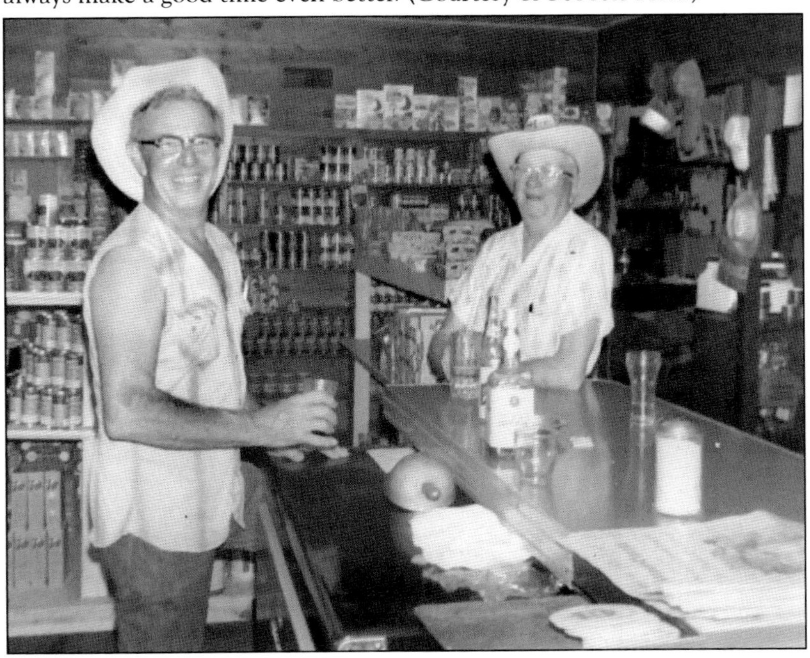

Any place is suitable for a drink with friends. Edward A. Johnson (left) and Mac McGregor get together to share a drink at Adolph's General Store in Lakehills. Today Adolph's is a restaurant and is still a gathering place for friends. (Courtesy of Burgin and Valli Johnson.)

Eight

UNIQUELY BANDERA

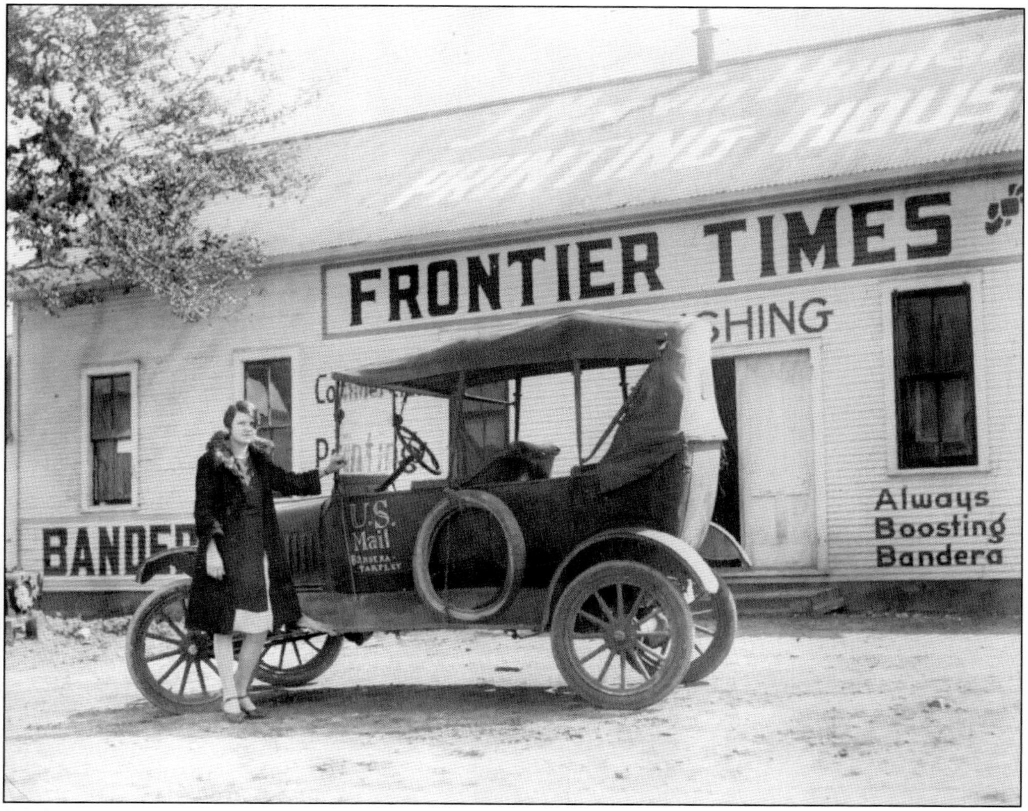

J. Marvin Hunter, a newspaperman and amateur historian, was fascinated with tales of the Old West. He collected stories of the characters that brought the frontier to life, and in Bandera, he found plenty to admire and write about. Bandera has seen the rise of unique businesses created by imaginative and artistic people, as well as by individuals who have chosen to live life as a tribute to the area's Western heritage. (Courtesy of the Bandera County Historical Commission.)

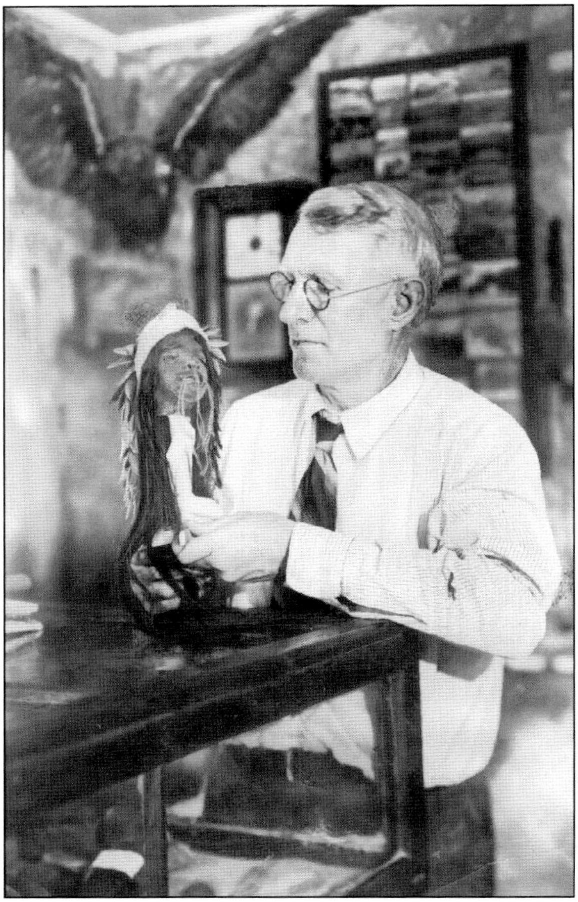

In 1923, J. Marvin Hunter published the first issue of the *Frontier Times Magazine*. Dedicated to "frontier history, border tragedy, and pioneer achievement," Hunter encouraged readers to send in their own stories. Along with their tales of frontier history, the readers also sent Hunter their family relics. Soon his New Era office was filled from floor to ceiling. After knocking down a wall and filling the larger office with more items, Hunter began thinking of building a museum. Despite the Depression, he was able to raise the necessary funds by selling his self-printed booklets on outlaw Sam Bass and subscriptions to his magazine. The museum opened in 1933. Wanting a fire-resistant building, he constructed it of stone gathered from all over the county and was even given stones from a fence that was built in 1878 to include in his walls. (Both, courtesy of the Frontier Times Museum Collection.)

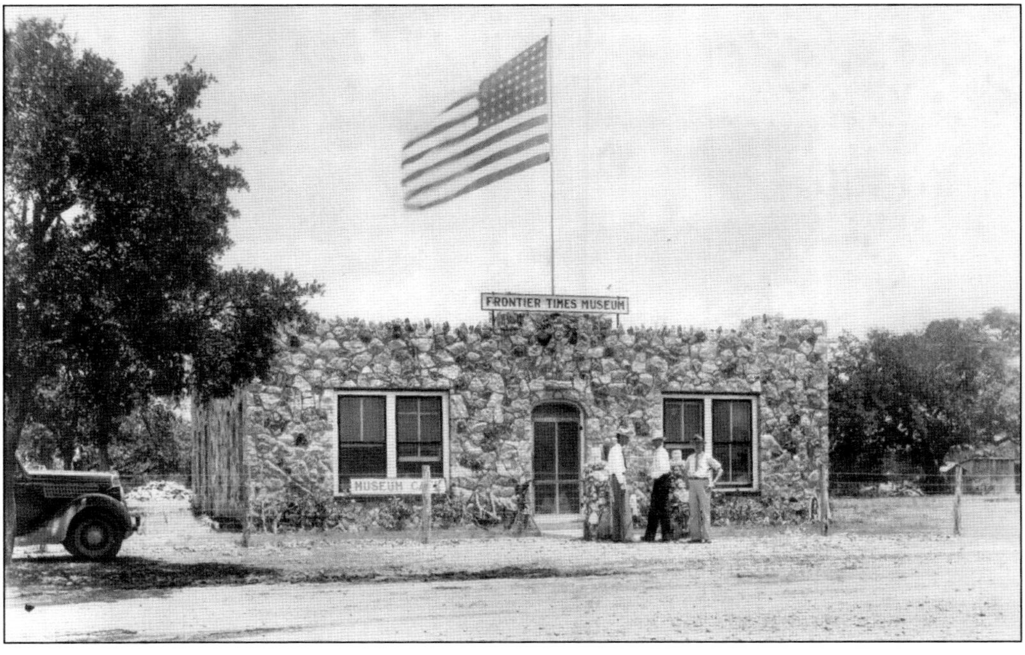

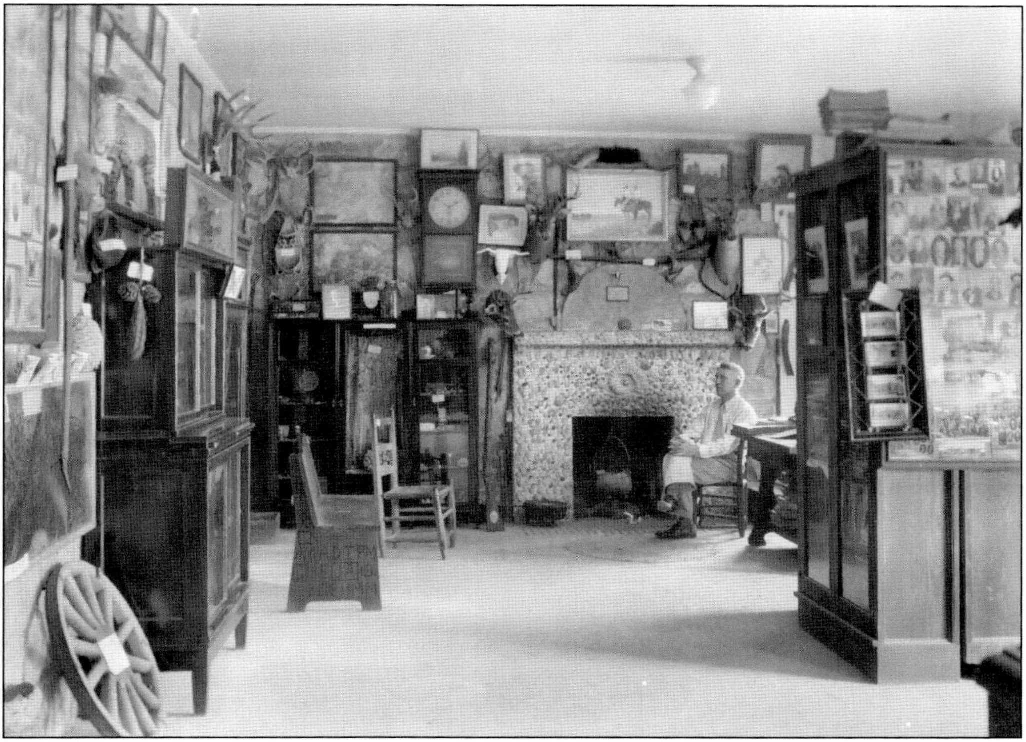

Hunter often said he did not collect items, but they collected him. The building itself became a collection, as petrified wood, fossils, and arrowheads were added to the walls and a large circular stone, used as a well covering, was hoisted into the wall to use as a window frame. The millstone from the Elder Lyman Wight's Mormon colony was set into the fireplace and is visible in this photograph. (Courtesy of the Frontier Times Museum Collection.)

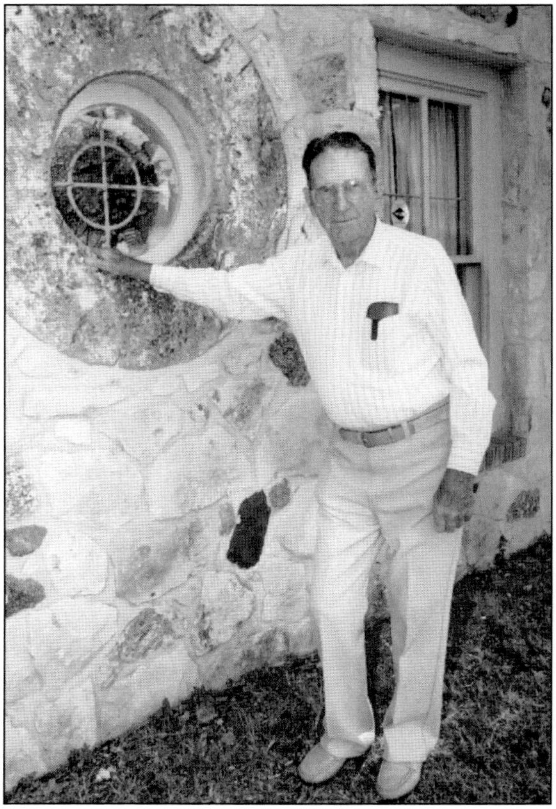

Hough LeStourgeon's training in fieldstone work came in handy when he helped build the museum. The use of fieldstone was not common in Bandera before the 1930s. His work on the museum influenced an iconic architectural style of rock buildings that is now found throughout the county. Hough is pictured next to the round window he built into the museum's north wall. (Photograph by Linda Palmer; courtesy of the Frontier Times Museum Collection.)

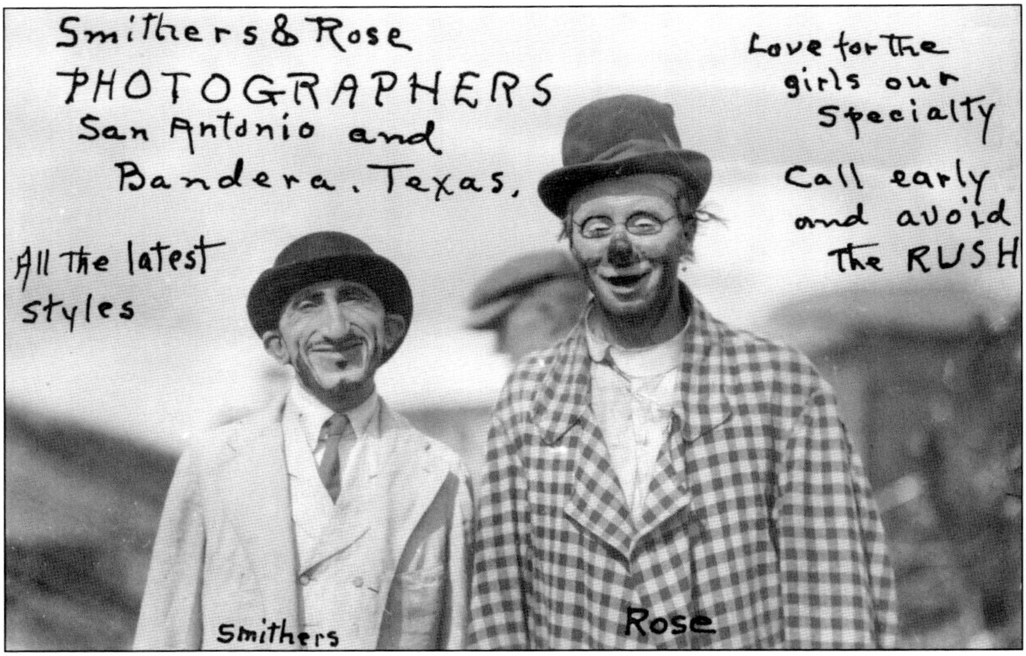

Despite their clownish appearance, W. D. Smithers (left) and Noah Rose were two of the most important chroniclers of frontier history. Rose amassed an impressive collection of original photographs from the Old West that he would rephotograph with captions printed by J. Marvin Hunter, producing copies to sell. San Antonian Smithers focused on the Texas frontier, capturing historical vignettes that were fleeting and almost lost. (Courtesy of the Frontier Times Museum Collection.)

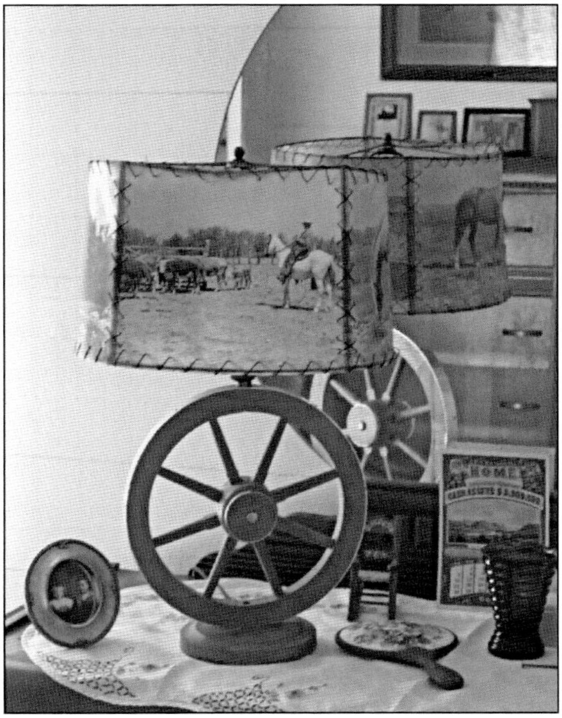

Smithers may best be known for lamp shades made from his Western images. After purchasing a photograph lamp shade at Rugh's Texaco in 1949, George Bradley built the original wagon wheel lamp stand in his backyard shop, and a new business was started. Bradley Lamps used the photographs of Smithers on translucent lamp shades placed on stands modeled on wagon wheels, oxen yokes, stirrups, and water pumps. The lamps were Western chic and continued to be made until the early 1960s. (Photograph by Lauren Langford.)

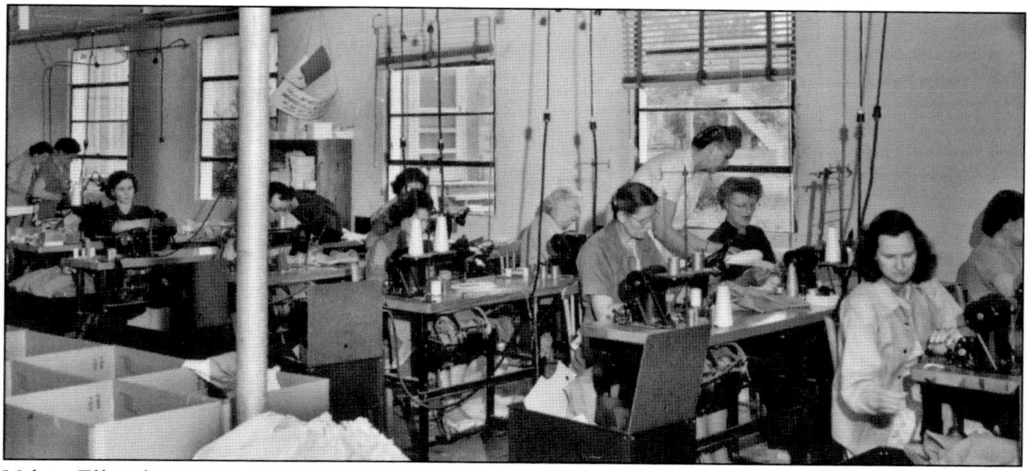

Velma Elliot began creating children's clothes while living with family on the T-Anchor Ranch outside of Medina. Her "Velma" designs were a hit at Saks Fifth Avenue, and she expanded her operations by opening a dress factory in 1951 on Medina's Main Street. She employed local ranch wives who needed to work because of the devastating drought. (Courtesy of the San Antonio Light Collection of UTSA's Institute of Texan Culture, L-4515-A.)

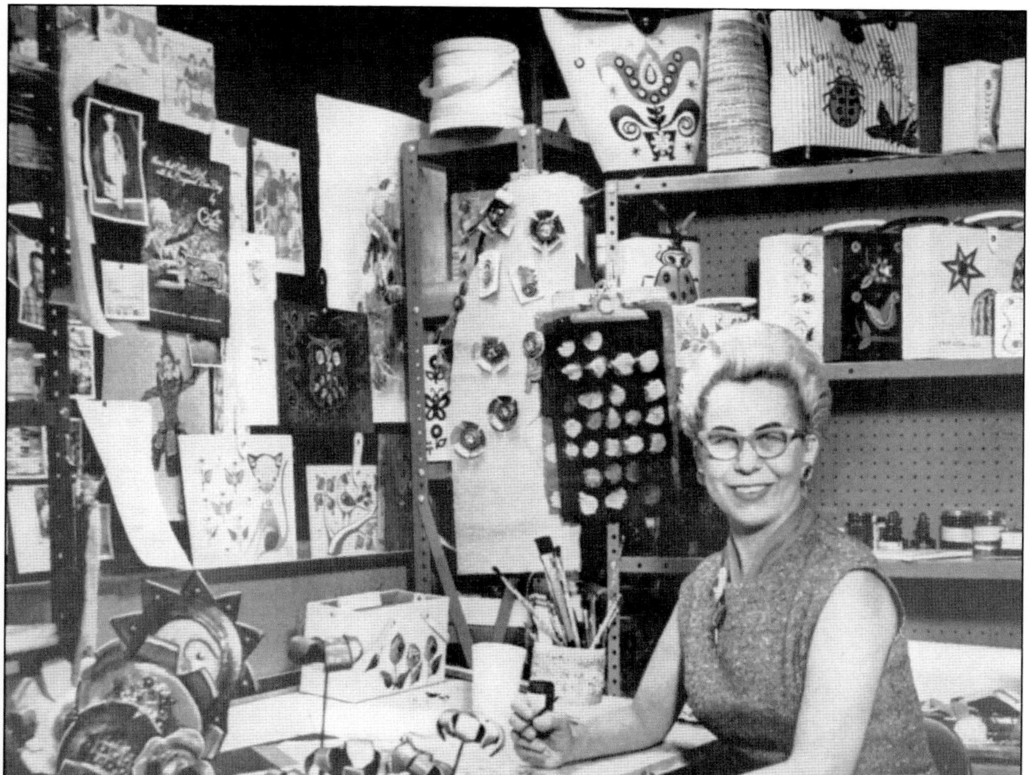

In the late 1940s, the gift shops of local dude ranches carried canvas and leather handbags designed by Enid Collins of Medina. When Nieman Marcus placed an order, her business exploded, and by 1958, a factory was opened with 80 employees. The canvas and wooden box bags, with their whimsical designs, were a big hit with housewives and celebrities throughout the 1960s. Even Lynda Bird Johnson was seen carrying a Collins bag. (Courtesy of Christian Collins.)

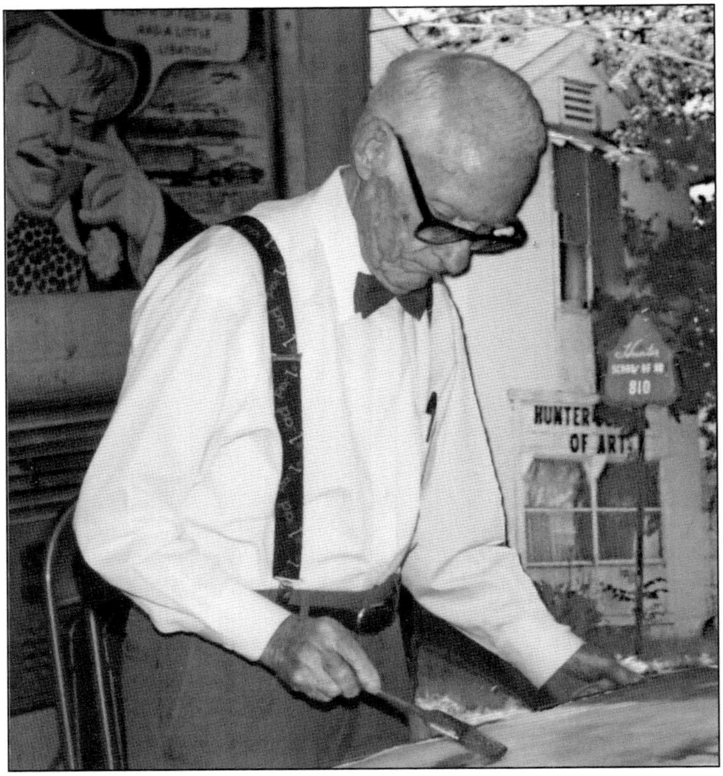

The son of J. Marvin Hunter, Warren Hunter was a painter, illustrator, and inspiring teacher. As an instructor, his art school was the training ground for many Texas artists, and he would later become the dean of the San Antonio Art Institute. His paintings reflect the beauty of the Hill Country, where he spent his childhood, and show a love of Texas that was inspired by his father. (Courtesy of Lauren Langford.)

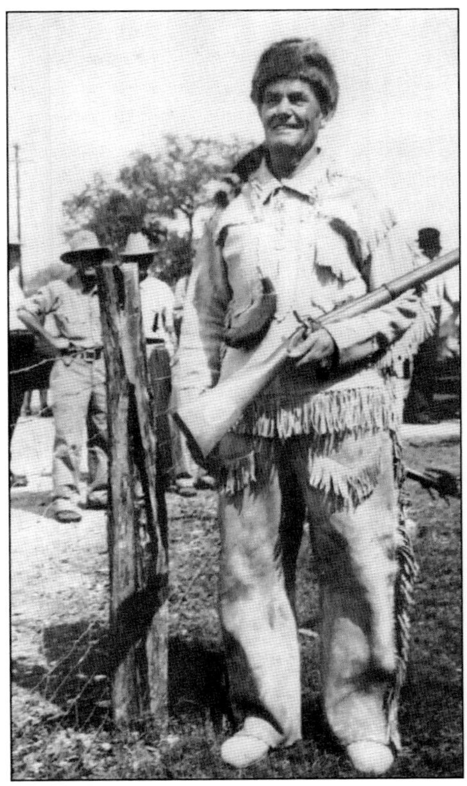

Bandera has always been home to larger-than-life characters, and Charlie Eckhart was one of the largest. Fascinated by Native American culture, Eckhart learned to tan buckskin that he regularly wore. He was an expert archer, carving his own bows and arrows, and was a skilled shingle maker. Eckhart was adopted into the Comanche tribe by Chief Baldwin Parker at the 1939 Settlers Reunion and given the name of *Tabikeenee* (Sky Eagle). (Courtesy of the Frontier Times Museum Collection.)

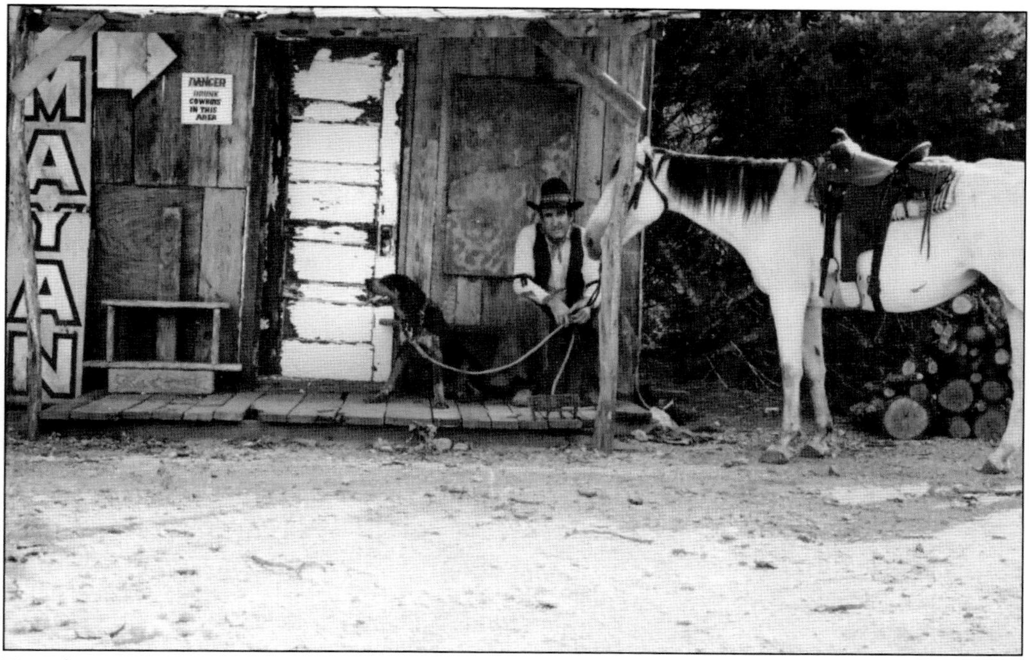

Travel on Main Street on Saturday and a visitor is likely to run into Kelly Scott cooking at his chuck wagon. An old-fashioned cowboy, he is one of the rare horseshoers left in Texas, a craft he learned at 16. He is frequently contacted to drive a stagecoach or supply animals and equipment for Western productions and has been used to add an authentic Texas touch to commercials and movies. (Courtesy of Kelly Scott.)

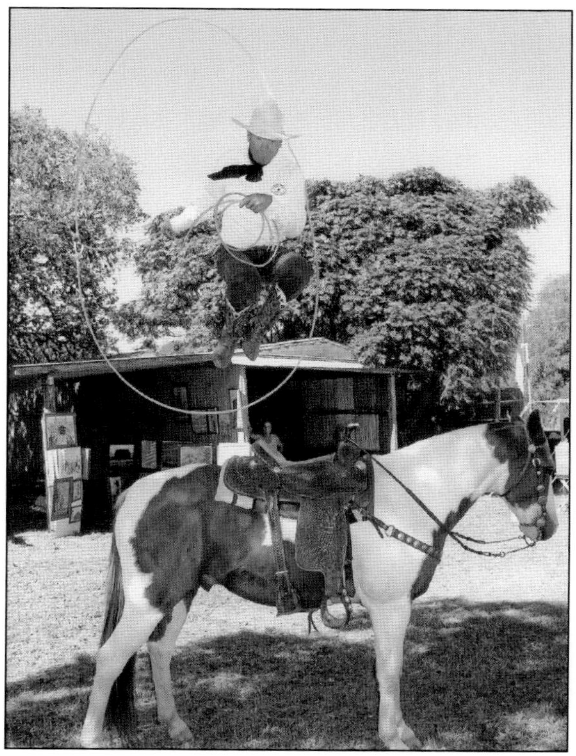

Often seen jumping on a horse while twirling a rope, Kevin Fitzpatrick is always a sight. After moving to Bandera in the 1980s, Fitzpatrick worked on several dude ranches, but his first loves were horses and trick roping. He developed his skills in trick roping after practice, practice, practice. It paid off, as he was designated the 2008 World Champion Trick Roper. (Photograph by Carolyn Rost; courtesy of Kevin Fitzpatrick.)

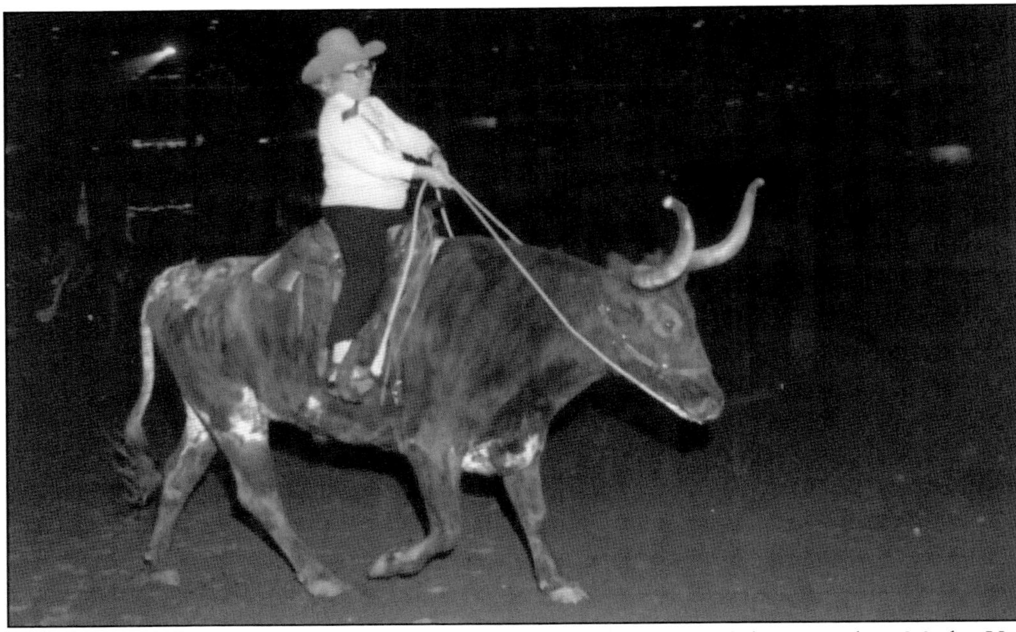

Perhaps no one has done more to preserve the longhorn cattle breed than Maudeen Marks. Her herd of longhorn cattle is one of seven foundation herds. She once said her idea of heaven was "to own Texas, stock it with Texas longhorn, staff it with Texas Rangers, ride from windmill to windmill, and have a dance every night." Her memory and her work have left a lasting legacy for Texas. (Courtesy of the Marks family.)

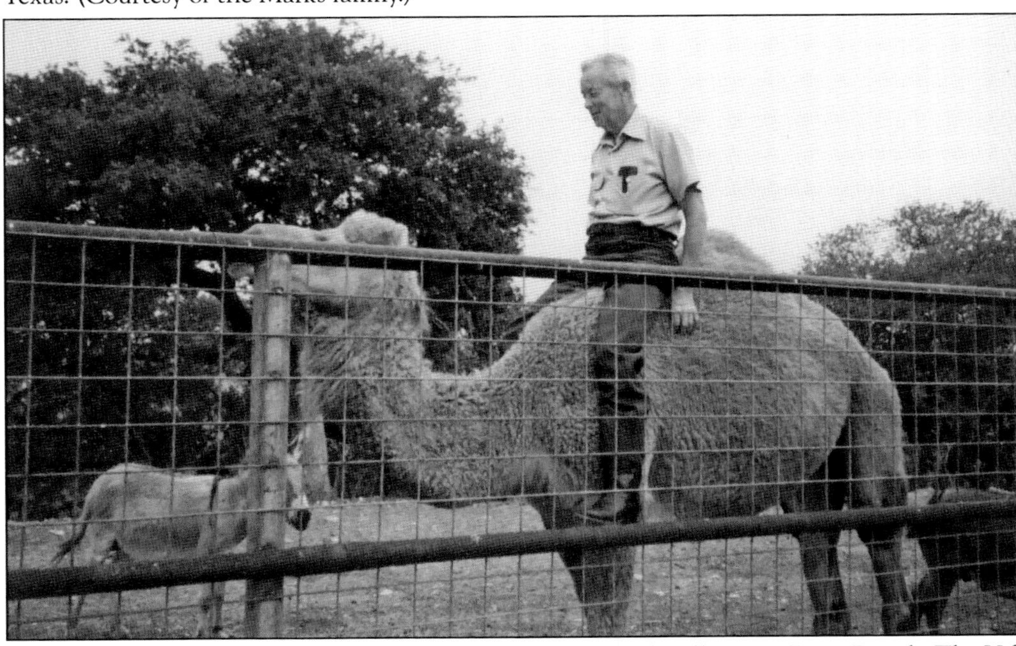

John Graham hitches a ride on a camel at his in-laws John and Nell Steen's River Ranch. The Hill Country environment is similar to Africa, and it is not unusual to find exotic animals roaming on a local ranch. *Bandera County Courier* reporter Stephanie Parker has written of Bandera's quirky past, such as Camp Verde's lost camels once living in the hills and the alligator found in Medina Lake. As Stephanie says, "Only in Bandera." (Courtesy of John and Jane Graham.)

Nine

A Life of Traditions

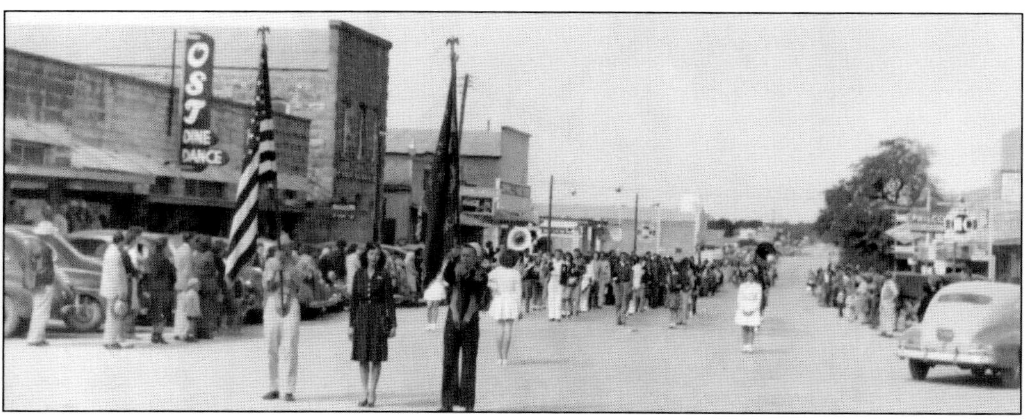

Give the residents of Bandera County an opening and they will throw a party, a parade, or host an event—and they have been doing that for a long time! In 1953, Bandera celebrated its centennial with three days of celebration. The celebration included a rodeo, a historical pageant, and a parade down Main Street. (Courtesy of the Frontier Times Museum Collection.)

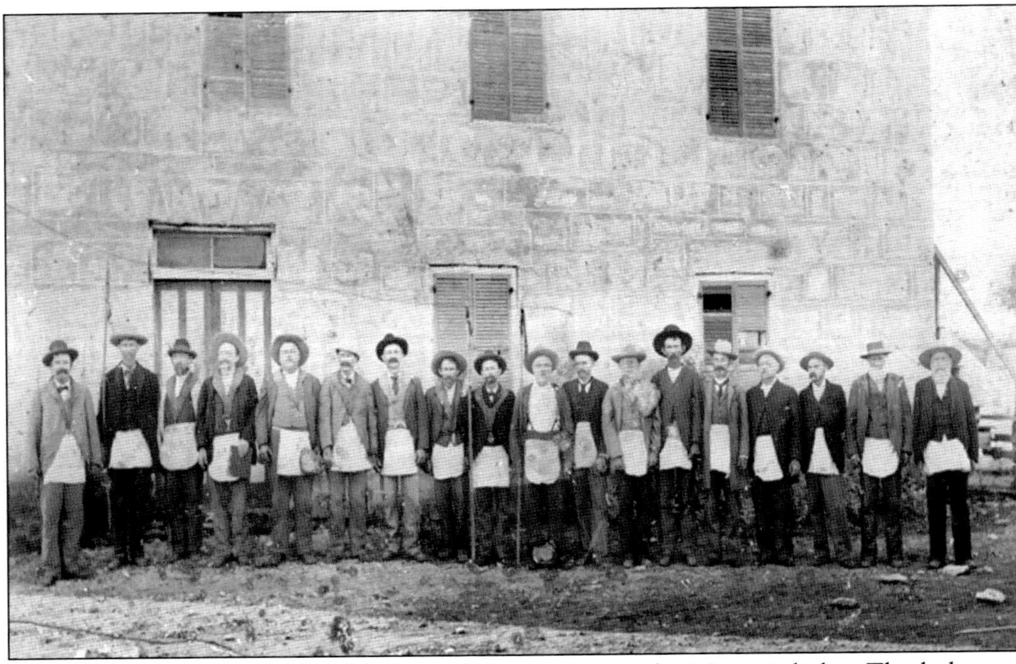

Bandera County, like much of the rest of Texas, organized a Masonic lodge. The lodge was chartered in 1870. The Masons are shown in 1888, posed in front of the county courthouse of that time. Stephen F. Austin was a Mason, as were 80 percent of the office holders of the Republic of Texas. (Courtesy of Lauren Langford.)

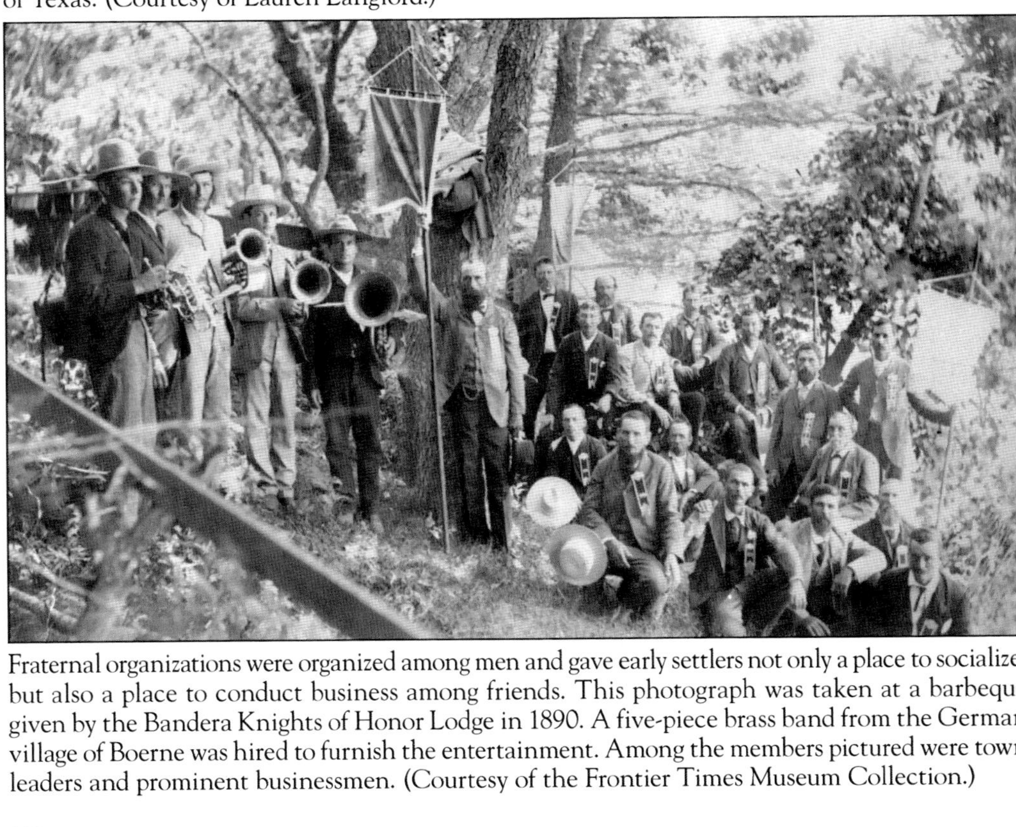

Fraternal organizations were organized among men and gave early settlers not only a place to socialize, but also a place to conduct business among friends. This photograph was taken at a barbeque given by the Bandera Knights of Honor Lodge in 1890. A five-piece brass band from the German village of Boerne was hired to furnish the entertainment. Among the members pictured were town leaders and prominent businessmen. (Courtesy of the Frontier Times Museum Collection.)

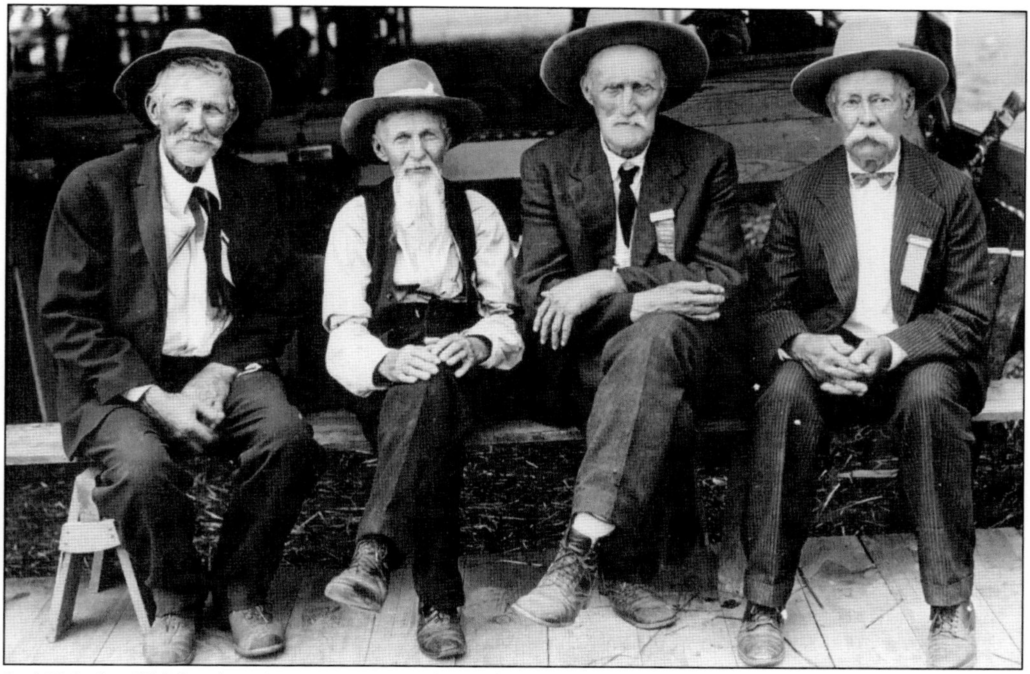

In 1924, the Old Settlers Association was formed to organize a reunion honoring longtime residents. Many had lived in the area for more than 70 years. The festivities took place in Bandera's Mansfield Park. This annual event was a highlight on Bandera's social calendar and would attract up to 5,000 visitors each year. Pictured here in 1926 are (from left to right) frontiersmen Eli Loyd of Medina, fiddler John Lane, Bill McCaleb, and Jim Walker of Medina. (Courtesy of the Frontier Times Museum Collection.)

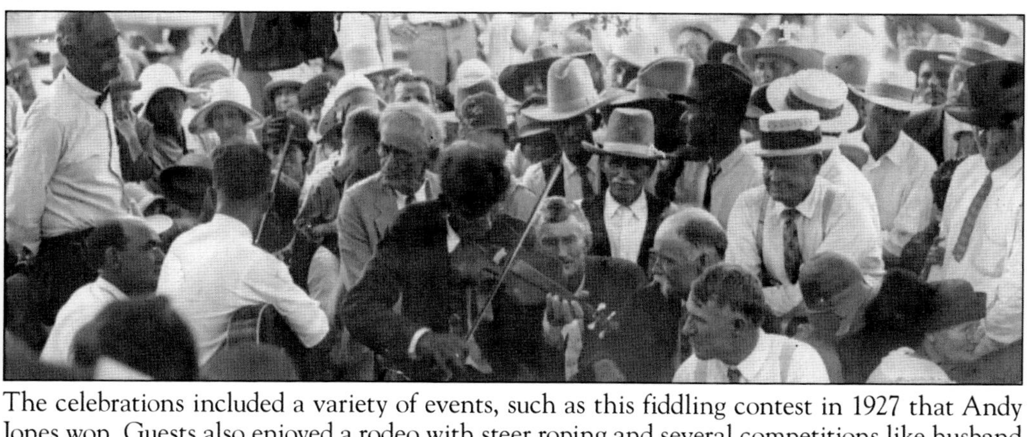

The celebrations included a variety of events, such as this fiddling contest in 1927 that Andy Jones won. Guests also enjoyed a rodeo with steer roping and several competitions like husband calling, pie eating, and coffee grinding. All this excitement was topped off with a barbeque dinner. (Courtesy of the Frontier Times Museum Collection.)

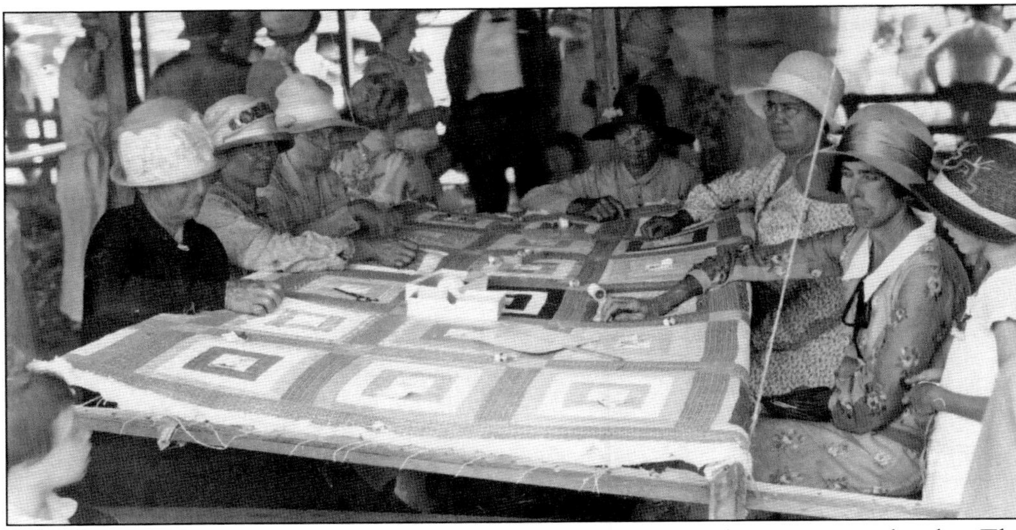

The surnames on the reunion registers are ones that could still be encountered today. The reunion offered a chance for women to engage in their own friendly competitions by showing off homemade cakes, pies, and preserves. Women also gathered at the reunions for quilting contests and bees, just as their female relations had been doing for generations. (Courtesy of the Frontier Times Museum Collection.)

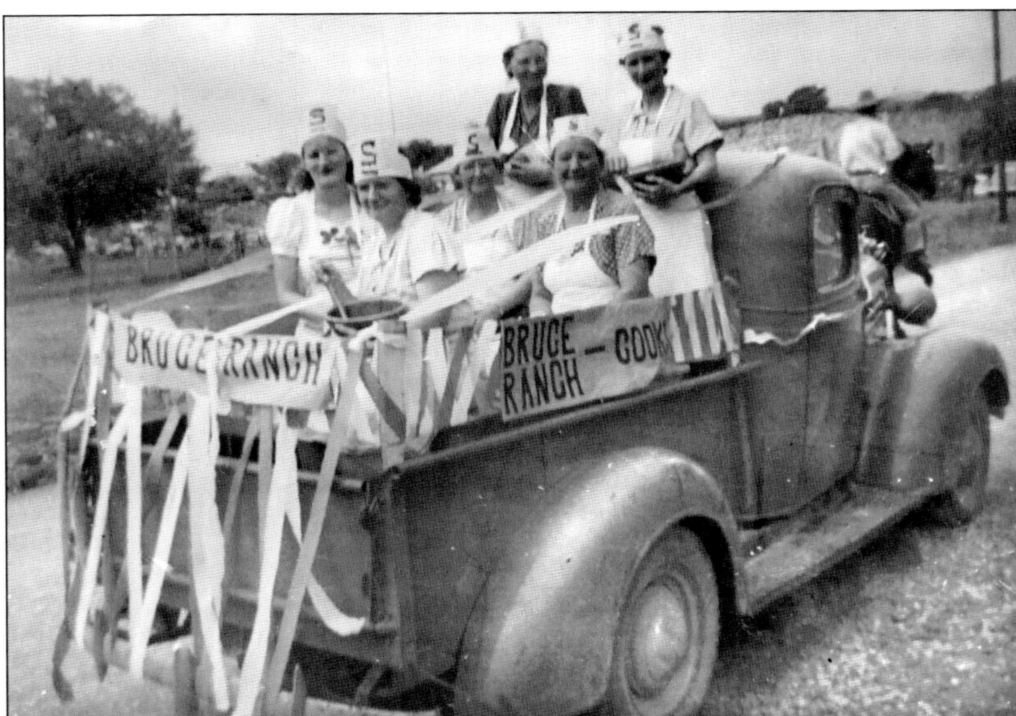

By the 1940s, the Old Settlers Association reunion was celebrated as the Old Settlers Jubilee. A large parade was held as part of the festivities. These cute cooks of the Bruce Ranch won third prize for their decorated truck in 1941. Friends, guests, and Mary Bruce dressed as cooks for their float. Ranch owner John Bruce is seen riding ahead on his horse. (Courtesy of John Hayes.)

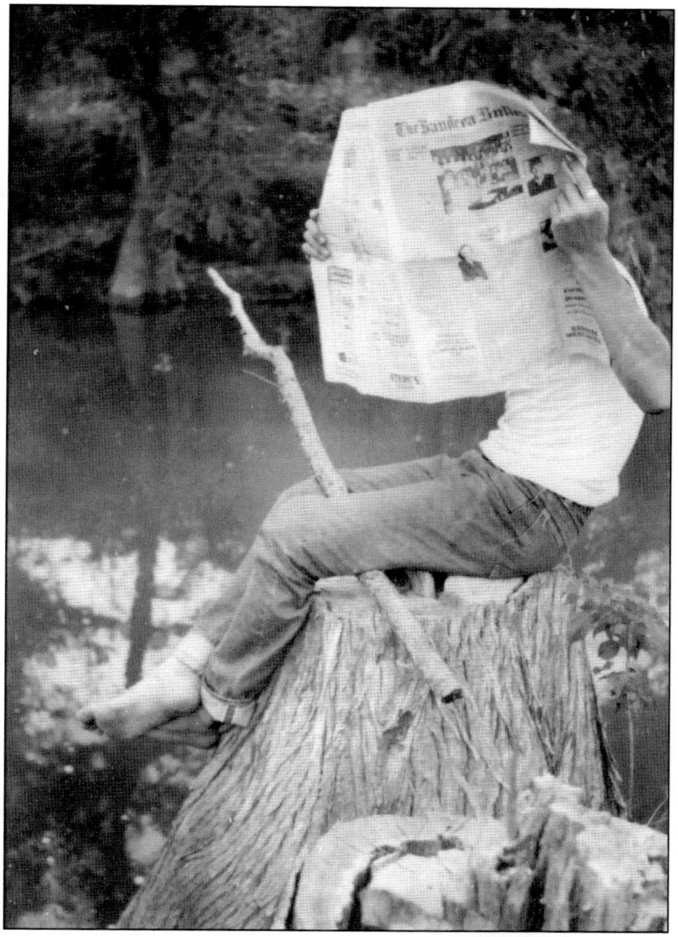

Flowing through the county, the Medina River plays a large part in the lives and hearts of those who live in Bandera County. In the past, the suspension bridge was a popular place to gather and to test one's courage. Brave souls went alone, and others ventured onto the bridge with several friends. Today Bandera's City Park is the site of the annual River Fest. The event began in 1998 and features the famous Great Hill Country Anything That Floats Regatta, where participants design their own water floats, which are often miracles when they actually do float. The river runs through the hearts of all, whether it is a party along the river or simply relaxing with the local newspaper. (Both, courtesy of the Bandera County Historical Commission.)

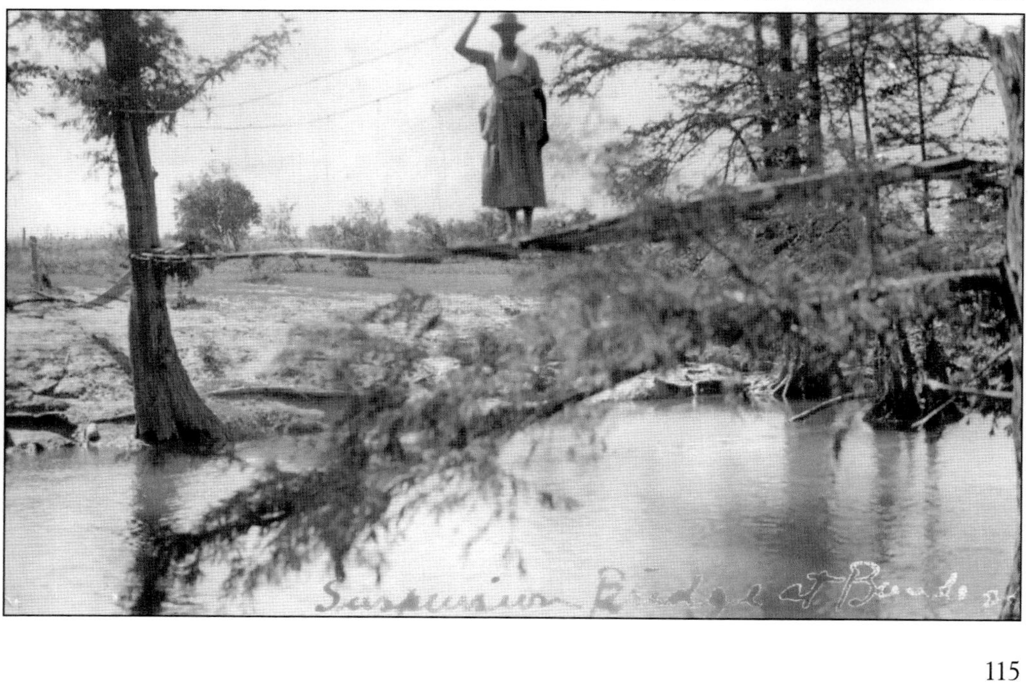

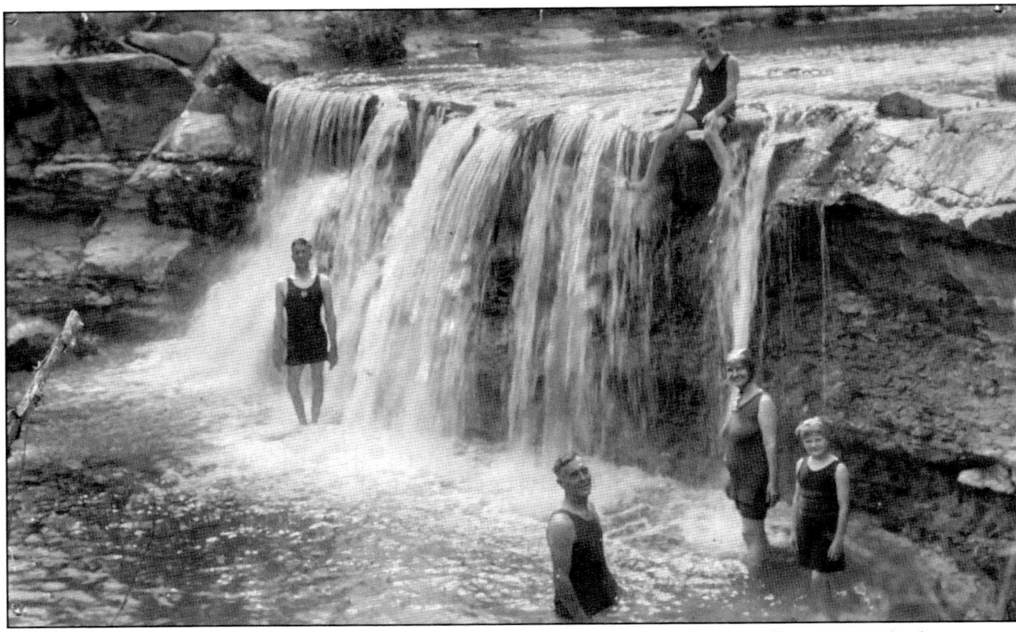

Swimming and tubing in the Medina River and in the many creeks that flow through the county is a great way to cool off in the sometimes brutal summer. Another early pastime on Sunday afternoon was taking drives down the county's scenic roads and ending at the Medina River. There it was considered fun to not only show off the car, but to also wash it in the river as well. The people above are finding the perfect spot to cool off on the San Geronimo Creek. Below, Mary Gladys Jureczki stands between sisters Beatrice and Theresa Dugosh, as they proudly show off their ride. (Above, courtesy of the Bandera County Historical Association; below, courtesy of Elenora Dugosh Goodley.)

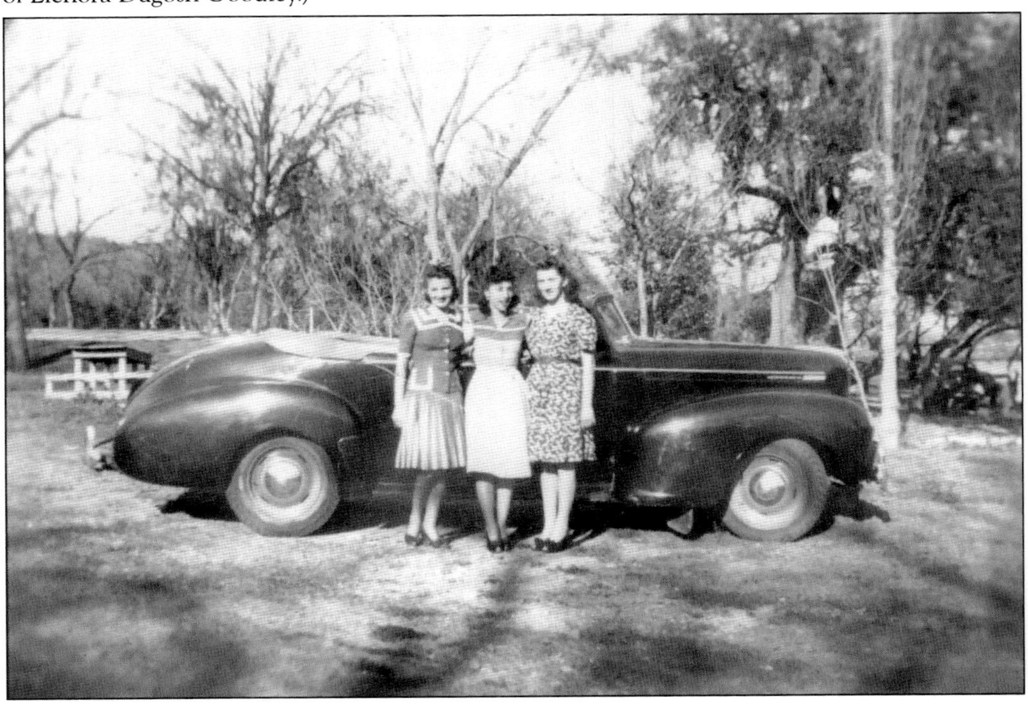

Weekend picnics and gatherings with friends are long-standing traditions that still bring life's simple pleasures. Old-timers spoke of gatherings that would last two or three days, when family and friends would take a break from work on the farm or the ranch to celebrate with music, good food, and drink. Polish wedding celebrations were legendary. Gabriel Anderwald recalled to J. Marvin Hunter the celebration of Tom Moravietz's marriage to Frances Haiduk. The celebration was three days of feasting and dancing all day and night. Albert Haiduk was the fiddler and kept playing as long as the crowd stayed. (Right, courtesy of Carr-Newcomer-Stanard family; below, courtesy of Bobby and Mary Stein.)

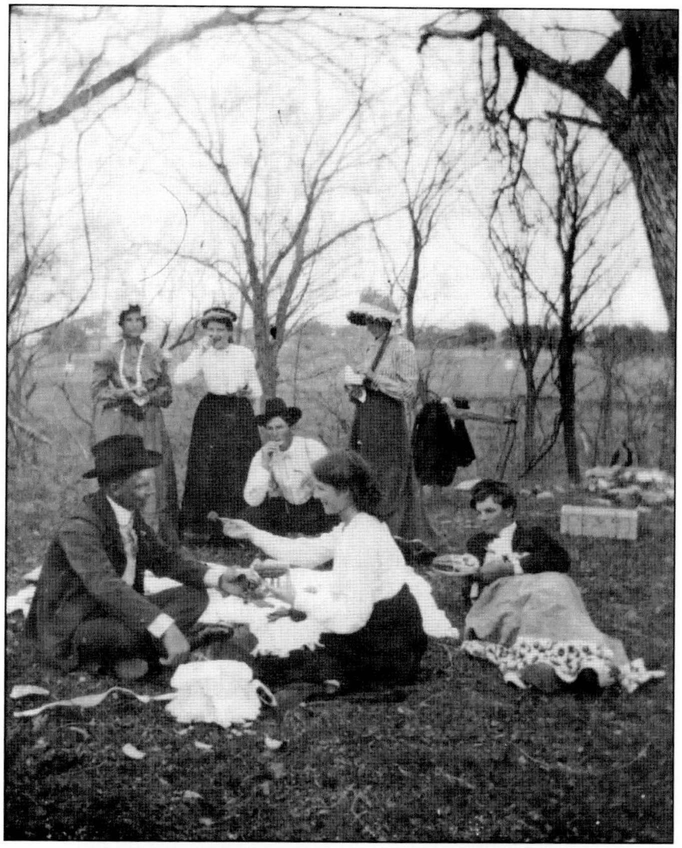

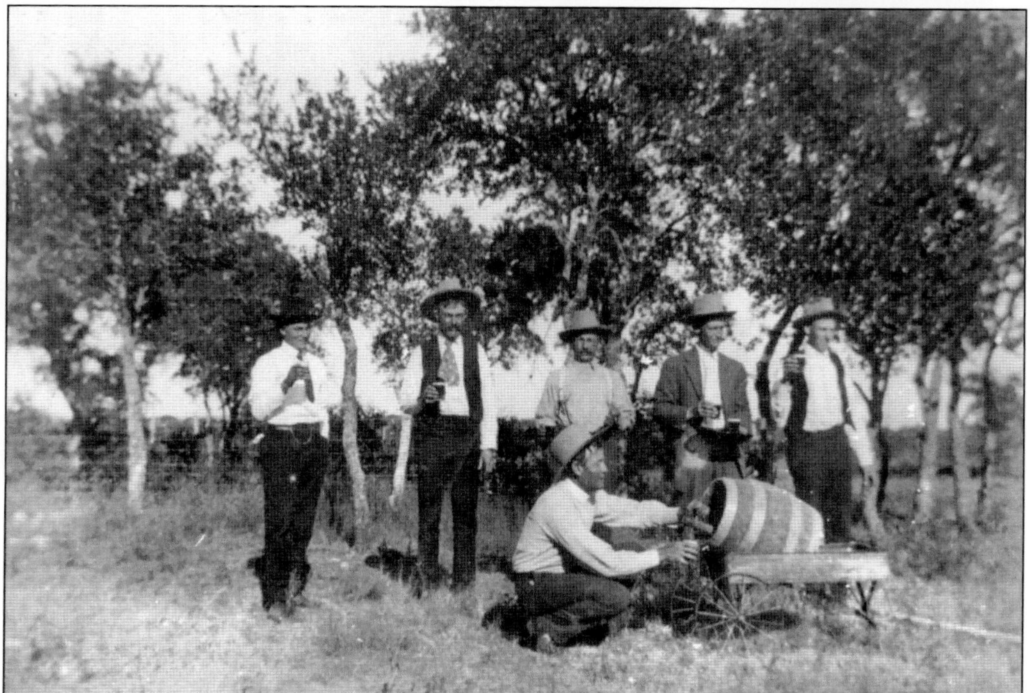

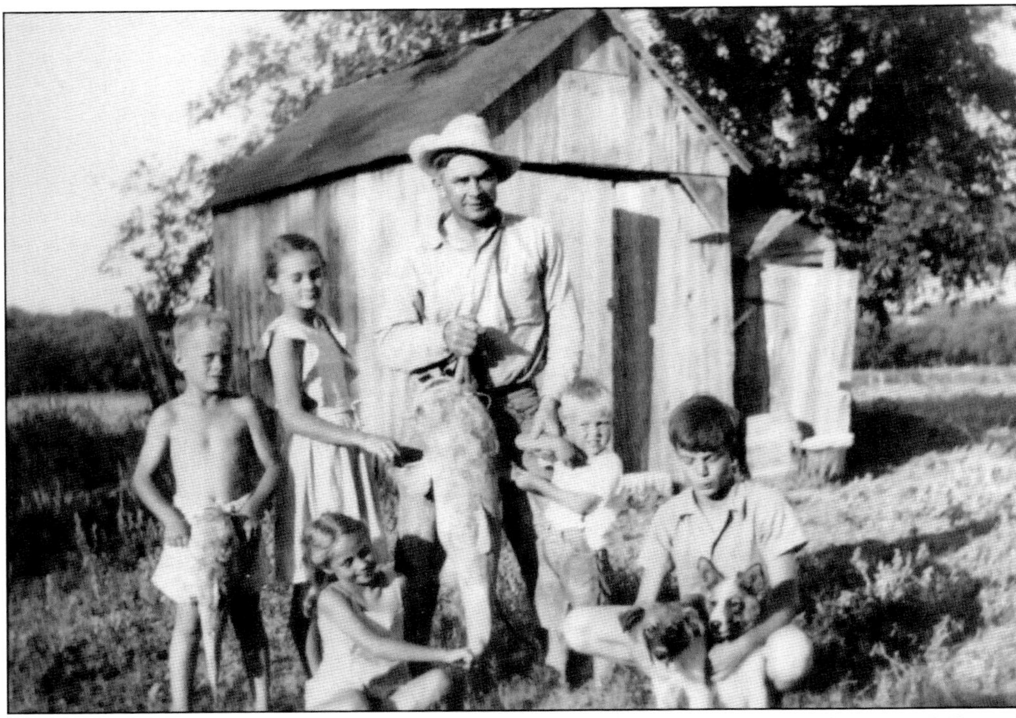

Fishing was not only a pastime; it was also done to place a meal on the table. Betty D'Spain's father poses in 1948 with a catfish caught in the Medina River near Bogey Creek. Betty recalled fishing for their Friday night dinner by laying out trout lines across the river and going back at night with flashlights to see if they had any bites. (Courtesy of Betty Laskowski D'Spain.)

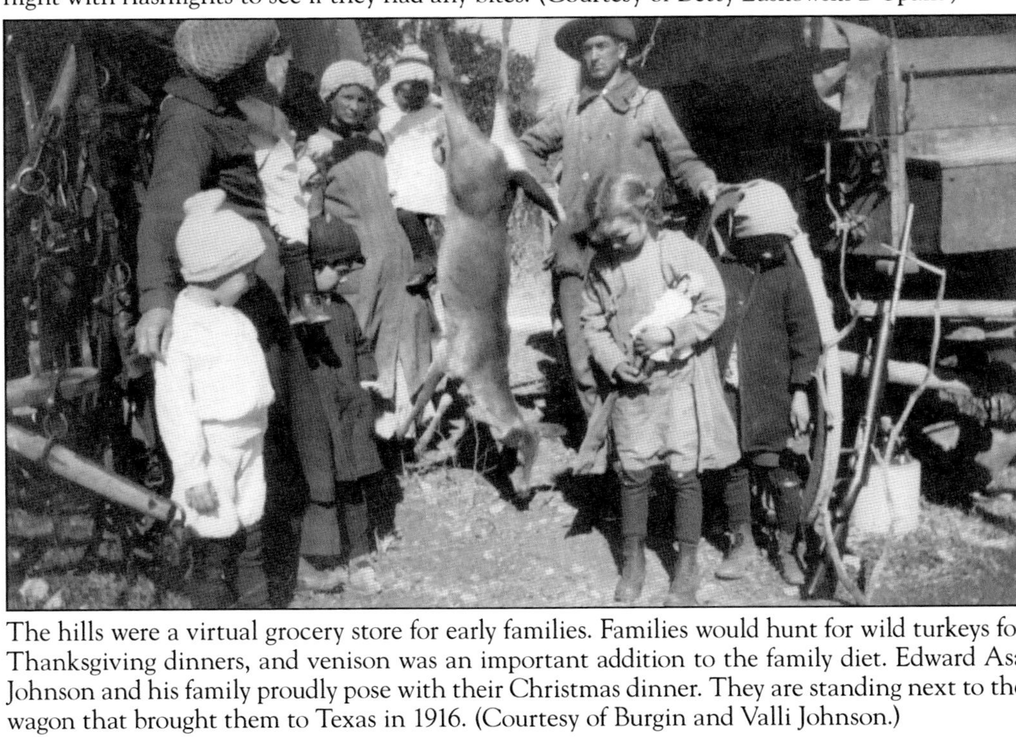

The hills were a virtual grocery store for early families. Families would hunt for wild turkeys for Thanksgiving dinners, and venison was an important addition to the family diet. Edward Asa Johnson and his family proudly pose with their Christmas dinner. They are standing next to the wagon that brought them to Texas in 1916. (Courtesy of Burgin and Valli Johnson.)

Today fishing and hunting are done more as a leisure activity and have become an important economic resource for Bandera County. Boating and fishing support many businesses around Medina Lake, and some dude ranches offer stock tanks on their ranches as an added attraction. (Courtesy of Marlene Leibold Grothues.)

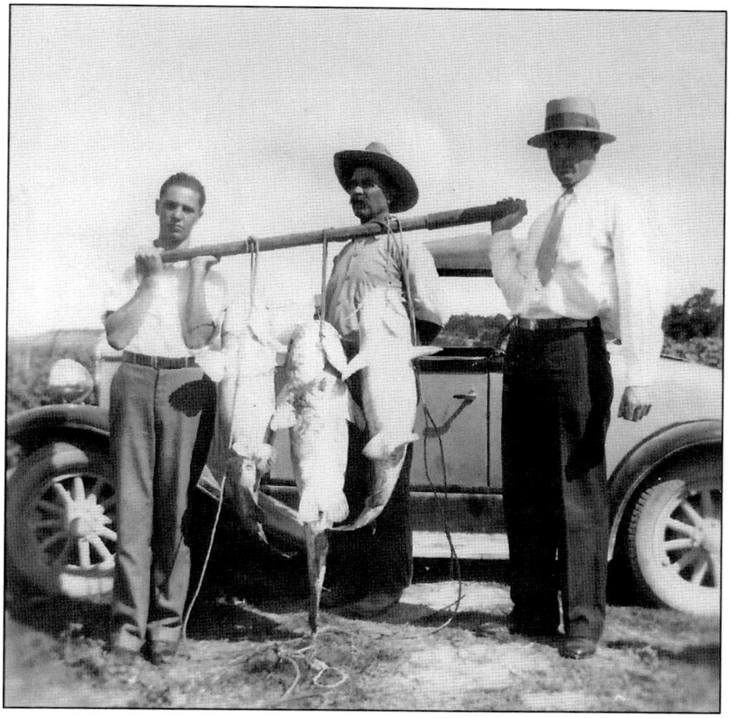

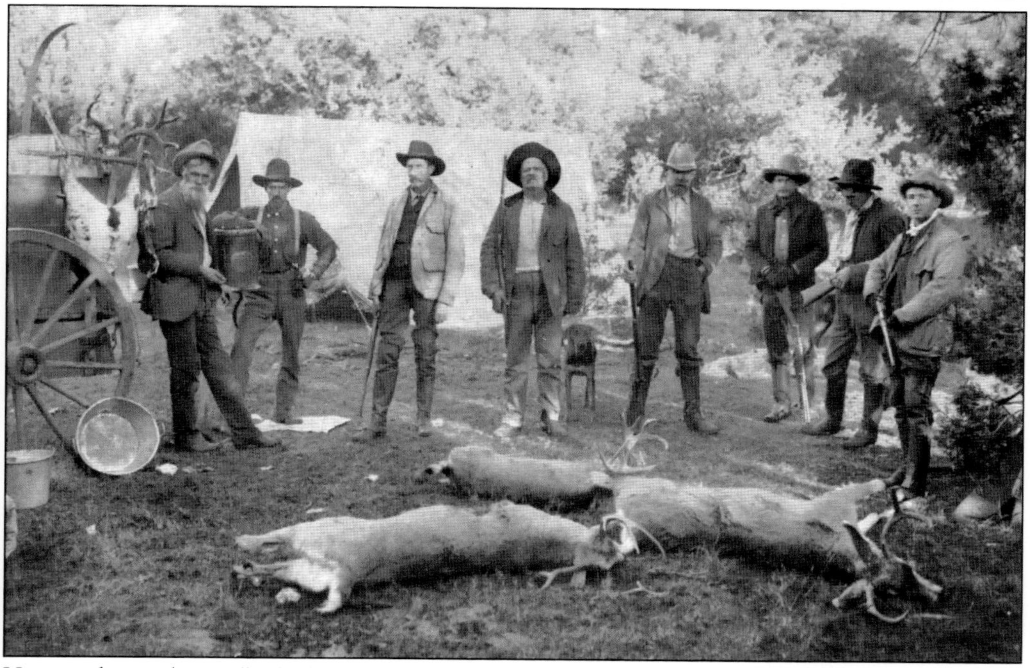

Hunters have always flocked to Bandera County, and this tradition is celebrated each year at the Hunters Bar-B-Que and Outdoor Exposition. In 1962, local businesses decided to sponsor a weekend to show appreciation for the hundreds of hunters who come each fall during hunting season. The weekend includes a hunter's breakfast, vendors, music, an auction, and a barbecue dinner, and serves as the annual fund-raiser for the chamber of commerce. (Courtesy of the Carr-Newcomer-Stanard family.)

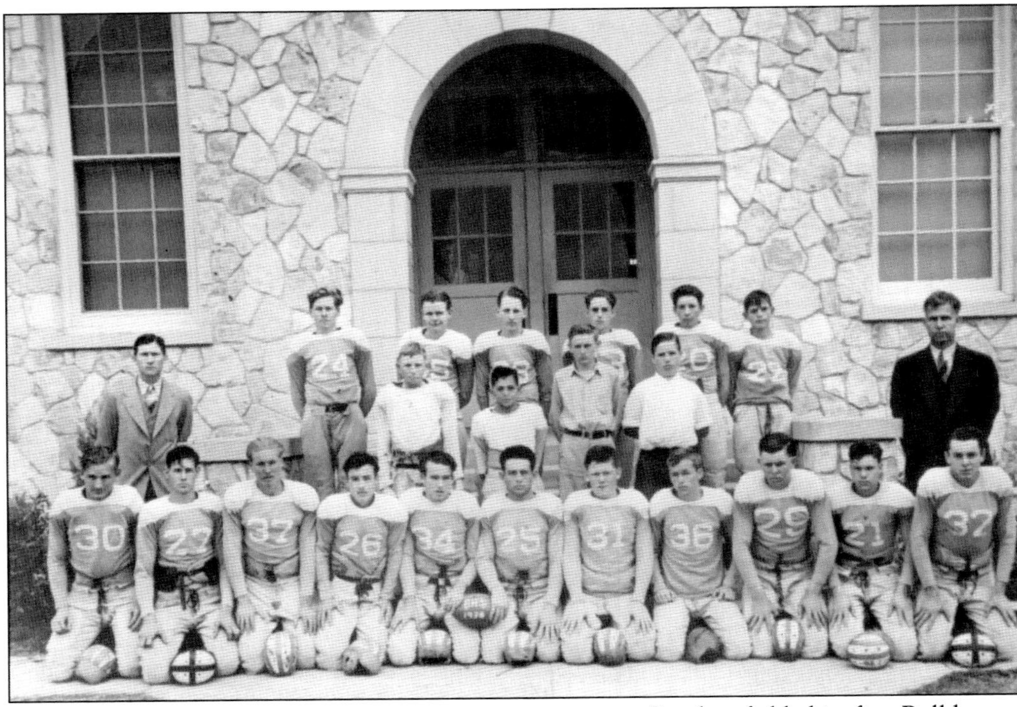

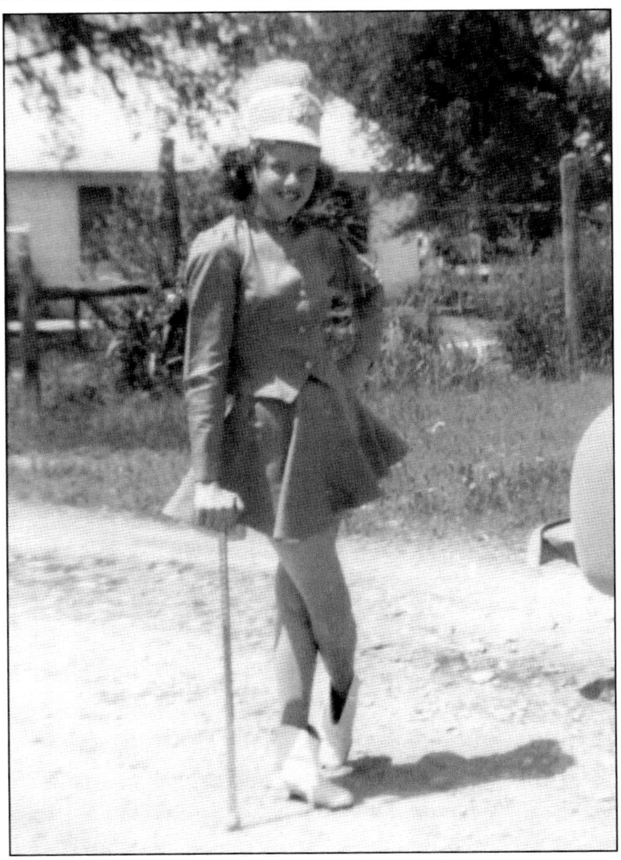

Bandera fielded its first Bulldog football team in 1936 in colors of burnt orange and white. School colors changed during World War II because of the shortage of orange dye, and today the colors are blue and white. With the game of football being so new, an early quarterback recounts that occasionally the officials would stop the game to explain the rules to the players. Today "Friday Night Lights" are an ingrained part of Bandera County schools' traditions. Spectators can no longer build bonfires at the end of the field, although officials still probably have to explain rules to players. In 2002, the Bulldogs became the state 3A champs, winning the final game in a triple overtime nail-biter. Above is Bandera's first football team. At left, Cecilia Carr proudly poses in her Medina School's majorette uniform. (Above, courtesy of Bandera County Historical Commission; left, courtesy of Cecila Carr Schmidtke.)

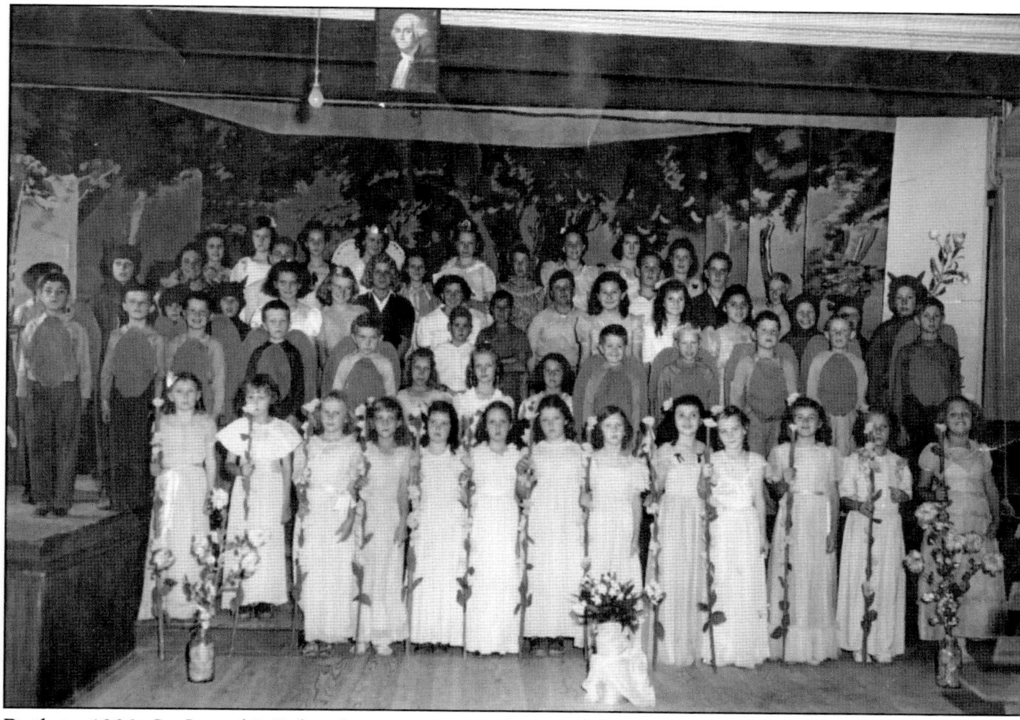

Built in 1920, St. Joseph's School was an integral part of the Catholic community until its closing in 1968. Many Bandera residents of a certain generation were students and remember the many traditions that were part of growing up in the close-knit school. The annual spring pageant was held near the end of the school year. The nuns would choose the theme for each year, and the students would perform in a variety of roles. Parents and the community were invited to attend, and it became a popular annual event. The above photograph shows the 1945 pageant, with hollyhocks on the front row, boys dressed as bluebirds, and even an angel and a queen. The theme of the play below had to do with the students' Polish heritage. (Above, courtesy of Annette Kalka-Schulte and Elenora Goodley Dugosh; below, courtesy of Betty Laskowski D'Spain.)

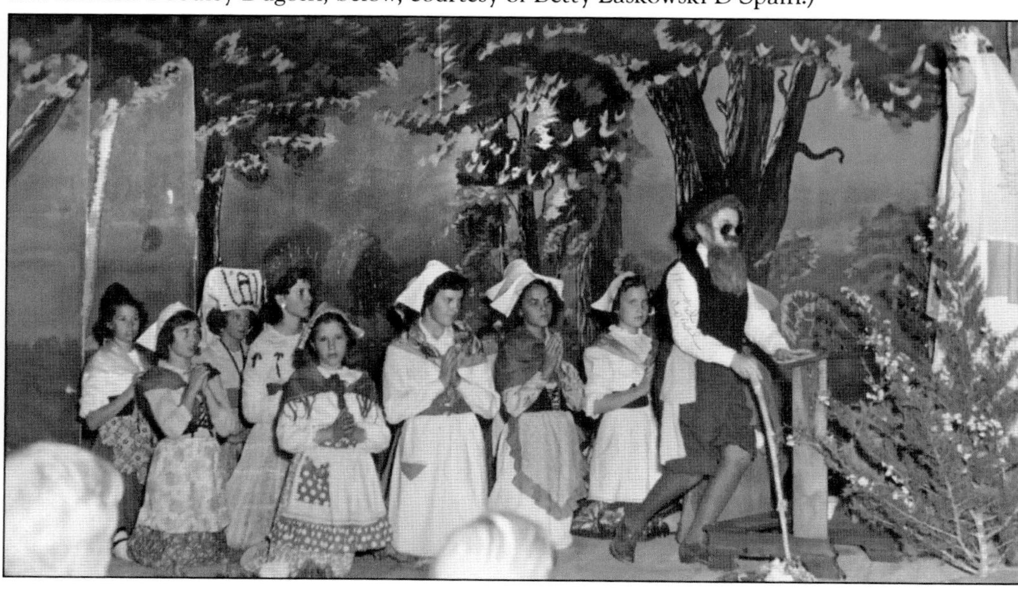

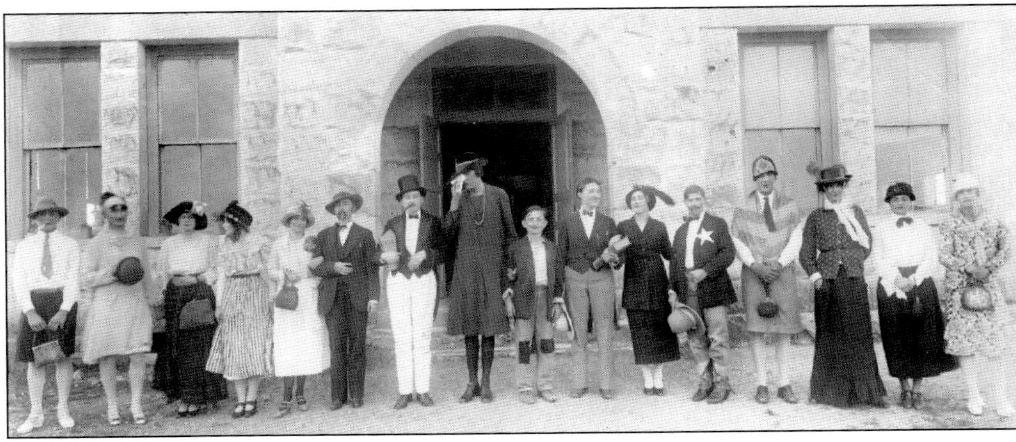

Residents of Bandera have always been able to find ways of entertaining each other. In 1926, local men put down their boots and work clothes to don dresses and hats in a citywide play that took an interesting look at marriage, love, and romance. The play was done in two parts. The first play to be performed was the *Womanless Wedding*, only to be followed by the melodramatic *Womanless Divorce*. The cast included the manly men of Bandera and a few of the ladies, who were dressed as men. The play was so popular that a large, formal portrait of the cast on stage was one of the first pictures to be put on display when the Frontier Times Museum was opened in 1933. (Above, courtesy of the Bandera County Historical Commission; below, courtesy of the Frontier Times Museum Collection.)

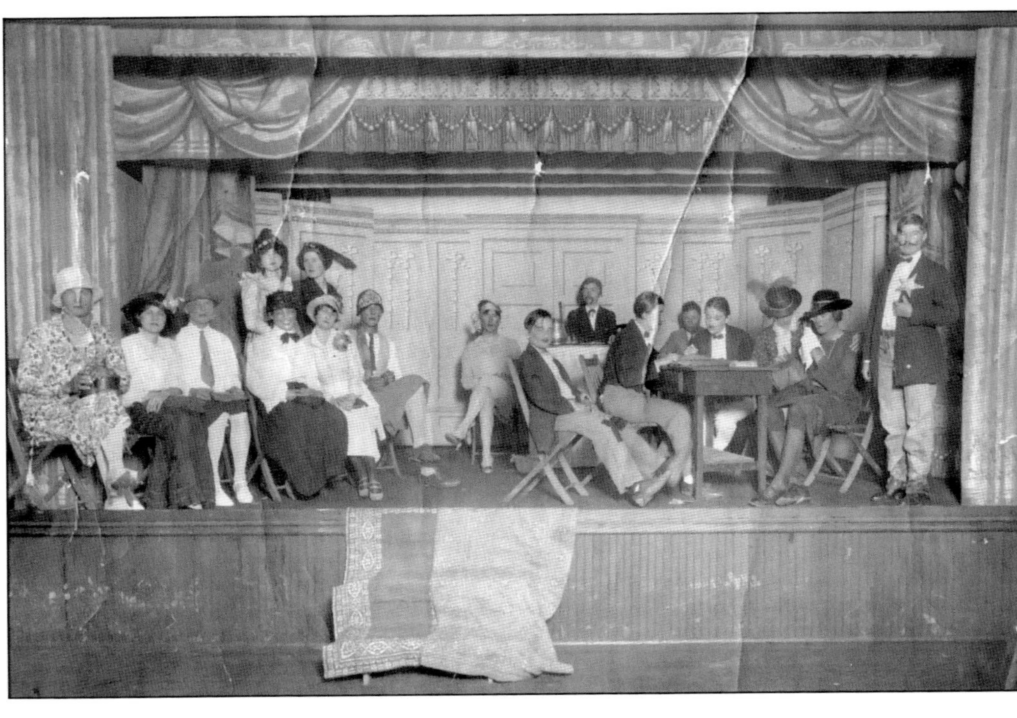

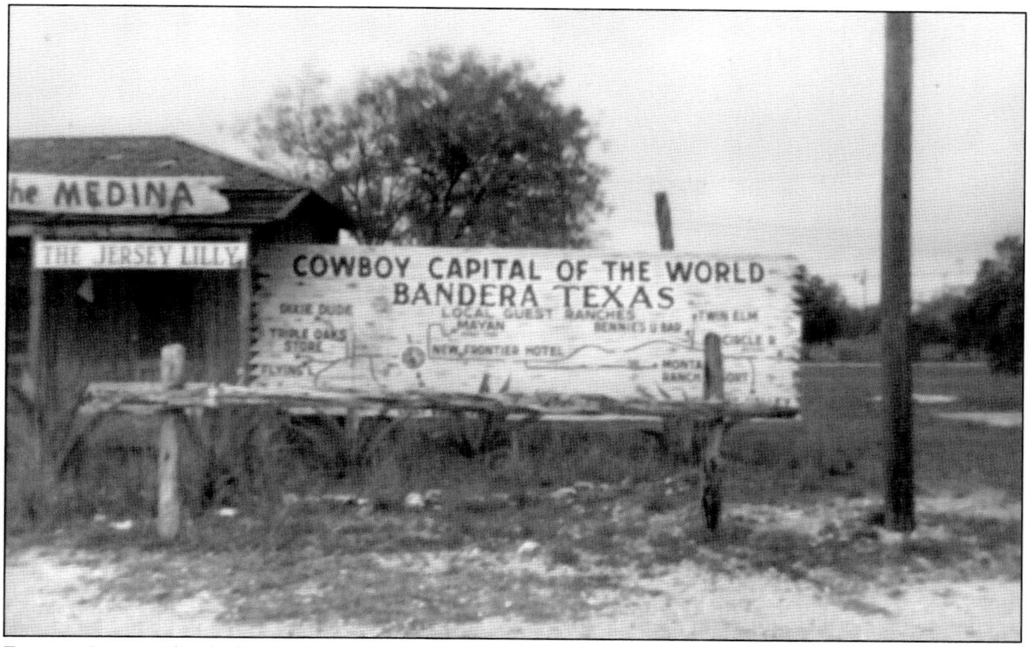

During Stompede, dude ranch owners declared Bandera to be the "Cowboy Capital of the World." The title refers not only to the many dude ranches, but also to the fact that the county has more rodeo champions per capita than any other place. To celebrate this designation and the Stompede, Lee Jeans donated an oversize pair of Lee jeans to fly as the flag of Bandera. While many prefer to recognize Bandera's heritage in sheep and goat ranching and its Polish heritage, visitors from around the country and the world identify Bandera with rodeos and cowboys on Main Street. Above is an early billboard next to the chamber of commerce building. Below, a young lady at this get-together somehow got to the wear the famed flag of Bandera. (Above, courtesy of the Frontier Times Museum Collection; below, courtesy of Scooter Fries.)

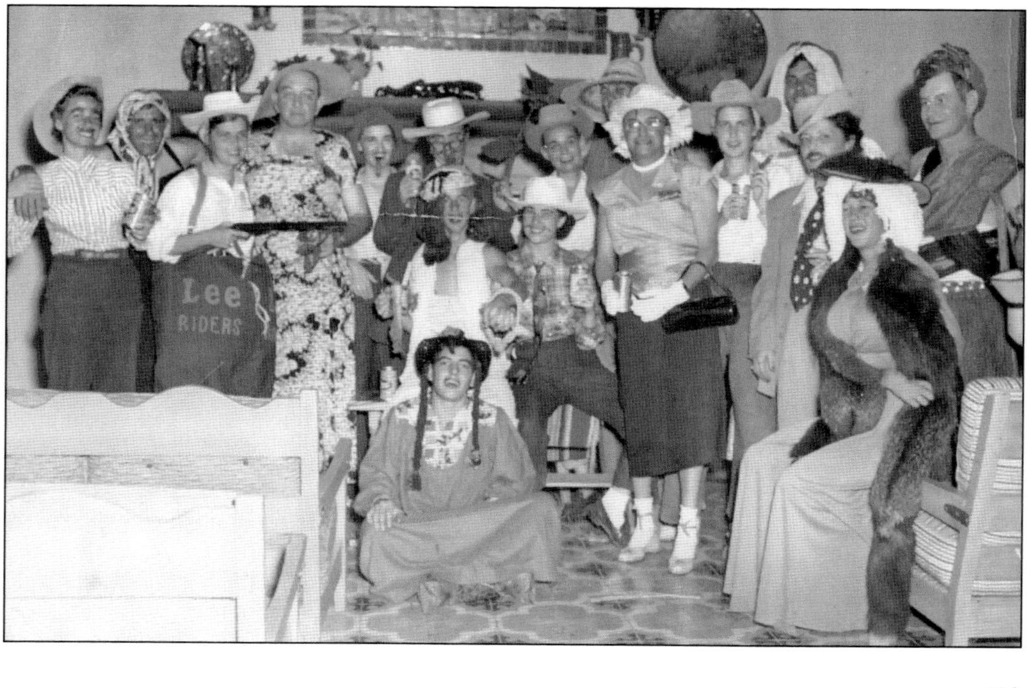

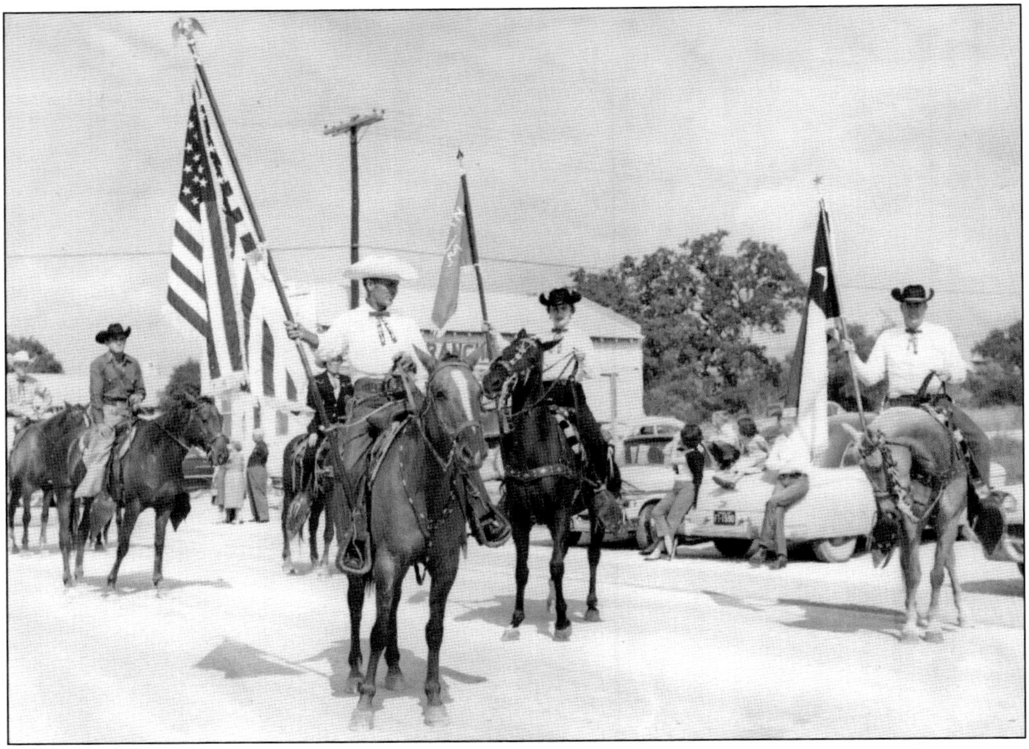

Bandera County continues to celebrate holidays and special occasions with parades, and the county can have up to five parades a year. Parades give an opportunity for patriotic displays of civic pride. Bandera's cowboy heritage is honored as well, as many participants partake on horseback or in wagons. (Courtesy of Judy Hicks.)

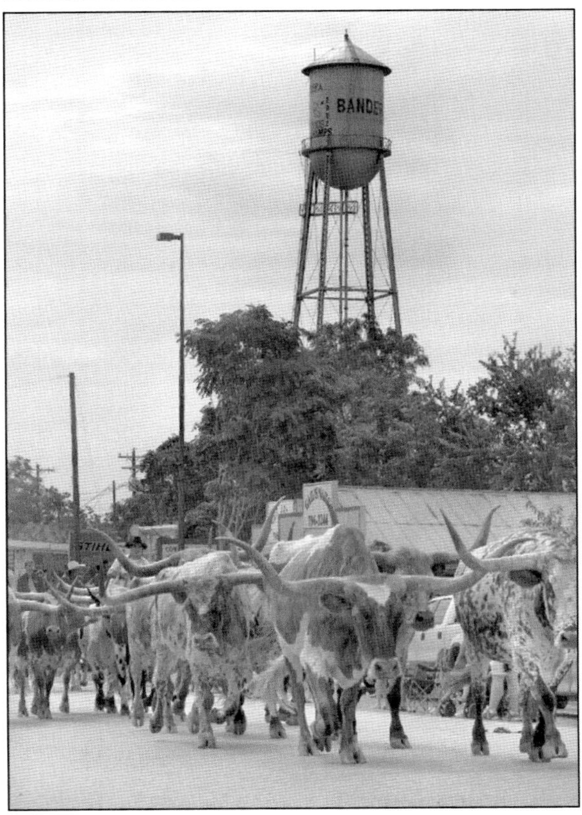

The Bandera Community Foundation sponsors the annual Celebrate Bandera every Labor Day weekend. Beginning as a one afternoon benefit concert to raise money for victims of the 2002 flood, it has grown to become Bandera County's major event of the year—a three-day festival that draws thousands of visitors from across the United States, as well as from Mexico and Europe. The Longhorn cattle drive down Main Street opens the event each year. (Courtesy of the *Bandera County Courier*.)

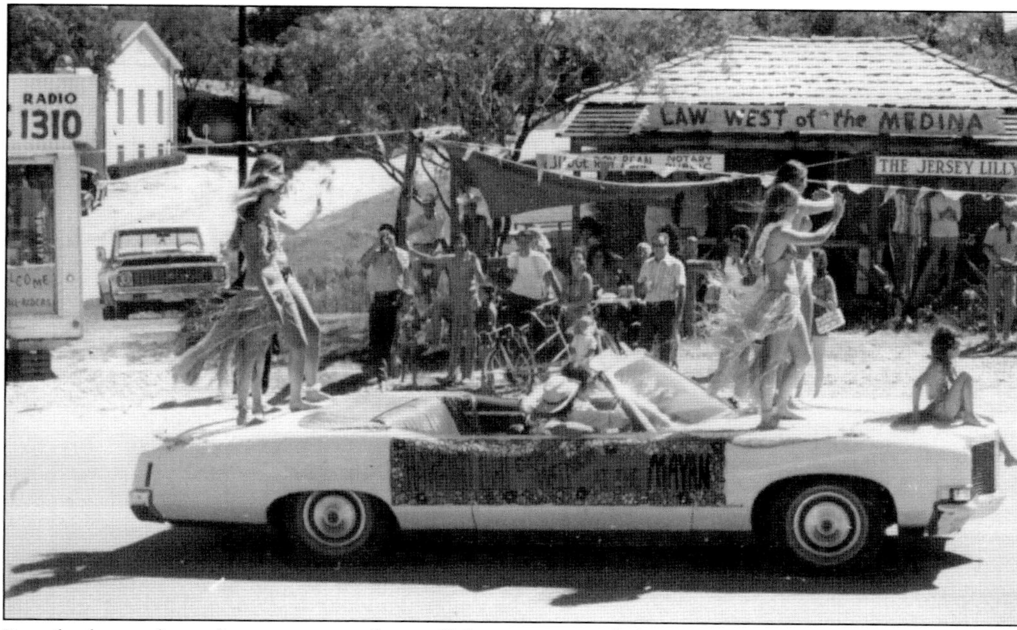

Parades have always been a way to show off the strange and the unusual. The Mayan Dude Ranch entered this parade float in an earlier celebration during the 1970s. What better way to celebrate Bandera than a Cadillac covered in Hawaiian hula dancers? The Cadillac is driving by the Jersey Lily and many admiring onlookers. (Courtesy of Judy Hicks.)

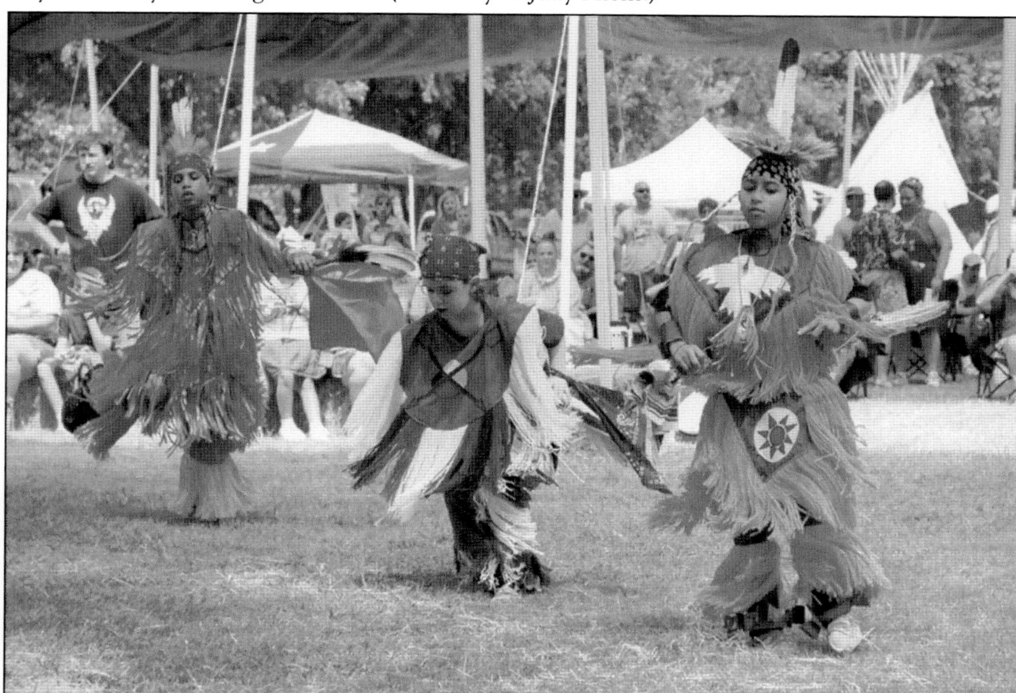

The Circle of Life Intertribal Powwow is held annually on Labor Day weekend during Celebrate Bandera. The powwow allows each Native American tribe to honor their ancestors by demonstrating and celebrating their traditions and culture. (Courtesy of the *Bandera County Courier.*)

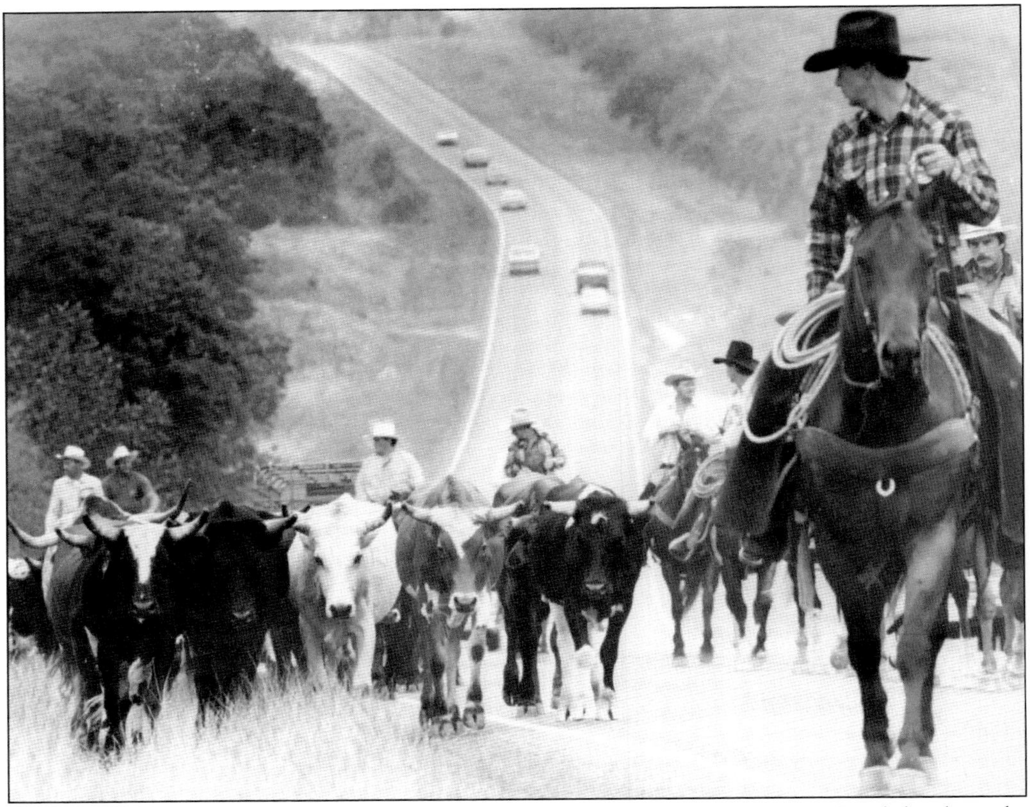

John Lytle of Medina County has been credited with establishing the Western Trail that brought cattle from points south through Bandera, up through the Bandera Pass and points north to Kansas. To honor the importance of the trail to Bandera and Texas history, Dan Wise and David Burrell organized a reenactment of the Western Trail in 2004. Horseback riders and wagons rode the 655-mile trail ride from Bandera to Dodge City, Kansas, in 48 days, retracing the steps of history. (Courtesy of the Bandera County Historical Commission.)

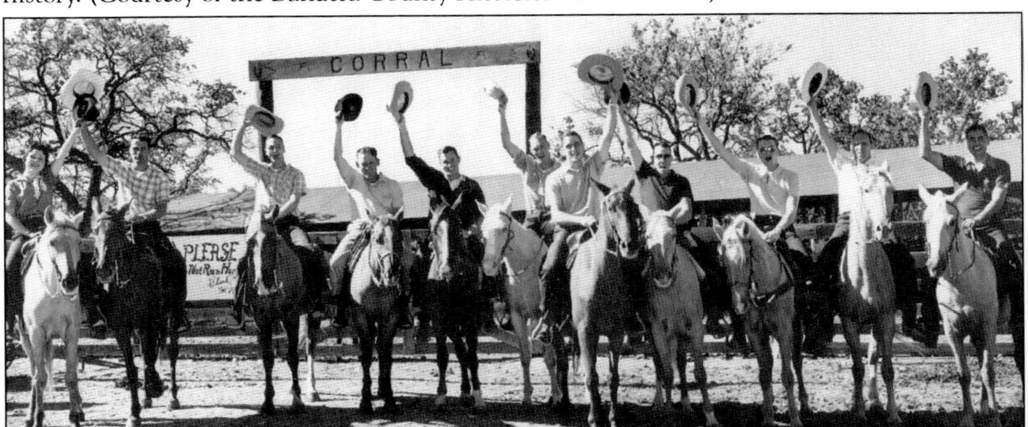

Bandera County remains true to its past, as it maintains its heritage and cultural traditions. As the future unfolds, its residents are determined to keep it an unspoiled place, where green hills surround the valleys and the clear waters of the Medina River flow, a wonderful place to live and a wonderful place to visit. (Courtesy of Judy Hicks.)

EPILOGUE

As it looks toward the future, the Frontier Times Museum honors the vision of its founder J. Marvin Hunter Sr., while preserving and interpreting the cultural heritage of Bandera County and the surrounding Hill Country. The museum will continue to serve our community, our youth, and our visitors by promoting the unique history of this area and its important contributions to the history of life on the Texas frontier.

DISCOVER THOUSANDS OF LOCAL HISTORY BOOKS FEATURING MILLIONS OF VINTAGE IMAGES

Arcadia Publishing, the leading local history publisher in the United States, is committed to making history accessible and meaningful through publishing books that celebrate and preserve the heritage of America's people and places.

Find more books like this at
www.arcadiapublishing.com

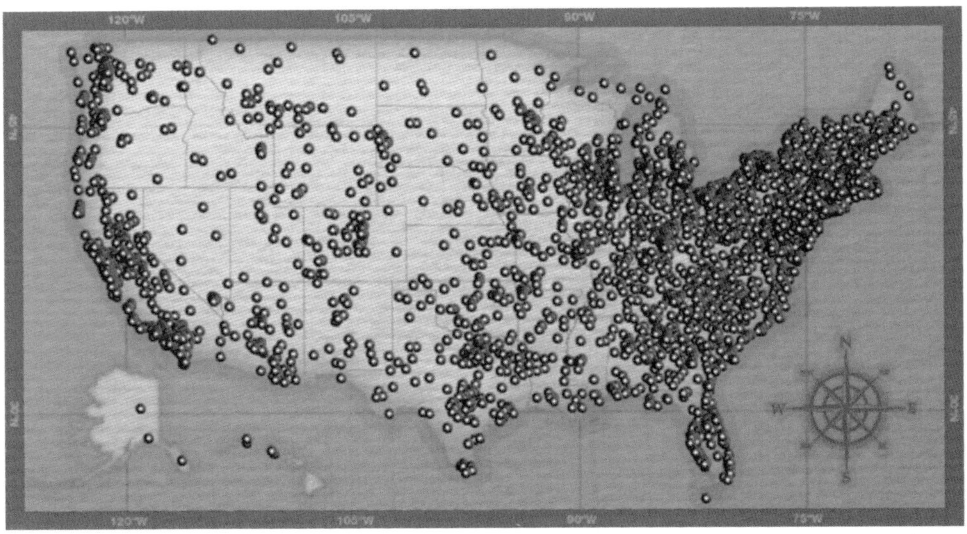

Search for your hometown history, your old stomping grounds, and even your favorite sports team.

Consistent with our mission to preserve history on a local level, this book was printed in South Carolina on American-made paper and manufactured entirely in the United States. Products carrying the accredited Forest Stewardship Council (FSC) label are printed on 100 percent FSC-certified paper.

MADE IN THE USA